The Writer's Voice

THE WRITER'S VOICE

CONVERSATIONS WITH CONTEMPORARY WRITERS

Conducted by John Graham
Edited by George Garrett

WILLIAM MORROW & COMPANY, INC.
New York   1973

Graham, John, (date)
    The writer's voice.

    Interviews originally taped in June, 1970, during the Hollins Conference in Creative Writing and Cinema for John Graham's radio program, The scholar's bookshelf.
    1. Authors, American—20th century—Interviews. 2. Authorship. I. Garrett, George P., (date) ed. II. Title.
PS129.G7   808'.02   72-10262
ISBN 0-688-00034-7
ISBN 0-688-05034-4 (pbk.)

ACKNOWLEDGMENTS

RICHARD WILBUR: The poem "Playboy," copyright © 1968, by Richard Wilbur, is reprinted from *Walking to Sleep*, by permission of Harcourt Brace Jovanovich, Inc. The poem "A Riddle," copyright © 1969, by Richard Wilbur, is reprinted from *Walking to Sleep*, by permission of Harcourt Brace Jovanovich, Inc. The lines from "Walking to Sleep," copyright © 1967, by Richard Wilbur, are reprinted from *Walking to Sleep*, by permission of Harcourt Brace Jovanovich, Inc. The poem "Dead Still," translated from the Russian of Andrei Voznesensky, copyright © 1966 by Basic Books, Inc., is reprinted from *Walking to Sleep*, by permission of Harcourt Brace Jovanovich, Inc.

HENRY TAYLOR: The lines quoted from "Three Snapshots for George Garrett" and "Things Not Solved Though Tomorrow Came" are from *The Horse Show at Midnight*, by Henry Taylor. Copyright © 1965, by Henry Taylor; reprinted by permission of Louisiana State University Press and by the author. "The Terrace," by Henry Taylor, copyright © 1970, by Henry Taylor, is reprinted by permission of the author.

JAMES SEAY: The poems "Let Not Your Hart Be Truble" and "Grabbling in Yokna Bottom" are from *Let Not Your Hart*, by James Seay. Copyright © 1968, by James Seay; reprinted by permission of Wesleyan University Press.

JAMES WHITEHEAD: The poems "The Politician's Pledge" and "Two Voices" are from *Domains*, by James Whitehead. Copyright © 1966, by James Whitehead; reprinted by permission of Louisiana State University Press and by permission of the author.

JAMES DICKEY: The poem "In the Pocket" and the lines from "Messages" are from *Eye-Beaters, Blood, Victory, Madness, Buckhead and Mercy*, by James Dickey. Copyright © 1968, 1969, 1970, by James Dickey. Reprinted by permission of Doubleday & Company, Inc.

DAVID SLAVITT: The lines from the poem, "Sestina for the Last Week of March," are from *Day Sailing*, by David Slavitt. Copyright © 1969, by David Slavitt. Reprinted by permission of the University of North Carolina Press.

R. H. W. DILLARD: The poem "Why Were the Bandit's Eyes

Preface

This book is an unusual, and unusually interesting, gathering of conversational interviews, "dialogues" if you wish, with a group of working writers about their craft and art. And I cheerfully recommend it to you and to your attention.

One reason I can recommend these interviews is that, as editor of record, I had very little to do with or to them. You can take my word for it that the texts have been very lightly, very slightly edited. They have been transcribed (from tape recordings), selected, arranged, punctuated for reading and to represent the spoken style. But they have not been revised, polished, "fixed up," or anything like that. Except for occasional and inevitable ellipses and run-of-the-mill, inadvertent boo-boos, they have been left alone to speak for themselves. Because they do that well enough.

Another reason I blithely break the rules of editorial intrusion and good manners, blowing a modest trumpet at the outset of this book, is that it is not my trumpet, not really. Except for this preface, for the short headnotes and such, and for the inconsequential bits and pieces of silent editing, I am not even *in* the book. It is the writers, and John Graham who talked with them one and all, who are at once the characters and the creators.

And for any doubters and scoffers, hard-noses who have earned their share of scars and kisses in the world, and especially in that rough and tumble battle royal we dignify by calling the literary marketplace, let me confess this much: the earnings, if any, coming by roundabout ways to myself, as editor, have already been signed over to go as a gift to Hollins College. Where these interviews took place. Where I was working at the time. Where I do not work any more.

I'm not assuming a pose of "purity." But it would be less than honest not to tell you that I am a more or less disinterested witness. And therefore I feel free to recommend this collection to you.

Even if I didn't feel that freedom, though, even if I were out here, up front, doing a buck and wing, whistling an accompaniment while I celebrate me, myself and I in the latest fashion, hustling for a buck and hoping for a big round of applause, even then I believe I would still feel free to tell you that I *like* these interviews and why I like them.

This coming from a man who, most of the time, doesn't like interviews of any kind or form, especially in published form. In general I think that published interviews are phony, contrived, duplicitous, misdirected, pointless and silly. Oh, I *read* them all right. Just as, being just as silly as anybody else, I may also stay up too late, my head humming from the leaden resonance of one-liners, my eyes bleary and bloodshot from the clever, continual shuffle of commercials, to see and hear the celebrities on the TV talk shows. With a profound contempt for myself, my own taste and the tastes of the times, I am nevertheless inclined to open a can of beer and settle back easy with the conned majority, knowing better, knowing it's all a shuck from the word go, and wait patiently for the canned wisdom, the plastic gags and tattooed aphorisms of the comedians, politicians, poets, movie stars, ball players, whores, gangsters and other public figures who are the ghosts who haunt our nights. And (I've already admitted it) I will read the fool things, too, almost any time. Which is just as well. Because you can't pick up a magazine, from *Playboy* to *Poultry Journal,* without bumping head-on into an interview of one kind or another. And in the drugstore, airport, bus station, there they are, too, bright in the weedy garden of paperback books. Practically an established genre, for Lord's sake! Right up there among the monthly blockbusters, the thrillers, the porn books, the sturdy westerns and the enduring nurse stories. I can pay my money and take a skim through the (apparently) accurate representation of the spoken words of pretty much the same public figures. Or I can settle for the more anonymous ones—for example, the airline stewardesses who tell all and then some about their private lives.

I am not sure why we Americans are so fascinated by interviews. I have some opinions, of course. Sometimes I think it's another sign of the sad necessity of our crowded, lonely lives, an urgent hopeless reaching out to touch something real, a deep hunger for something authentic when everything seems false, a desire to believe at least in the possibility of naked truth. We have a lust for contact. And yet at one and the same time (for aren't our deepest feelings always *mixed?*) we like to know that what we are being given has been carefully retouched, airbrushed, wrapped and packaged, that even in seeming nudity the truth is still in disguise, a trick done with mirrors.

And we seem to need to know, to realize, as almost invariably we come to, that these people, the characters we encounter in the various forms the interview takes, are, you know, really very much like us, not any wiser or braver or more virtuous, not even smarter or more skilled at whatever it is they do, but maybe more clever, certainly luckier than the rest of us.

Which is one of the reasons, I believe, why most of the time these people are permitted to talk about anything and everything—except what they do well.

Another voice in myself tells me that this is a traditionally *American* contradiction and compromise. From the beginning until now (and honestly I don't think it has anything much to do with the *Puritan ethos* and all that) we have preferred *fact* to fiction. Or, to put it another way, we prefer to have our fiction justified by a sheen or scum of hard facts. As Americans, we like to pretend we are *learning something, improving ourselves* and having fun too. I don't want to belabor this basic little point. I just want to observe the obvious—that we place a premium upon the "authentic" raw materials of fact and "real life." But there's a paradox. We don't care that much about raw reality. We don't rush out to read the transcripts of most trials, for example. We call that "research."

Still another inner voice reminds me of the undeniable truth that both the interest and the form have been around a very long time, through all the ages we know about. After all, it is by this means, the dialogue, that we know something of the character and wisdom of Socrates.

Enough said. The interview is a very present form, in all its forms, today. Those forms range from the disguised interview, the piece *about* someone, itself based on a series of interviews with a subject and others, the kind of thing Tom Wolfe does as well as anyone alive, to the transcription, with varying degrees of inaccuracy, of tape-recorded or written questions and answers.

And, as I said a while ago, generally I read them, but I don't really like them, either as an idea, in theory, or in fact, as I find them.

These talks here are an exception to my general rule and reaction. They have a reason and a special context which distinguishes them from other interviews with writers. Most gatherings of literary interviews, even the best of them (and the volumes of the *Paris Review* interviews are a model for the best) are anthologies of literary celebrities, a little firmament of big stars. That is not exactly the case here. There are some people who would or will qualify for star billing. There are some others who do not and, as the world goes, may not enjoy that kind of status. Who knows? I wish them all well, and if "well" includes literary stardom, may they all burn brightly and long. But celebrity is not the point. The point is that all of these people were together, in a brief community, working together in a common enterprise at the same time and the same place. All were participants, full-time staff or visitors, at the Hollins Conference in Creative Writing and Cinema, which took place between June 15 and June 27, 1970. This was a very unusual (it may prove to have been unique) gathering of poets, novelists, critics, editors, film-makers, etc., together with some 268 students (age range fourteen to sixty-eight) of writing and film, coming from forty-eight of the states for an intensive, almost round-the-clock series of classes, formal and informal, lectures, readings, panels and socializing. It was a wild time. Some of us are still recovering from it. The students were first-rate and consequently demanding. The staff was large, excellent, experienced, and various. The result was a no-nonsense directness about the art and craft of writing. The result is evident in these interviews, coming out of that particular community and that special context. What you have, then, is rare, more so than may be at once apparent. You have good and serious writers talking in their own distinctive voices about themselves, their works, their art and craft, with an almost absolute minimum of . . . guile and disguise (I wanted to say, and will, *bullshit*). Talking directly and candidly about what they know best and care most about.

Since some time has passed, in a sense these interviews are "outdated." Or are they? All the writers interviewed have been writing since the summer of 1970, and all are working now. They have continued, grown, and developed. Some have changed direction slightly. But the directness and integrity of their views is as valid now as it was then. For neither art nor craft are (as you'll see) entirely at the mercy of time and place. It was a time and a place that brought these artists together and made these conversations happen. And that is not likely to happen in the same way again. But I believe that there is much more here than a record of that time. Given the time and the place, there was a good chance for this kind of directness and, yes, honesty. Other things served to make the possible become more likely.

John Graham, of the University of Virginia, came down from Charlottesville with a couple of sound engineers and a lot of equipment, to record all the public events of the Conference and, if possible, to tape-record some talks with writers and visitors for a radio program, called "The Scholar's Bookshelf," which he has done for some years at Virginia. The public events were duly recorded. And, together with his expert colleague and engineer, Rod Collins, Graham managed to tape some 110 separate broadcasts, each a fifteen-minute segment, of usable, professional quality, during the twelve days of the Conference.

The interviews printed here are taken from some of those broadcasts, transcribed and edited for reading purposes. Not everyone, by any means, could be interviewed. A good number of good writers who were there simply couldn't find time in the hectic schedule. And, of course, there are others (even talks with some of the same people) which couldn't be used for this book for one reason and another, mostly because it would have been unmanageable as a book if everything were included. Where more than one of the separate, fifteen-minute interviews with an individual writer has been included here, I have presented them in the chronological sequence in which they were done; and the text is divided into numbered sections to distinguish the limits of each unit as a part of the whole.

First, I think it is important to remember that the idea for a *book* came later, after the fact of the taping and the radio program. That's part of the special context. The writer being interviewed came directly from a classroom or lecture hall to a small quiet room in the Hollins library. Graham and Collins were waiting with tape recorders and the clock which all three were fighting. The situation was somewhat relaxed in that it was to be a taping, not a live broadcast. As broadcast it might work and it might not, but the burden was on Graham and Collins. At the same time it was intense, if not tense, because of the clock, not only the exact time limit for the program, but also the fact that the writer had hurried from somewhere to do this and would very soon have to hurry off to another scheduled event or appointment. It was stolen time, and there was no time to waste.

After Graham gave a brief explanation of the method, they went to work. There was a brief music cue, Collins announced the program, then John Graham opened with a standard introduction—"My guest today is Manny Gumbo, poet and teacher and *blah-blah-blah,* and we are at the Hollins Conference in Creative Writing and Cinema." After which he began the conversation, working toward questions which might give the guest an opportunity to talk freely.

It was just that simple. But the success or failure of it as a program (and here, in this form, as an interview) depended on Graham's ability to get the guest writer talking easily, freely, and in his own distinctive voice and style.

Which is why I have put the interviews in sequence for this volume, as they were made, in the order they were done. For they tend to "build" a kind of structure, overall and individually. In one sense Graham appears at a slight disadvantage; for he was concerned with the individual fifteen-minute broadcast.

The last thing on his mind (if the notion ever occurred to him at all then) was how *he,* as interviewer, might appear in some printed, sequential version of the talks. His primary purpose, then, was to assume spontaneously any role or stance, any mask necessary to elicit from the writer a good conversational broadcast. He must be protean in hopes of allowing the writer to present himself honestly. So it is a sort of little drama in which the interviewer succeeds or fails, most often by establishing his own vulnerability. In that sense the sequence of interviews is *psychologically* interesting. And the sequence gives an outline of this drama. It's worth remembering that for each writer each interview was a separate occasion. Only Graham and Collins had any sense of the whole.

Another aspect of the character of the interviewer is significant, though not readily apparent in the broadcasts or transcripts. Unlike most interviewers, Graham knew his guests quite well. They knew him, and he had their professional respect, as a teacher, critic and writer himself. And he, too, was actively involved in the selfsame context of the Conference. He was one of them, a familiar member of the same brief and odd community. Ate his meals with the staff and students in Hollins' old octagonal dining room. Drank his drinks with them nightly in the dormitories and apartments. (Hear the record players? Sniff the sweet flat scent of pot?) The point? They knew him. The writers wanted to help to make the programs work. Graham is too good at the game and craft of the interview not to have used this, too, not to have been willing to take a stance of helplessness, from time to time, if that stance could cause the writer to speak up and speak well and honestly. The reader will notice, more than once, a simple and harmless device (among a number of similar ploys, some quite subtle), where Graham professes outright ignorance of some work or other by his guest. Not surprisingly the guest comes to his rescue, time and again. Out of friendship if nothing else. Of course, it isn't *true.* Graham had, in fact, read nearly everything by all his guests very carefully. He had done his homework and then some. But his little lies are always aimed at getting at the truth—the truth of his subject, getting his subject to talk truly in his true voice.

In this he succeeds admirably. Nothing can (or should) precisely represent the actual spoken voice of each writer here. I know their voices and can attest and affirm that I can hear their tones and styles, distinctive and precise, in every page of the transcript. But I believe that I would feel much the same way if I did not have the echo of the writer's voice in my mind. That is, I honestly believe that the character and the voice of each of these writers come across naturally, dramatically and with clarity, in the transcriptions of their conversational interviews. And I believe that this has interest and value, not just because they are talking openly about what they know best, minding their own business without apologies, but because, as American writers, they are each and all profoundly concerned in their work with the use, abuse, the energy and limits of the *spoken language,* the living and changing lingo which, even in our highest rhetorical flights and fancies, gives American writing, our kind of English, a special and an influential character.

To put it another way, I believe that the *styles of speaking* of all these artists, when, as here, they are speaking easily, openly, honestly and out of their true vocation, are a valid representation of their characters and creativity.

For those interested (as, to a degree, all readers of interviews must be) in character, in "personality," it's there. But not at the expense of or separate from the art and craft practiced by the speakers.

I know of very few interviews about which I could say this—that they are very true.

Another (and final) truth I'd like to mention. Some, a goodly company, of these writers are very well known, sufficiently so that their interviews could be legitimately included in an all-star collection of literary celebrities. Others, younger and newer or, at the moment, out of the public spotlight, are not so well known. It pleases me to note that the interviews are of an even quality, that the value of interest, the extent of the artist's commitment to his vocation is not a factor of fame or fashion. It seems to me that the interviews are equally interesting in different ways. And so it seems to me that this gathering, coming from a brief time of community enjoyed by a variety of writers, of different ages and at different stages, is an accurate reflection of the larger community of American writing. Which is not, finally, a marketplace or a stockmarket and not a horse race or a track meet, but a community (of the dead as well as the living) of gifted, dedicated, intelligent, talented individuals, each and all engaged with, captured by the joys and pains of a lonely craft hard to learn in a lifetime, and an art worthy of all craftiness and a lifetime's dedication.

GEORGE GARRETT

Contents

The Writer's Voice

R.V. Cassill

BIOGRAPHICAL

Born: 17 May 1919 in Cedar Falls, Iowa.
Education: B.A. Iowa 1939, M.A. Iowa 1947.
Occupational: At this time he is Professor of English at Brown University. Has done many things, but chiefly he has been a teacher/writer, a pioneer literally in the creation of that professional category, serving at the Iowa Writers' Workshop 1948–1952, 1960–1966. He has held posts elsewhere, including Purdue. He is founder and, until his recent retirement, long-time president of the Associated Writing Programs.
Books: Novels—*Eagle on the Coin* (1950), *Dormitory Women* (1954), *The Left Bank of Desire* (1955), *The Wound of Love* (1956), *Clem Anderson* (1961), *Pretty Leslie* (1963), *The President* (1964), *La Vie Passionnée of Rodney Buckthorne* (1968), *Dr. Cobb's Game* (1970); short story collections—*Fifteen by Three* (with Herbert Gold and James Hall, 1957), *The Happy Marriage and Other Stories* (1966); essays—*An Iron Time* (1969); text and anthology—*Writing Fiction* (1963); editor of *Intro* (vols. 1–4, 1967–1971).

Nobody, except Cassill himself, knows exactly how many novels he has written or under how many names; because way back he wrote a lot of original paperbacks, to pay the bills and keep his basic craft exercised.

He regularly has written important criticism for a variety of publications including *The New York Times, Book Week, Chicago Sun Times,* etc.

An accomplished artist, he has had successful gallery shows of his paintings and drawings.

SNAPSHOT

No *way* to do Verlin any justice even here in the context of these quick blurry personal impressions.

Except that he hates the word, I'd call him the *Dean* of us. Maybe the *coach*, except Verlin's a playing coach and a top performer.

He's a good man, passionate in all his work, a tough but merciful judge, a generous *giver* of all he's got to his work, to students, to others.

Like his own Dr. Cobb, he knows a lot about things of the dark, powers of darkness. It's some solace that he's not afraid of what he knows.

I see him as good-looking in an honorably rugged, weatherbeaten way, wearing a wealth of dark hair, shaggy whether cropped or cut long. He seems not so much casual (even in a tuxedo, I guess) as rumpled, suit and skin. His deep voice is always a surprise; his style of talking—real sentences which loop into complex grammatical shapes, then unsnarl, like a rodeo lariat—astonishes, then is just right.

He's got a celebrated temper which will scare the wits out of the average and turn any bully into a counterpuncher. But it's reserved for the phony, duplicitous, hypocritical, and for responsible wickedness.

He's also the possessor of perennially youthful, almost boyish charm, warmth, enthusiasm, energy.

He's a patient master-teacher.

As poet, novelist, story writer, *as writer,* he's the complete pro in every detail. Not the cliché "old pro," though. He never stops learning and growing.

Best I can do is give him a salute (and mean it) when he goes by.

I. *I mean, there's no use in technique unless it contributes somewhat to the meaning of the novel.*

GRAHAM: I have in front of me a rather flashy paperback with the not enigmatic title, but questionable title of *La Vie Passionnée of Rodney Buckthorne.* I'm afraid I'm going to start with the obvious now, Verlin: Who? Why?

CASSILL: Why? Well, for years one of the things that amused me when I spent time in France, was that all melodramatic, sensational, cheap and flashy biographies were apt to bear the title *La Vie Passionnée* of somebody—*La Vie Passionnée of Pablo Picasso, La Vie Passionnée of Rabelais, La Vie Passionnée of Manolete the Bullfighter* and so on. And for years I thought that I would some day write an autobiography with the title *La Vie Passionnée of Wimpy Cassill.* When I was a pre-teen boy I was called Wimpy, for reasons I won't go into here. And then I put this novel together, it seemed to me there was an odd, funny discrepancy between the pretense of *La Vie Passionnée* and the rather ridiculous name of my hero, Rodney Buckthorne. It seemed to me that kind of joke title set the tone for the book as a whole. It's an artificial comedy, and I hope the title indicates that and leads off strongly suggesting what it's going to be.

GRAHAM: It is a very funny novel. I see it as a rather sharply critical novel of a certain type and certain themes and beliefs. But one thing that I feel very strongly about the novel, now that, along with the satire, I get a clear sense of your fondness for all of your characters, even the bad ones in their foolishness. Is this a fair reading? I see a dry smile—I am being too . . . ?

CASSILL: I am about to respond professorially and say "Yes and No." That the young man, Nickie, is just a bad guy.

GRAHAM: And yet you rather like his raw energy.

CASSILL: I'm amused by it. Oh, yes, I find this fascinating. It's colorful, it's constantly surprising.

GRAHAM: Isn't he one of a long tradition of rather pleasant, not really terribly clever con men?

CASSILL: He's a con man. I think the end of his con, though, is rather deadly.

GRAHAM: All right, what is the title of that last chapter? "The End of the World"? This great staged happening with damned mattresses and old tires . . .

CASSILL: . . . hung all over this old abandoned hotel that's been turned into a flophouse, and it's Nickie's great idea to make it a museum without sending the people away who are using it as a flophouse. He simply moves his art in with them. This is, of course, an exaggeration, a satirical comment on some of the tendencies in art and art promotion that we've seen in the last few years in this country.

GRAHAM: Rodney Buckthorne, I can remember any number of the movements that this aging professor was involved in in the thirties, and he, is he not, is a kind of predecessor of Nickie?

CASSILL: Exactly. . . .

GRAHAM: He's on the edge of things.

CASSILL: But the point of the whole novel is that though Rodney is a con man—an extremist running off in many directions, marrying many women—that there's something redeeming about his whole career. He is a quixotic character, and Quixote is the great hero of all Western romance. He's the fool and believes in myths and illusions, but he's a hero.

GRAHAM: He's a mythmaker about every one he gets near.

CASSILL: And Buckthorne constantly misinterprets things, over-interprets all sorts of signals from his environment. But then Nickie is a counterfeit of this. He espouses the same causes—art, love, political reform and so on—but there's no redeeming ennobling excess of goodwill about Nickie, as there is about Buckthorne.

GRAHAM: Vivian is a very engaging character.

CASSILL: She's a good girl and he treats her very, very shabbily.

GRAHAM: Shallowly, too!

CASSILL: Yes, well, the egocentricity of Nickie, the juvenile selfishness here, is in definite exaggerated contrast with the sort of boundless generosity that Buckthorne feels, at any rate, whether he's able to do anything about it or not.

GRAHAM: Buckthorne does genuinely try to help people. He may be a bungler, but there's a lack of self-interest in him at times.

CASSILL: When he deserts his wife, his wife and a friend—female —are talking this over. This is early in the book. The wife is unhappy about being deserted, but in some way she understands. And she says to her friend, "Women will always respond to Buckthorne." And the friend says, "I don't see why." And the wife says, "Because he cares about us." Meaning about women, and he does.

GRAHAM: I may be making problems for myself here, but to

grab at terminology very quickly, Verlin, it's a realistic novel in many ways, and yet we have the mysterious landlady we never meet directly, and we see her in the opening chapter, and then we see her in the closing chapter, manufactured, if you will, in Rodney's imagination. But there is this web, then, of mystery over the whole thing. Did you see that as . . . as almost a technical problem?

CASSILL: Technical problems and technical devices should be part of the meaning of the thing. I mean there's no use in technique unless it contributes somewhat to the meaning of the novel. I said this was an artificial comedy, and part of the device or trick, if you will, is to keep old Miss Brule out of sight.

GRAHAM: I started to believe in her, you see, and so I get a little angry. . . .

CASSILL: She is, in many ways, a creation of Rodney's imagination. He lives in her apartment, he snoops around and reads her books and plays her records, looks at the photograph albums. She becomes very real to him, and in a very peculiar sense he falls in love with her. She's the great love of his life, as long as he never lays eyes on her. And the trick there is to show how the imagination works. And I said it a while ago, he's a quixotic hero, whatever his stature may be. This is his mold. He's a hero of the imagination. This again distinguishes him from Nickie. Rodney lives by the imagination.

GRAHAM: Rodney is not really interested in money. He's going to make do someway. But Nickie's whole pursuit of the foundations, the rich foolish widow who may fund this grotesque happening where New York's finest are supposed to come in with their horses to break it up—that is probably the most chaotic scene I've read in any novel.

CASSILL: I pull out the stops. I started from what I read in the newspapers and multiplied by three, in all cases, for that final chaos. But back to Rodney's imagination about women—another technical device of the book is to keep suggesting that this very beautiful young woman and the obviously aged Miss Brule may be the same person, sort of creeping back in different disguises. The directional mind rejects this, and properly so; so that the technical problem is to adjust the language so one never says definitely that this is so, but keeps it at the level of "What if it were so?" When you write about magic or the supernatural, it seems to me that the obligation on the writer is to say to himself, the only magic I can really rely on is the magic of the writing itself. I can't make the reader believe that something happened by extranatural causes, but I can write in a way that will enchant him, that will overcome his rational objections.

GRAHAM: Not to switch too sharply from Rodney Buckthorne, but one of the writers here tells me that a book of yours that I've really got to read is *Clem Anderson*. What's that all about? He was so enthusiastic about *Clem Anderson*.

CASSILL: It's a novel about a writer—a very, very long novel, and I think a rich one. It intends to show how writers grow in their role, how they gather up their past and make something of it, and what it costs them to do this. In a very, very loose sense, the figure of Clem Anderson is modeled on Dylan Thomas. Clem Anderson is an American, but starting from a small-town background, he goes up like a rocket, and consumes himself in the process, burns himself out dead and dry as he moves.

II. *I think we are at the end of an age, and the magicians have always appeared at the ends of ages.*

GRAHAM: I understand, Verlin, that you're in print with a new novel. Is it that close to home?

CASSILL: Yes, it is. I finished it last fall and it'll be published in this coming October [1970]. I'm at a stage now where the work's all done. I'm simply waiting for the returns.

GRAHAM: They're not going to annoy you with any more page proofs or anything?

CASSILL: That's all done. Everybody's working now on promoting the book. It's called *Dr. Cobb's Game.* "Game" is an ambiguous word, a simple one, referring to his style of life and also his intervention in power.

GRAHAM: Is he another con man that you have written on before, in *Rodney Buckthorne?*

CASSILL: Not exactly. For one thing, he's developed realistically, and he is a man who moves in a realistic social situation. A doctor, who dabbles in magic. It's not exactly my version of the Faust legend. But here the general large thematic concerns of the book are the nature of power in the modern state, the modern collective society, and the resources that an extraordinary and gifted individual may bring to bear on these mechanisms of power.

GRAHAM: I don't mean to be cheap in this remark, but it sounds incredibly "relevant"; as we're all now asking ourselves how can we effect changes in public policy.

CASSILL: And I think many of us have the sense that the machinery of the state and the machinery of modern technology have run wild. They've got beyond human control altogether, and at times like this historically it is true that belief in magic, or reliance on magic, or a search for magical, nonscientific means as an alternative have been very, very popular.

GRAHAM: The Astrology crises, which I just can't take in. I accept your historical. . . .

CASSILL: This is true. I have really done a good bit of reading about magic, and I think we are at the end of an age, and the magicians have always appeared at the ends of ages. The cults of magic, the groups that define their coherence, their relation to each other, in magical terms, appear when the mechanisms of society get out of control, and when they become hostile.

GRAHAM: A kind of despair of rationality?

CASSILL: Yes, it's the thing that succeeds despair. Hope begins to re-form, and it re-forms along magic lines. Magic very often is a return to knowledges and styles of life that have been abandoned while the civilization was flourishing and growing up. But when the civilization drys and rots, people search around, sometimes rather wildly, for those old ways of being human. And that's what Dr. Cobb, the main character in the novel. . . .

GRAHAM: It's a little like a deathbed repentance, then, isn't it?

CASSILL: Except that it starts with a sort of presumption of the death of an age. He's, in a way, a kind of Noah, seeking a new world, and I might say—if this sounds cheap, let it sound cheap —but he goes in his search for renewal of power where people have always gone, through magic, associations of magic, to sex. I mean sex is the origin of all religious rites. Somewhere in the

relationships are found the origin of the forms that develop
into religion, that develop into moral codes, and so on. So his
sexual explorations, and his guesses, and his experiments—some
of which are ruthless and drastic and eventually disastrous—
are all part of this attempt to find a way out of a collapsing
general situation.

GRAHAM: With *La Vie Passionnée of Rodney Buckthorne,*
sexual magic there was chaotic and mocked, really, was it
not? Is this true with *Dr. Cobb's Game?*

CASSILL: No, no, the central ideas are probably the same, but
not intentionally. I say they're probably the same because
they're my ideas. They would naturally be the same from book
to book. But *La Vie Passionnée of Rodney Buckthorne* is an
artificial comedy. It's treated satirically and lightly, I hope, in
places. In the new novel, it's straight-on. And although it has
comic passages, it's intended as a massive, serious, and realistic
novel. And the magic thing is not affirmed by the novel. We're
not affirming that he has magic powers, but that he's seeking
for life-styles, new means of intervening in the power struggles
of the world by magical means. He's trying to find a way, and
this is dead serious for him. He is a character represented as
someone who walks among us, a man in a real situation.

GRAHAM: It is laid in America?

CASSILL: It's partly laid in America; it starts in America. But
a great deal of the action takes place in England, and the
implications are global. The story is narrated by a man who
works for an American think-tank, a kind of intelligence-
gathering agency; and he's watching this man, wondering what's
happening, as he sees some of the effects on figures in prominent
political positions, and knows that they must have a cause
somewhere, and begins to examine further to see who this man
is who seems to be sending out the waves. That's a technical
device.

GRAHAM: Who tells the story?

CASSILL: The American intelligence man.

GRAHAM: So his sense of discovery then is ours, and his sense of confusion and mystery.

CASSILL: Yes, that provides some of the suspense of the telling. As he learns more and more, the reader learns more and more.

GRAHAM: In talking about *Dr. Cobb's Game,* my experience with your work, in contrast to a great number of novels I've been reading lately, indicates you want your novels to open out into a public world, don't you? I mean, you're not talking about, you're not essentially interested in, the sort of one-to-one relationship of a grating marriage, let's say, or a son's relation with his father. You're more interested in society at large.

CASSILL: The novels have moved in that direction, partly intentionally, partly because one's lifetime is not enough to do everything that one has in mind. I've written quite a few novels and a great many short stories, and many of them have been about domestic situations. It's just that now, probably sharing the overwhelming public concerns that dominate so much of our life, I've tried to open the domestic out into the public. The new novel is not searchingly psychological; but it does examine the minute, particular night minds of some of the characters and tries to make some correlation between those and the irrationality of society and the technological world all around us.

GRAHAM: I'm not—not for a minute—suggesting from what you told me that you are writing a polemic, but with your own experience as a novelist, and with your experience teaching creative writing, is it true that younger writers are thrusting more towards the polemic, toward the manifesto, draining off some of their creative energies for poetry and what you and I might call nonargumentative fiction?

CASSILL: I don't know. I suppose we all go with the spirit of our times. And we know that there is a great deal of political argument in the world, and perhaps in some strange way, I'm doing what everybody else is doing, in turning directly to an examination of magic in this new novel. This wasn't quite a conscious decision. I just felt it was there, something that was looming, as a kind of shadow, of considerable importance and interest to me. And as I was working on the novel, not before, I began to be aware of more and more interest, as you put it a while ago, in astrology and magic.

GRAHAM: What you just said is interesting in connection with your book *Writing Fiction,* where, by way of encouragement for the young writer, you are insisting that fiction must be a voyage of discovery for that young writer and—are you not saying that this last novel of yours, *Dr. Cobb's Game,* was something of a voyage of discovery for you?

CASSILL: Oh, sure it was. I think this happens with each novel. As I said, I have written a great deal, and I never knew when I started a novel quite where I was going to end up. I may have known where the story would end, but I didn't know what dimensions and colors it would accumulate as it went along.

GRAHAM: Does writing fiction get easier?

CASSILL: No, it doesn't get easier.

GRAHAM: You still sweat?

CASSILL: Yes. You sweat about different things. You clear up certain problems that made you sweat once upon a time, but this tends rather to get you in deeper waters, so you sweat about harder problems as you get over the easier. I don't think it gets easier at all.

GRAHAM: Three o'clock in the morning is still the grim hour when you can't move it?

CASSILL: Sure. I don't write at night, though everybody has his own peculiarities there. I write in the morning when I'm still groggy—my mind is livelier.

William Peden

BIOGRAPHICAL

Born: 22 March 1913 in New York City.
Education: Both undergraduate and graduate study at the University of Virginia; received his Ph.D. there in 1942.
Occupational: Has taught at Virginia, Maryland, and Missouri. Since 1946 has been on faculty of the University of Missouri where he is Professor of English. He was Director of the University of Missouri Press from 1958 to 1962; regular critic and book reviewer for *The New York Times Book Review, Saturday Review,* and the *Virginia Quarterly.*
Books: Short stories—*Night in Funland* (1968); novel—*Twilight at Monticello* (1973); historical studies and editions—*Some Aspects of Jefferson Bibliography* (with Adrienne Koch, 1942), *Life and Selected Writings of Thomas Jefferson* (with Adrienne Koch, 1944), *Selected Writings of John and John Quincy Adams* (1946), *Increase Mather—Testimony Against Profane Customs* (1953), *Thomas Jefferson—Notes on the State of Virginia* (1954), *Collected Stories of Hubert Crackanthorpe* (1969); texts and anthologies—*Twenty-nine Stories* (1960), *The American Short Story* (1964), *Short Fiction: Shape and Substance* (1971), *Golden Shore: Great Short Stories Selected for Young Readers* (1967).

SNAPSHOT

People, friends and strangers alike, tend to call him "courtly." And they have a point. He's soft-voiced, a gentleman by any

13

measure, old or new, exemplary in manners, good manners that seem to *mean* something, not idle gestures thereof, very neat and trim in bearing and dress. But Bill Peden has got the body, and with that the spirit and confidence, of a professional fighter who has kept himself in shape. And so he has, though without making a big thing about it. He's also possessed of the patience of a distance runner (which he was), who knows pains by name and hurts by heart, but has learned long since to keep them to himself.

For all this and more, he is one of America's great teachers. Has lost track of how many books his many students have published. And he is a beautifully compassionate man. The darkness, chaos, absurdity and anarchy of flesh and spirit, which you can find in full measure in his short stories, prove he's earned a lion's share of wound stripes and ribbons. But he'd never wear his medals. He carries the weight of courage, of unbroken integrity, with a casual modesty (like a coat lightly over one arm) which manages a ritual camouflaging of both. And that is pure *style*.

He's one of the few living men I know whom Queen Elizabeth I would have liked and understood at first sight.

I. *Generally speaking, I think my characters are very nice people who lead very unhappy lives.*

GRAHAM: William Peden is the author of *Night in Funland and Other Stories*. Now this was issued in 1968, wasn't it, Bill? This is a good time for me to catch Professor Peden and talk a little bit about some of his stories. In general, Bill, I do want to say the stories were shaking stories, really. I got turned in on myself a little bit. As you and I were talking the other night, we've got sort of two worlds that we've got to learn how to read: the world of actuality perhaps, and the world of language. And it seems to me you've produced here a number of stories about people who don't know when they're misreading the world of actuality. They may be concerned about the same thing, but from such different points of view that I find the stories are disturbing.

Could you talk with me a little bit about one aspect of technique that I'm very interested in, and I've always wanted to get hold of a short story writer and ask him about this. I'm thinking about the second story, "Wherefore Art Thou Romeo?" It's not a long story at all, but I think with the compression through allusion and metaphor, what you wind up doing is expanding that story out into the past, and into a future that's just going to get bleaker. You refer to Dylan Thomas from the past, and this poor dog, which is dying—it's a grim smelly beast —but we get flashback and anticipation. It's a little fifteen-page story, but yet we get a much bigger story than that in Time. I'm not talking about depth, now. Is this a conscious process, your use of metaphor to compress, to get allusion, and—through metaphor and analogy—to get other worlds within the world that you're directly talking about?

PEDEN: I'm not sure that it's a matter of metaphor. It is true that that particular story is very compressed actually in chronological time. The story concerns two or three hours in the life of what I consider a rather attractive but hopelessly alcoholic woman, married to a rather pedantic . . .

GRAHAM: Self-centered man.

PEDEN: Kind of a jackass intellectual. But the main focus, I think, in the story is not on those three or four hours of elapsed time, where very little actually happens, externally, in the story. The husband and wife have lunch; the husband goes off to a series of lectures on contemporary literature; the wife is left alone; she drinks too much. She's unhappy in a great many ways. She had met the poet Dylan Thomas some years ago on one of his tours of America, and had had a brief coming-together with him, which is far more meaningful to her than her present life with her husband. And throughout the story I have tried, maybe not consciously, to counterpoint or contrast two different kinds of reality. And the reality of the past is much more real, much more vital, to the woman than the actual, drab, unresolved blankness of her days. This curious thing you mention, the dog, is the one . . .

GRAHAM: You do some terrifying things with animals. I'm going to come back to this.

PEDEN: I've always been interested in animals, dogs and horses particularly; and just as a purely personal statement I would say that the dog is the only character in the story that is based on actual experience and observation. To me he exists first of all as a dog in the story. He's simply a sick, objectionable dog who's lived too long; and on a kind of semi-symbolic, if you wish, level, he suggests something about the whole useless-ness of the woman's life. It's not a pleasant story, although I am always surprised at the criticisms made of the story. The woman is seen by a good many people to be a thoroughly un-desirable, objectionable character.

GRAHAM: Oh, I didn't get this. Even her husband is attracted to her, he touches her during the meal.

PEDEN: She's really a very nice person, who, unfortunately, is married to the wrong man. She has a drab life, but I conceived of her as essentially very decent, but an unhappy, wasted kind of person. But two or three critics have had words that I cannot repeat here. And that saddens me a little. I thought she was a nice person. I really liked the dog, too. But it is, looking back on it, a rather drab story, I'm afraid.

GRAHAM: Could we shift a little bit, following a lead you've given, to this one other story, "The White Shell Road"? A man and a woman are having an affair in a motel. I think they're shallow people, both of them, and yet they're not bad people; they're rather simply at cross purposes. They remember, for instance, the island they both went to with their families, as children. But they remember it in such a different way that we can see—can we not?—from that past, that their future is at best very limited?

PEDEN: They are, they are shallow people. This must say something about my own attitude, I guess, towards people. If I were to attempt to reconstruct my own attitudes in terms of some of my stories, I'd really be faced with a dilemma; because a good many of my stories—I guess the majority of my stories— are concerned with people who are unhappy rather than happy, or unsuccessful rather than successful.

GRAHAM: But I don't see . . . basically they're not bad people.

PEDEN: I don't think there are many bad people in my stories. There are one or two contemptible people, I think, in the story, "The Gunner and the Ape-Man," which is as close, I guess, to a melodramatic story as I ever wrote. There is a character who, I believe, is the "I," the *persona,* the narrator of the story, who simply sits by and watches his friend . . .

GRAHAM: This gross fat man . . .

PEDEN: Very gross fat man commit a kind of atrocity. But he is the only, I think, really despicable character whom I have ever created. Generally speaking, I think my characters are very nice people who lead very unhappy lives.

GRAHAM: I do think from my reading of these stories in *Night in Funland,* I do think you like your people. I would want to hold one story in reserve, though, and that's "The Pilgrims"— these two young instructors and the wife. May I ask why that title, which is driving me wild? I see these people as cripples, incompetents, not really knowing how to have any fun. I don't think they really understand their relationships with each other at all. We've got a grim, dying banty rooster in there, that is also rather funny, mind you—and this dog with the bad leg. Why do you call this "The Pilgrims," and aren't these people that we almost don't need to know?

PEDEN: Well, the title is used ironically. The story, as you said, is about a few hours in the lives of two graduate students and the wife of one of them, who is, in a certain way, the mistress of the other one. They're not very pleasant people, and they do go on a kind of pilgrimage that day. They have won a dog and a bantam rooster at a raffle the night before and waking up in the cold light of day . . .

GRAHAM: It was a dreadful morning.

PEDEN: They want to get rid of the rooster. And they take the rooster out to a countryman to try to get rid of the rooster, and that is the extent of the pilgrimage. So the title is ironic. Actually, this is a very interesting thing, and a very curious thing, in a way. The story was based on a story that a friend of mine had told me, something that had actually happened. That is, a couple and a friend had won a rooster at a raffle—at some kind of party—that's the only factual thing in the story. And as the story was told me, and as I began thinking it over before I began writing it, it was essentially a humorous sort of thing. And as I wrote it, I thought it was basically humorous and to a certain degree burlesque. Not until I reread the story a few weeks ago did I realize that it's really a rather distasteful group, a rather unpleasant group of people. This is one of the hazards that you face when you write. Actually, although I have talked about the business of being so "knowledgeable about your craft"—and I think I am that—you don't really see what you've done until some months have gone past, after the thing is published. There's a difference between reading something in manuscript and then seeing it in cold type some months afterwards, and I'm sometimes surprised. Basically, I think I'm a brotherly, optimistic person—I'm surprised at the depth of the pessimism in some of the stories I've written, particularly in that story "The Pilgrims." It is, I think, really a rather decadent group of people.

Margaret Sayers Peden

BIOGRAPHICAL

Born: 10 May 1927 in West Plains, Missouri.
Education: B.A. University of Missouri 1948, M.A. Missouri 1963, Ph.D. Missouri 1966.
Occupational: Associate Professor of Spanish at the University of Missouri.
Books: Translations—*The Norther* (novel by Emilio Carballido, 1968), *The Golden Thread and Other Plays* (plays by Emilio Carballido, 1970); *Paper Flowers* (play by Egon Wolff, 1971); *The Siren and the Seashell* (with Lysander Kemp, essays by Octavio Paz, 1972). Forthcoming: a collection of short stories by Horacio Quiroga; a biographical and critical study of Emilio Carballido.

Has had articles and translations in such magazines as *La palabra y el hombre, Hispania, Mundus Artium, Tri-Quarterly, Modern Drama, Latin American Theatre Review, Modern Language Journal, Journal of Modern Literature.*

SNAPSHOT

Petch Peden is tall, slender, very graceful. A beautiful woman whose American Indian heritage (she is part Cherokee) shows itself in the fine angles of her facial bones, in a calm gravity. Her Spanish is easy, fluent and impeccable; and she can wear the bold Latin colors and jewelry without affectation. Deeply sympathetic with the contemporary writers of Latin America, she has dedicated herself to the task of translating their work into our own language and idiom. It's true, she seems to be too good-looking to be a scholar, a critic, a creative translator, but she is all three brightly and with style. She is also, without the least conflict of roles, the wife of William Peden.

I. *If you are a writer, you're something of a hambone. You're an actor, you want to hold the stage as long as you possibly can; and so you go on madly describing things that you could do without.*

GRAHAM: I have before me a very handsome copy of *The Norther,* by Emilio Carballido. It's a short novel that Professor Peden has translated, and translated, I might note, as an English reader, very well indeed. But why don't I know more about Mexican literature? I am interested, and I've read a lot of French literature, a lot of German literature, I'm not a boy any longer. Now, why?

PEDEN: Why not Mexico?

GRAHAM: Why an absolute blind spot?

PEDEN: Well, I think the first thing I'd do is probably not separate Mexico from Latin America. I tend to think of Latin American literature. And my first reply is a very happy one, from my point of view, and that is, you're going to hear a great deal about Latin American literature, because something absolutely exciting and fabulous is happening in Latin American literature. There are lots of . . . I can go into reasons if you want to.

GRAHAM: I wish you would, really, because I'm very curious about this blockage of mine.

PEDEN: The fact is that it just suddenly exploded, as if there were a marvelously delicious infection going around.

GRAHAM: Is Borges giving this? Are people getting confidence from this?

PEDEN: Borges is an icebreaker, a pathmaker, pathfinder. Borges is discovered, and then someone considers the possibility that there might be another writer in Latin America. And on top of that, Latin America's writers are just getting better. It's as simple as that. I think probably the simplest statement is that Latin Americans have been too busy getting themselves settled to have time to write.

GRAHAM: Is it a matter that a bright young man is almost shanghaied into political thought rather than aesthetic activity?

PEDEN: Actually, it's almost the opposite. There's always been a tremendous affinity for literature among the aristocracy, but, you see, the aristocracy has traditionally been extremely small in proportion to the population in general. One of the things that's happened in this century is that there's beginning to be a reading public in Latin America.

GRAHAM: You mean just a rising base of literacy gives a man reason to write?

PEDEN: That's one thing. Another thing is that Latin America is undergoing what some writers tend to call "a crisis of identity." Instead of thinking that Spain is really their home, really their culture, in this century different countries at different times begin to think, "No, maybe I'm an Argentine, whatever that is." They start investigating, "Well, what does it mean to be an Argentine?"

GRAHAM: This is curious, because in a way, this is a hopefully fruitful dilemma that the black writer is going through in America.

PEDEN: Yes, I think maybe there is an analogy there. I shouldn't be surprised. What the Argentine wants to know is who he is; in fact there is a term in Spanish that translates roughly as "what are these beings," "what is my being?" What am I, by being a Mexican? Am I a Spaniard? Is that my heritage? Am I Indian, is that my heritage? And it's had a very salutary effect upon the literature because people have turned inward upon their own cultures.

GRAHAM: Certainly the Mexicans have had an enormous sense of identity in terms of plastic arts—painting and sculpture.

PEDEN: Yes, but that comes from underneath. I mean that comes from the people, that was there with the Mayas and the Aztecs. You think of Aztec sculpture, for instance, their buildings. They had the sense of texture and feeling. But literature has been imposed upon them from above, from the Spanish aristocracy.

GRAHAM: They're always trying to imitate that literature.

PEDEN: That's right, and that's what's been wrong, I think, with a lot of what's been written. And after they broke away from the Spanish in their wars for freedom—literal freedom from—then instead of worrying about who they were, they turned to the French. And for a while, oh, everything was French. The good families sent their children abroad. In the meantime, there's absolutely nothing going on in literature in that country, because everyone tends to think of themselves in terms of Europe. That's what changes, you see, in this century. And, as I say, they turn in upon themselves, they let themselves, if you will, *become* themselves. Instead of an imitative culture they begin to have their own.

GRAHAM: When you say, in this century, was there a crisis point on this?

PEDEN: Take the case of Mexico, which is perhaps one of the simplest things. It is indeed the country that I know, that I feel most at home in talking about. I know it best. We tend to forget that they're in a bloody, messy revolution from 1910 through 1920; they don't have political stability until the thirties. So the result is you don't have any literature. That, coupled with the isolation that the Second World War brought about—they had to depend upon themselves for printing which they hadn't done before.

GRAHAM: You mean the raw technical matter then, of printing presses in Mexico, is a serious matter?

PEDEN: That was one of the things.

GRAHAM: What about periodicals—fairly serious periodicals—is this an outlet for a Mexican writer now?

PEDEN: They're great lovers of the little magazine. They love literature, they really do. It's such a different kind of thing from our culture. Businessmen love poetry. They write poetry. The statesmen tend to be literary people. Almost every famous Latin American writer has at one time been in some embassy. So there's a great respect.

GRAHAM: There's not the sort of schizophrenia that we have, if you're an engineer, you cannot possibly be a poet also?

PEDEN: Absolutely not! Almost every Latin man who has any education is a poet.

GRAHAM: Does this expand out into music and painting? I mean, is this an organic kind of thing?

PEDEN: I think so, because it is not unmanly to be artistic.

GRAHAM: I think probably we're still hung up on that stage very much.

PEDEN: And it's a shame. It's sad and tragic.

GRAHAM: I mean, Archibald MacLeish was kind of a freak almost in American political or government service.

PEDEN: But there are any number of Mexicans who are good poets, who are doctors. I just translated a play by a Chilean who's a chemical engineer, and he's a darn good dramatist. And this is not the exception.

GRAHAM: You have for a long time responded very warmly to that integration of life, and it's a delightful piece of new information for me.

PEDEN: They're exciting people. They have incredible potential, because they do have this openness about literature, this receptivity. So that it seems to me that as the level of the reading interest rises to meet what's there for them, there's going to be a tremendous audience for the arts. Maybe one thing contributes to another, maybe that's why there are more good writers. But most of it is caused by an interest in exploring who they are, rather than being imitative. My husband did an article, read a paper recently at an international James Joyce symposium about the influence of James Joyce on Latin Americans.

GRAHAM: They're choosing the right people to be influenced by if they're going to Joyce.

PEDEN: They are, they are. And they're reading other people, but they're not imitating anymore. In other words, in order to be arty or to be literate, they don't have to do so in the French manner now, as they did at the turn of the century. Indeed that's looked upon with disfavor. So, as a result, you've got people who are doing these exciting things. I don't know whether that's the complete explanation or not, but the fact is that something "untoward" is happening in Latin America.

GRAHAM: It sounds as if everything is working together at once.

PEDEN: It is, it is, and one would think "Renaissance," but that's not the correct term, because there's never been anything to redo. It's the first time. Oh! The point I intended to make— I tripped myself up by talking too much—the point that my husband made in that paper on Joyce is that for the first time this is an original literature. And, of course, I think if you don't have an original literature, you don't have a good literature. So that's why perhaps Latin American literature hasn't been internationally known. And your mention of Borges. He's undoubtedly the first. But you know, it's an interesting thing about our perception of Borges. We did not get that from Latin America. We picked that up from France.

GRAHAM: Which again indicates that there's a very high wall for the direct flow, and that's one thing I wanted to ask you about. I see that this novel, *The Norther,* which you have translated, was published by the University of Texas Press. In its "Texas PanAmerican Series." Can you tell me a little about that series, because I will never be the audience for Spanish. What are you people going to translate for me?

PEDEN: That's exactly what I think the value of translation is. I get a little defensive at times because, in academic circles, translation is seen as something you do with documents, you know, with your left hand. But I'm so pleased that Texas has gone out on a limb, really, to sponsor this sort of thing. The purpose of the PanAmerican Series is precisely this—to introduce Latin American writers to an English-speaking audience.

GRAHAM: Petch, I read *The Norther* today and enjoyed it very much. It's got a kind of control in it. The blocking, I think, on the novel is very exciting as points of view shifted. It's a very simple story, wouldn't you say, basically?

PEDEN: Very simple. Actually this was one of the things that attracted me about it, its simplicity. And the fact that you picked up the word "control" is very interesting to me, because that's exactly the right term in regard to the novel. It's a controlled novel.

GRAHAM: We've got an old story, really, of a clearly very attractive widow who falls in with a very young, seventeen-year-old boy. They have what I guess should be called an affair, he's a kept kid.

PEDEN: Not a pretty situation.

GRAHAM: Not pretty, and one of the things that interested me was Isabel's self-awareness. What is handled so well in the novel is her relationship to the cleaning women. There's a succession of cleaning women. She doesn't want to be judged. She doesn't want to put a name on the affair.

PEDEN: Then she would have to realize herself what is happening.

GRAHAM: And yet she doesn't have any moral sense about this, does she? It's more of a social thing. Or is it even that?

PEDEN: Is it that she wants to hold off time somehow, by not naming things? If you name things, you place yourself in time, and it seems to me that that's the thing she's trying to hold back —time.

GRAHAM: She talks about grabbing a rope at some point, and this boy is the rope that will keep her from falling into the well of time.

PEDEN: Does the boy strike you as being unpleasant or mercenary?

GRAHAM: Now the word I want is "unformed." He is not very likable, and I'm not going to argue he's got a great potential. But I understand from the very useful introduction that you offered that the author is upset because of at least one critic noting a clear homosexual line or potential in this.

PEDEN: Potential.

GRAHAM: But I want the word "unformed" here, because I don't think he knows yet. He's not set, and I think that's the whole argument of the novel, isn't it, that the boy's not set?

PEDEN: What you did not mention, and it is a necessary part of our talk about what's in the novel, is that there is a third leg of the triangle.

GRAHAM: And a formidable one.

PEDEN: Perhaps the most interesting character in the whole novel, I think. Max is his name. He's just one of those things that comes in and out of a life, and changes a lot, without any plan. He's a fascinating character to me. Did you—did you notice or enjoy what he had done with the time sequence in the alternating chapters?

GRAHAM: Yes, that's rather what I think I mean by "control." The blocking is not as artificial as I thought it was at first. The thing that impressed me was—and this is why I want, I think, to go to Aristeo as "unformed." The widow goes to the movies. That's where she heads all the time; that's her reality. But Aristeo is excited by the sea. He wants to move around the town. He has not eaten in very many restaurants. He's experiencing things. I mean, for you and me to go and have a soda at Howard Johnson's is zero. For my four-year-old daughter it's just wildly exciting. And that's where Aristeo is, almost.

PEDEN: That's obviously why they don't have anything to "say" to each other, because they're both experiencing reality as a completely different thing. Their perception of reality is absolutely different.

GRAHAM: I've got just one line here on Max. When Max first comes in, he just walks into the scene, really, having met Aristeo (but no names exchanged or anything) the night before, and Aristeo and Isabel are on the beach. She's doing her embroidery

—wonderful disparity of actions—and he's playing like a wet puppy in the surf.

PEDEN: But he's got to do it.

GRAHAM: But Isabel, being rather properly reared, says to him, to Max, this stranger, "Are you from around here, Mr. Uh, Mr. Uh—" "Call me Max. No, I'm not from here." And that's the end of the chapter. The chapter endings are very dramatic. They pitch you forward, wanting more—

PEDEN: They do, and interestingly, there's an inevitable movement. They come together at just the right moment, and sort of move around on their own axis and there's no direction.

GRAHAM: The axis breaks, really, and they fly off.

PEDEN: I think, as it should be in anything important, that happens to human beings. None of them—no, I take that back—neither the young boy nor Isabel are going to be the same. Max, I think, is going to be always the same. He's one of those people who change lives, but maybe he himself is not going to change.

GRAHAM: Sort of goes through the world rather carelessly.

PEDEN: Very carelessly.

GRAHAM: We hear talk of Havana, New Orleans, Mexico City, Vera Cruz, and there is a sense that he's a damager.

PEDEN: I was going to say, he's a "destroyer." You've got it exactly.

GRAHAM: I thought of Conrad at times while reading *The Norther*. Is there any meaning to you in that?

PEDEN: I've never spoken to Emilio Carballido about Conrad. I know a few of the people that he admires. The conventional ones. I don't think he reads English, though, and I don't think there are that many translations into Spanish.

GRAHAM: Of Conrad? I read *Lord Jim* again not too long ago, and Conrad does have these rather evil characters there. There's one little paragraph that picks up some of the things we're talking about. Again this is a chapter ending: The affair commenced:

> The old servant watched him leave without being able to believe her own eyes, and when Isabel looked at him from the cynicism of her pleasure, the old woman packed her things and announced that she was leaving. Isabel was very pleased, and the next day she acquired a young girl whose face was pitted with pockmarks.

PEDEN: Yes, that paragraph tells a lot.

GRAHAM: It seems to me to be so loaded. Does he write this way, or did you tighten up in your translation?

PEDEN: I didn't tighten a thing. I try as nearly as I can to be exact. I guess every translator does try to get inside the skin of the person he's translating, and do what he's doing as nearly as he can approximate. The word "translation" almost is out of favor in my mind. I think "approximation" maybe is a better term. You know why I think he writes that way is that he is basically a playwright.

GRAHAM: These are scene directions, almost.

PEDEN: I think he's seeing things in terms of a play taking place before him.

GRAHAM: And yet, he is awfully good with details—that hotel room, the restaurants, the sea, the wall.

PEDEN: But very, very briefly. It's a novella. It's not a novel. He's written two other novels, but still it's the same thing. He uses almost a kind of shorthand, it seems to me, when's he's describing things. He has a perfect eye. He has the perfect gift to transmit what he sees in his writer's eye for you to be able to perceive, but he spends absolutely no energy on superfluous detail.

GRAHAM: You know, just in the last week I probably read ten novels and five or eight books of poetry. And with each of the novels I couldn't help feel that they could have been say a third . . .

PEDEN: Shorter?

GRAHAM: And profited by the cutting. I think a great many writers may fall in love with their writing.

PEDEN: I think it's one of the pitfalls of the novel. You have all this room, and if you're a writer, you're something of a hambone. You're an actor, you want to hold the stage as long as you possibly can; and so you go on madly describing things that you could do without. That's something Carballido does not do. He's very economical, but at the same time I think a whole character comes through. But if you could, read that novella again, not so much for the story but just noticing how little he really does use. There's a great deal of conversation, there's a great deal of musing on the part of the characters. It's the playwright in him.

GRAHAM: This is helping me a great deal, and yet I am impressed by his capacity to get the visual aspect, and for that matter, the tactile and the olfactory aspects.

PEDEN: The very end of the novel, when you get the feeling of the boy running into the darkness—you taste the salt, you feel the wind stinging your face . . .

GRAHAM: Notice the roughness of the path. He's very conscious of the rockiness and stickiness of the path.

PEDEN: That's right. I think, really, Emilio is a tremendously talented man. I hope that he's going to be recognized in this country.

Fred Chappell

BIOGRAPHICAL

Born: 28 May 1936 in Canton, North Carolina.
Education: B.A. Duke 1961, M.A. Duke 1964.
Occupational: Various miscellaneous jobs; proofreader for Duke University Press; since 1962 has been writer-in-residence at University of North Carolina at Greensboro, where he now directs the Graduate Writing Program.
Books: Novels—*It Is Time, Lord* (1963), *The Inkling* (1965), *Dagon* (1968), *The Gaudy Place* (1972); poetry—*The World Between the Eyes* (1971). He has received, among other awards and honors, a Rockefeller Grant and a grant from the National Institute of Arts and Letters. While still a teen-ager he was among that select company who wrote for *Weird Tales,* but nobody knows the name he wrote under, and he won't tell.

SNAPSHOT

Broad powerful shoulders hunched forward, a little slumped, with a slight sure-footed crouch like a good welterweight fighter; his face lean and angular, all planes and angles like a one-eyed jack, and you remember, or *think* you do, little scars; they aren't there (I believe), but they ought to be. Fred was once described by a friend as "a guy who looks like he's just getting ready to knock over a gas station." Which is silly, but has some comic truth in it. Silly because Fred is so honestly gentle, deeply so, and full of love and sweetness, proving these things can still co-exist, be wedded to pure virility. The only truth to the image of danger being that Fred is fearless of men, fears no living man, though it's clear he fears God and knows, too, how fearful the invisible powers of darkness can be.

Of all the writers in this collection he is the most *intellectual,* though you have to read and reread his works to see the signs of all that. He doesn't let it interfere with feeling, energy, imagination.

Once (we were both drunk enough to speak up without inhibition) I asked the great teacher William Blacksburn of Duke one of those half-baked journalistic questions. "Bill," I said, "you have taught a lot of really good ones, people like Mac Hyman, Styron and Reynolds Price. Tell me, who's the best writer you ever taught?"

The answer wasn't half-baked or even qualified.

"Fred Chappell," he said. "He's the best of them all."

I. *I tried to keep this deliberately obscure and ambiguous to myself in the novel, just because I think the more ambiguous some things are, the scarier they are.*

GRAHAM: Fred, I started your most recent novel, *Dagon,* at about nine o'clock one night. This was my first mistake of the day—it was a very good day—because I didn't finish it until about two in the morning, and my dreams were not too good. I find it a novel that is inclined to take the skin off of one. But I need some help on it. We've got a novel here about a kind of—would you call him an ordinary man? He's an ordinarily cranky man who takes the real full-depth plunge into self-discovery. Though I'm not sure of that because I don't see . . . *Is* this man a self-aware man?

CHAPPELL: He is and he isn't. That's a cop-out, I realize. He's aware of himself. He knows exactly what kind of limits there are to his personality at this point. He's a man who doesn't know his past history fully and doesn't know how he stands in relationship to—not only to society as a whole, but even to other people, even someone as close as his wife. These things he never knows. You want to speak of it as an educational novel. You're right, he never learns. He's the wrong protagonist for that, because he *can't* learn. He becomes, you notice, more and more passive rather than putting learning to any use. And I think finally he doesn't learn. Hopefully *we* learn.

GRAHAM: This helps me a great deal. He doesn't, in the process of his degradation, his dehumanization, or his humanization, understand. I like the opening very much, as he explores this old house, trying to understand the past, not being able to read the letters or understand what they could possibly mean. But the thing I liked, in what I thought was a rather strange opening chapter, as he explores the house of his grandparents, was that he keeps getting reflections of himself in the paintings, in the front of French doors—and he's fragmented in these reflections, always.

CHAPPELL: He's always distorted and always torn apart. Of course he's looking at the true image of himself at that point, but he doesn't know it. He doesn't understand all the way through. If he could perhaps read this little sign, perhaps he wouldn't have to suffer the whole thing that he does suffer. Peter Taylor once told me, in connection with the house, "If you'd ever get a house right, you'd get all the characters of the story right."

GRAHAM: Taylor's acute and you've got to listen to that kind of thing.

CHAPPELL: I listen to him. As a matter of fact, Peter Leland, the protagonist, is a little bit modeled on Peter Taylor's consciousness. Not Peter Taylor, the personality, but on that wonderful Puritan acuity he has.

GRAHAM: And the incredible sense of place and of family that he has working all the time. I've heard him say that that is what one has: family. Good or ill, that's what one is given.

CHAPPELL: That's right. Peter often—you'll notice the characters in Peter Taylor's stories—their identity is connected and grows out of their family and their background. I wanted to try to do the same thing except not let the man know what his background was.

GRAHAM: In your novel *Dagon,* this pursuit of "background" that he becomes obsessed with is always—I'm sure this must have been conscious—it's always dust-filled. Everything he's involved with is filled with dust.

CHAPPELL: Sometimes the dust is so thick it obscures things that are important for him to know, that he should be able to read, but he can't wipe it away without obscuring, without griming things even more. One of the scenes I tried to make very frightening was the attic scene.

GRAHAM: That was terrifying. When he put his toe into the stack of old newspapers, they are so dry, so gone. And the dreadful discovery that he traps himself in there, the strange chains.

CHAPPELL: The chains, which of course belonged to his family earlier; and there's some hint that he has seen this as a child. I tried to keep this deliberately obscure and ambiguous to myself in the novel, just because I think the more ambiguous some things are, the scarier they are. This is really a horror novel, almost a pulp-fiction horror.

GRAHAM: Let me ask you about the conception of it. I'm almost inclined to call it "a philosophical novel" rather than a psychological one. I think it's very difficult for us now in 1970 to read philosophical novels because we are so—whether we choose it or not—so trapped, if only by indirection, through Freud, in psychological analyses, that we're not very good at these larger patterns.

CHAPPELL: Part of the reason for it is the fashion. It's been the fashion in fiction, I guess since Chekhov and Henry James, to be, you know, psychologically oriented. We had the philosophical novel before, in the eighteenth century, but the trouble with the philosophical novel, with the exception of *Candide,* is that it gets to be so abstract and dry and dull. I've written two novels which are philosophical novels. They're not easy to read. None of my books are easy to read. But what I try to do, and I wasn't able to do it completely in *Dagon,* what I try to do is let the philosophical structure stand behind the novel, and the drama that the philosophical notions generate just takes place in it. And if you follow the story perhaps the system would be intimated to you. But if you don't ever get the system, the story may just appear to be nonsense.

GRAHAM: This was a difficult novel for me to read; in a sense I had to learn to read this, and I was unprepared. Could I hit you on one or two things that confused me? I couldn't grasp why he needed to kill his wife, really. I could see his departure, I could see living in the tenant farmer's shack, and drinking and drinking and drinking with this devil of a woman. I mean to congratulate you on this, now. She's the most unattractive character I've read of. But why'd he *need* to kill his wife? Did he have to do something absolute?

CHAPPELL: He doesn't know it yet at that point, and I think the reader doesn't know it. I hope the reader does, hopefully, find it out. But he's already under the subjection of that priestess, "Dagon." He is already her thrall, actually her sacrificial slave at that point. He doesn't know it yet, he doesn't know what happened. He's not even sure—I hope this was clear —but he's not even sure he's done that.

GRAHAM: Yes, this is it. Everything becomes so muddied, so dusty in his mind that it's a long time before he can raise his throat to the sacrificial knife that must be borne.

CHAPPELL: He dreams of killing his wife before. He's dreamed it, and then, when it happens, it's almost exactly like the dream. There's very little difference, and I wanted to make the reader think that perhaps he did it the first time, and now he's dreaming. Or perhaps now he's carrying out the dream or—to leave it like that—perhaps it happened, perhaps it didn't happen. Of course, it really did happen in the literal terms of the book. He does kill his wife, he does go and become an absolute slave to this priestess. But the literal events of the book take place from his point of view, from his sensibility, so we're never quite sure.

GRAHAM: Now this brings up a problem. I don't mean to cheapen it by calling it a technical problem. I think for instance of that dreadful long automobile ride, as they go to find the house for this tattooing that takes place over many days, weeks, those dirty little coastal plain towns that they go through, and the lovely touch of those peanut butter crackers and the cellophane paper. Now, all of this is so realistic, to grab at a standard term, and yet we are in a philosophical novel. We are in a dream world—or we're in a world where reality, actuality, fantasy are muddled. Did you have problems with how much concrete detail to use?

CHAPPELL: It's a real one, and one of the hardest problems I had working out. I had to test a great many sentences just to see what was happening in regard to realistic detail. Suppose we wanted to stick labels around? Would you call it a surrealist novel? Unfortunately, to an American the word "surrealist" means goofy and unreal.

GRAHAM: Or so displaced that . . .

CHAPPELL: That there's no point. It's pointless. I wanted . . .

GRAHAM: I think we think of data rather than . . .

CHAPPELL: Well, our great Titan, Dreiser, has shown us what can be done; and, fortunately or unfortunately, that's how most Americans think of the novel. When they think of a novel, they think of nine hundred pages of impenetrable fact. That's not the way, for me, the novel should be. I like a novel that you can read at one sitting, like you read a good detective story. I like to keep that tension, keep driving and pushing. I don't like novels—I say this—I don't mean to sound so authoritative— I don't like novels that take six months to read. I really forget where I am.

GRAHAM: I've read many novels where I know if they were cut a third, they'd be better. I'm being careful with "a third."

CHAPPELL: As a matter of fact often—I've done it with *Dagon* and I've done it with the new book, and I think I might do it from now on—I just write the new novel on the back of the old novel. It's a form of discipline. You can't possibly get any longer than the novel before.

II. *And it's like a car you've been trying to get to run, an old Hupmobile, that you've been looking for all the parts for, for the past thirty years, and, one of these days, you know you're going to take it out on the highway.*

GRAHAM: Fred, I have just finished reading your very, very fine short novel, *Dagon*, and basically, I think, what I'm asking is, what are you up to now? I enjoyed the novel in a rather perverse way. You write both fiction and poetry. Am I going to get anything from you next?

CHAPPELL: Like most writers, I have more projects on hand than I'm ever really going to finish. I do have a novel that I'm working on very hard now, and it should be out next year. It will be called *The Gaudy Place*. I've also been working on a book of poems for a long, long time, about twelve years now. And I keep fiddling with it. Maybe one day, that'll turn out. I'm working on short stories, essays, even a little scholarship here and there.

GRAHAM: You're working on a number of things concurrently. Do they get in the way of each other? Do they seem to stimulate each other?

CHAPPELL: You do get hung up often, and it's nice to have something to go to instead of wasting your time drinking or something. It's nice to have something that you can work on that is refreshing and is different, is very different from what you're currently working on. It's not like before, I didn't use to work this way. My first two novels, each of them took me five weeks to write, and I sat down and I just wrote. But then I got to get more and more commitments. People would commission me to do articles and stuff.

GRAHAM: Life just plain got busier and you just learned how to handle it?

CHAPPELL: That's right, that's right. Also, after your third novel, I don't think you're as uptight about everything as you were.

GRAHAM: That dreadful anxiety of trying to discover whether you can in fact become a writer must happen while you are in the process of a novel. Did you just say that you wrote your first two novels in five weeks each?

CHAPPELL: Working four hours a day, writing a thousand words a day.

GRAHAM: I can hardly believe you.

CHAPPELL: In a way, it was easy because those novels came to me all in one flash, just like taking dictation. All I had to do was put the words in the right place and remember to punctuate sometimes. On the other hand, the novel I'm working on now . . .

GRAHAM: That takes my breath away! I'm afraid I have meekly become very self-conscious listening to you because the very thought . . . ! If I could ever produce a thousand words a day, I would go to bed as a hero. To think that you were able to write that quickly is hard. But, you do get blocks? What do you do when you do get blocks?

CHAPPELL: Often what I do is to read something different from what I'm currently writing. I'm reading a book on Greek tragedy while I'm writing a novel, or reading someone's poems while I'm writing a short story. And I find that if I just drop it and quit writing and spend a day reading about hummingbirds or sea turtles or a lost city, that my perspective is changed. I feel a little bathed.

GRAHAM: I never know what to do. I'm basically an uncreative person. I'm doing scholarly work and what I end up doing frankly is just butting the head against the wall, and maybe I need to make some of these shifts you're talking about.

CHAPPELL: It's different in the scholarly stuff. I think that in scholarly stuff, the little I've done, you have to keep butting your head against the wall because once you're there, you do break through. What happens there is not so much a problem of style or presentation, but there's a piece of information that you don't have that you need, and you don't know what it is.

GRAHAM: But isn't that true of the creative writer too a lot of the time? Don't you know that there is something right there that you can, in a sense, find?

CHAPPELL: That's true. You notice this especially when you begin a novel and you're not quite sure yet. You've left out something just as big and invisible and powerful as love that you were about to put in, you know. Yes, but there's a case where you have to go away for a long period, at least I do, for a long period of four or five weeks.

GRAHAM: Just let your—I've been avoiding the word "subconscious"—but let your subconscious go to work and dredge it up?

CHAPPELL: That's right, yes.

GRAHAM: With this new novel, the major thing that you are working on, *The Gaudy Place,* is it going to be like the novel I've just finished, *Dagon?*

CHAPPELL: No, it's not supernatural at all. It's almost a little crime novel in a way. I was in Italy. I was working on a long, picaresque, not very funny novel. I finally threw it away. The new one is a novel about the South. My wife and I belonged to CORE, you remember that, the Congress of Racial Equality, one of the first civil rights groups? It was a corrupt group in the town we were active in. It was a corrupt political group. It really didn't do that much. That's why it died, I'm sure. There's no CORE now, at least as far as I know. And I thought, I'm going to do a long satire about civil rights and how corrupt sometimes it is at the beginning, though the great organizations like SNCC, NAACP, those are fine. But then, Mr. King, Mr. Martin Luther King, was assassinated while we were in Italy. And you couldn't write any satire on civil rights anymore. It would break your heart to think about writing something like that. So I got taken with the notion of how a violent act occurs. And this new novel is about a guy getting shot through the collarbone—not a terribly violent act, you know, no death, but violent enough. I wanted to follow it from the very beginning, the full act itself. How it came about.

GRAHAM: In talking with novelists, I've found they like to trace back, don't they? They believe in cause and effect, and they want to find out how far back you have to go to find out why you and I are sitting here now.

CHAPPELL: I don't know whether a novelist believes finally and philosophically in cause and effect. I don't frankly philosophically believe in it. I've studied too much urban charading here to go with that. But, in human terms I think there is a cause and effect. In sub-atomic physics, I'm sure there isn't.

GRAHAM: Let's try "order" instead of cause and effect, some kind of order.

CHAPPELL: That's right.

GRAHAM: There must at least be an art.

CHAPPELL: And it may be in events themselves, or it may be just something you see and impose. But it is there. It's as real, if you impose it yourself, as it is if it really happened as far as I'm concerned.

GRAHAM: How far back do we have to go to find out about this bullet wound in the shoulder?

CHAPPELL: We have to go all the way back. The novel is built on a sort of economic ladder. It starts with the lowest possible economic thing I could think of in the city. And the final cause is not the poor people who do the shooting, but the very rich people who cause the whole thing. I wanted to place the responsibility not on the people in Watts or whatever. This is not a novel about race, by the way; it's just a novel about a criminal act of violence, not by the people in the poor part of town themselves, but the people who own the poor part of town, the people who crush down.

GRAHAM: And ignore, and by ignoring or by overt acts . . .

CHAPPELL: That's right. I think that's where the responsibility inevitably lies. The novel begins with a person who's trying to be a procurer for a prostitute. He's only fourteen years old, and that's his goal in life. That will be the highest place he can get on the social and economic ladder. And it goes on up to the man who owns a construction company and rezones parts of cities, ghetto parts, for his own profit.

GRAHAM: In other words, simply manipulating people's lives. It's nice and clean. But isn't there a wonderful ballad, "some men rob with a six gun and some with a fountain pen"? It's "The Ballad of Jesse James."

CHAPPELL: That was made up not at the time of Jesse James, but during the thirties when people really saw right. I agree with that. This is a fountain pen robbery. How does the line from Dylan Thomas go? "The hand that signed the paper felled the city." That was a wonderful line!

GRAHAM: Where are you in the novel? Do you know the beginning and end?

CHAPPELL: I've written it once and sold it and then got cold feet. I didn't think it was well enough done and took it back from my publisher and tore it all down and started from the ground up. I'm about one third of the way through it again.

GRAHAM: That takes nerve, to my mind.

CHAPPELL: Takes nerve to face up to my wife and say I'm not going to take that money.

GRAHAM: This whole business of writing and rewriting. You say you have spent ten or twelve years building up a book of poetry, playing with the poems, a touch here, a touch there. I think I can imagine doing that. I find it very difficult, however, to understand how a writer—is this the right word—avoids "boredom" in terms of rewriting a novel. Do you ever get bored with your own work when you're at a very advanced stage, when you know everything that ought to be in the novel?

CHAPPELL: Well, you're a teacher, too. You can tell whether you get bored with the sound of your own voice or not. Of course, you do. But hopefully you work at it long enough, and it becomes so impersonal and so much an object that you're working on that it's no longer the sound of your own voice. And it's like a car you've been trying to get to run, an old Hupmobile, that you've been looking for all the parts for, for the past thirty years, and, one of these days, you know that you're going to take it out on the highway.

GRAHAM: To a certain degree then, and I'm not cheapening things here, to a certain degree at some point, what *really* can take over is your craftsmanship, your desire to finish this table that you're trying to build and get a good stain on it.

CHAPPELL: There's nothing cheap about craftsmanship. It's one of the things in America that's getting quickly lost in our culture, and we'd better begin to value it more and more and more. Verbally, manually, and whatever way! I think craftsmanship is rapidly becoming an obsolete value in America rather than a means to an end.

GRAHAM: So, the story has got to be there, and then the work of refinement just has to take place. Would you argue that your work in poetry is particularly useful for you in the novel? There must be a transfer.

CHAPPELL: Yes, there is.

GRAHAM: I'm thinking in terms of craft, refinement.

CHAPPELL: Poetry is very good for a novelist if he's interested in it. Some novelists are not and they don't need it. For a novelist, the study of poetry, either as a reader or as a writer, is good for his diction, I think. It helps you find the phrase, the word that Flaubert was so in favor of. There are some novelists who don't need the word. I hate to pick on Dreiser again, but someone like Dreiser, James T. Farrell, they don't need the word. They got so much other juice that they can get by without the word.

III. *Also, a lot of young girls try haiku because it can be a sentimental form, and it doesn't look sentimental and you can get by with it. It's a gentle way to cheat.*

GRAHAM: Fred, what I would like to do is to get you to help me in the sense of what else should I be reading that I haven't heard of? Poetry, prose, anything. . . .

CHAPPELL: I think that the best novelist writing today who you've heard of and everyone's read is Georges Simenon. Even the Maigret stories seem to me to be great stories. But, outside of that, there are hundreds of other novelists who we all know. I'd like also to mention my students. But I think that just for variety's sake and to get new ideas about fiction, you might try Bertha Harris, who is also a North Carolina novelist.

GRAHAM: I've not heard of her. What's she done?

CHAPPELL: Her first novel came out last year and her new novel will be out soon. Her first novel was called *Catching Saradove*. A wonderful story about past and present. The South . . . she's from North Carolina . . . and the protagonist of her novel goes to Greenwich Village and lives there. So that you have the South overlayed on the bohemian North, the very old on top of the very new. And there's all kinds of sexual adventures, but mostly, adventures of sensibility, new ways to see things. A way to see New York that's shocking, yet familiar at the same time. And a way to bring that kind of sensibility, that juvenile kind of sensibility she has, onto the South that we know and love and hate so much. I recommend it very highly.

GRAHAM: Would you say you discover the protagonist or New York or the South or everything all together in this novel by Bertha Harris?

CHAPPELL: Everything all together because the identity of the protagonist in *Catching Saradove* is also the identity of New York and the identity of her southern background. The protagonist is called Saradove, and the novel *Catching Saradove* is about trying to understand her and see what she is. And she's a mixture of everything. I don't mean to make her sound passive like a movie screen which all these impressions are flashed upon. She's not. She's a very hard-edged person in her own right. But, everything works together. It's a brilliant novel, and *Confessions of Cherubino,* her new novel—I've only read parts of it—seemed to me to be even better, even more brilliant than the first one.

GRAHAM: Is it a realistic novel or a fantasy novel or a surrealistic?

CHAPPELL: Psychological realism, for the most part. The first novel has a lot of fantasy escapes, childhood fantasies, and adult fantasies which are generated from memories of childhood fantasies. It's wonderful.

GRAHAM: You're talking about a first novel here, and you're talking as if one of the things you admire enormously about it is the *craft* of it.

CHAPPELL: The craft of it. She's different from most other first novelists you've read. She's got absolute control of technique. I think Eudora Welty might have started this way. Just fullborn out of the head of someone. Out of her own head, she's got a nice one. Other writers . . . Yukio Mishima, do you know him?

GRAHAM: No, is he Japanese?

CHAPPELL: He's Japanese . . . I don't know how old he is, I think he's in his thirties, but he's already written something like four hundred books, I believe.

GRAHAM: Oh, Fred!

CHAPPELL: No kidding . . . !

GRAHAM: Even the speed you have described to me of the writing in your first two books is not going to permit that kind of production.

CHAPPELL: Not all of them have been published in English, of course. I think only about twenty or so have been published in English.

GRAHAM: I can't imagine how I have missed someone who is this prolific at that age. What sort of thing does he write?

CHAPPELL: He writes psychological novels, which are strange. You wouldn't think that you could be remotely interested in a Japanese psychological novel. And yet, a novel called *The Temple of the Golden Pavilion* is really one of the most searching sort of intensely interior novels I have ever read. If it were written by an Englishman or an American or a Frenchman, I don't think I would be so much in favor of it because it's full of almost Freudian things, which I think is death for the novel, for the most part. Fortunately, his cultural difference from Freud, and the way he reads Freud, transforms it into some rare magic flower. You just almost don't believe it. The cultural differences . . . there's something . . . there's something. . . . I don't even know how it would be in Japanese, but something changes, something radically changes.

GRAHAM: If we can back up just a little bit. You say that maybe twenty of them are in English. Are they in paperback?

CHAPPELL: Some of them are in paperback. *Confessions of a Mask,* I think, is in paperback from Avon, and I think that Avon also published *The Sailor Who Fell from Grace with the Sea,* which is a short novel and a very good one. There are also books of short stories in hardcover, and there are some little plays.

GRAHAM: In general, since when—1955 or so—we've gotten interested in Japanese writing, haven't we?

CHAPPELL: I think that's about the time. New Directions started a great deal of it, of course. They've been and are always very good about other cultures, especially French.

GRAHAM: I think that New Directions and Knopf have done nothing but favors for us in America with their wonderful translations.

CHAPPELL: That's right, Knopf publishes the hardcover editions of Mishima. And there is a company that publishes wonderful

Japanese literature of an earlier period before the contemporary writers. The people who started the modern renaissance, who we don't know as well as we should. And Charles Tuttle's books unfortunately don't get the distribution they ought to have. You can say that about a number of things.

GRAHAM: In talking about this different sensibility, dealing with things we feel we do know something about, all of my reading experience, frankly (and I think this is a very common failure) is Western civilization. By Western, I'm eliminating Spanish, Latin American, and certainly Japanese and Chinese. Will it be, because I'd like to get at this man, much of a leap for me getting into a Japanese writer? Am I in danger of taking false steps by reading as an Occidental?

CHAPPELL: No. It's not really the same cultural shock that the first Western man who read a *haiku* must have experienced. He must have felt this is nonsense. What in the world is this about? No, as a matter of fact, what caused the renaissance in Japan was their introduction of Western literature to them.

GRAHAM: So we're sort of going around the pylon there.

CHAPPELL: That's right. We have tended to get sophisticated in our literature, get more and more allegorical and symbolic and very artifistic—is that a good word? I don't mean artificial.

GRAHAM: I like it.

CHAPPELL: At any rate, they are discovering the novel as this kind of form rather than the chronicle—which was their first novel form, and one they've continued—so that they sort of get back to the sources of the strength. It's almost a new discovery. Of course the Western literature has been there for forty years, but, it takes time to absorb a form. How many good *haiku* are there in English?

GRAHAM: Everybody and his brother's uncle does try them because it's such an attractive, brief, compressed thing. We like them. We should do them. But we can't carry them off.

CHAPPELL: I'm sorry to say that a lot of young poets begin trying *haiku*. I don't think they should because it's not a form congenial to English. In the first place, we always cheat. We just use the syllable count for our *haiku* and the Japanese have a wonderful pitch pattern that we don't even mess with. Also, a lot of young girls try *haiku* because it can be a sentimental form, and it doesn't look sentimental and you can get by with it. It's a gentle way to cheat.

GRAHAM: I've got two writers now. Can you think of anyone else that I'd like to read?

CHAPPELL: It's hard for me to just choose one out of a bunch. I think the most famous of my favorite current writers is Jorge Luis Borges, the short story writer.

GRAHAM: This has been an explosive development, now, hasn't it?

CHAPPELL: It certainly has. For those people who haven't read his work, it's a wild and wonderful rediscovery of the short story. He's the one short story writer who gets back to the beginnings of the short story, assuming, if you do as I do, that Poe invented the short story form and it never got better. It also never got worse than Poe, either. But Borges—we were talking on an earlier tape about the philosophical work. This seems to me to be one of the places where philosophical literature really does come through brilliantly.

GRAHAM: He's fascinated, is he not, by language?

CHAPPELL: He is.

GRAHAM: You know that fantastic situation of looking into the mirror, looking into the mirror, looking into the mirror? He does things like that, doesn't he? He's so self-aware about language—a little like Alice in Wonderland. Was that fair?

CHAPPELL: I think that's fair, yes.

GRAHAM: Just this absolute fascination with what happens when we start talking with each other. Normally, we ignore it.

CHAPPELL: It's a way to manipulate as in a chess game. He would love these metaphors that we're using—chess games, reflections, and stars, that's the kind of thing he loves and the kind of thing he can treat and not many people can.

GRAHAM: He has been the man who's been the battering ram for Latin American authors, I understand. There's a whole wave now. I was talking with Petch Peden, and she's just so excited because she's in Spanish—she teaches Spanish at Missouri—and she says it's so wonderful now that you don't really have to be so sort of protective or self-defensive about Latin American authors because they are all growing up, almost overnight, with Borges leading.

CHAPPELL: I think that's absolutely true, and there's a Latin American disciple of Borges who is almost as good as he is. Bioy Casares is his name. And he and Borges have actually collaborated on stories which are wonderful stories to read. But I hope that it brings in that whole slew of forgotten acres of Latin American literature that we don't normally read, all those people that we need desperately.

Brian Moore

BIOGRAPHICAL

Born: 25 August 1921 in Belfast, Ireland.

Education: St. Malachy's College.

Occupational: Proofreader, reporter and rewrite man for the *Montreal Gazette,* 1948–1952; since 1952 has been a full-time writer.

Books: Novels— *The Lonely Passion of Judith Hearne* (1956), *The Feast of Lupercal* (1957), *The Luck of Ginger Coffey* (1960), *An Answer from Limbo* (1962), *The Emperor of Ice Cream* (1965), *I Am Mary Dunne* (1968), and *Fergus* (1970). Nonfiction—*Canada* (1963), *The Revolution Script* (1971).

Moore has written a number of screenplays, including the adaptation of his own *The Luck of Ginger Coffey* and, for Alfred Hitchcock, *Torn Curtain.* He has received awards and honors in England, Canada and the United States. Some of them are: Author's Club First Novel Award (England 1956), Governor General's Award for Fiction (Canada 1960), a Guggenheim Fellowship (1959), and a fiction grant from the National Institute of Arts and Letters (1961).

SNAPSHOT

He still has a piece, a good, solid piece of his accent left, though the idiom he talks now is almost wholly American. On-stage, speaking, reading from his novels (which are written, I think, to be voiced and heard, too, savored by tongue and ear), he can seem diminutive, puckish, cherubic, almost a stage Irishman. Which he is not by a long shot. And the words he says and reads don't fit that false illusion. Still, enough of the illusion remains and becomes a kind of charm. And that gives his fine and subtle sense of humor, equally present in his life and his novels, a chance to work its spell. Compassionate, sympathetic, and quite serious, Brian is also, at the same time, a very funny man. You have to listen, though. He won't flash italics and exclamation points to get your attention.

Truth is, from my angle, he's tall, tall enough, dark, and with angular, strong good looks. And a very Irish smile when it comes.

One thing he is completely serious about—the skill and craft of writing. And everything he makes is, to the last detail, made with care and has every chance to last.

I. *I never wanted to write any journalistic novel, probably because I am an ex-newspaperman, and I know the dangers of journalism.*

GRAHAM: The novel I've just finished, Brian, is *The Emperor of Ice Cream*, which came out in 1965. I think it's a fairly straightforward novel, is it not? It's not really your *I Am Mary Dunne*—flashbacks, the insets—but rather it's very straight chronologically.

MOORE: It is. It's what the Germans call a *Bildungsroman*.

GRAHAM: Right, I've got the name down here.

MOORE: It's the sort of book most guys write when they're twenty or twenty-four. I've waited 'til I was forty-four before I wrote it, because I was afraid that if I did write it when I was twenty-four, as it just happened to me, I wouldn't be able to handle the—let's say, extremely strong material at the end. The book ends, if you remember, with people . . . with the blitz in Belfast in Ireland, which was a tremendously heavy series of air raids on a place which never expected to have any. There were seven hundred German bomber raids, and I was at that time eighteen years old, and I found myself being punched from adolescence into a volunteer job coffining dead bodies for weeks. And that experience naturally had a strong effect on me. And my father, who was a surgeon, an old man, really died of a heart condition he got during one of the—well, he was helping people in the blitz. So if I'd handled it when I was twenty-four, I probably couldn't have written it. And if I had tried to handle it then, I would have been too emotional and too off-balance. Because what I really wanted to do was to deal also with the silliness of that period, which people seem to forget.

GRAHAM: Well, the thing about the closing section of the novel —tremendously interesting, what you said—because it almost should have been so grim that the grimness would have dominated the character, really, and I got no sense of that. And the young man, Gavin Burke, I guess you could almost say his surprise that he could handle the job that he was given, the surprise that he could stay up all night carrying bodies, and this fearful mutilation that suddenly—some of it is just because they are so tired, isn't it? All of a sudden it's silly, isn't it?

MOORE: Yes, I don't know if you remember, if you're old enough to remember that period.

GRAHAM: I do indeed.

MOORE: But the thing that happened. . . . Well, first of all, let me say this about the book. If you write a book which has an historical happening in it—a journalistic happening, which this was at the time—as you said, the journalism, the events tend to kill the characters. I've always been afraid. I never wanted to write any journalistic novel, probably because I am an ex-newspaperman, and I know the dangers of journalism.

GRAHAM: I see . . . the advantages you get out of newspaper work are coupled with others.

MOORE: You lose if you make the incident important, so the only way this incident could be handled was by making it almost historical. It was, to English reviewers who read the book. They were sort of very interested historically to (a) realize that Ireland had ever been bombed and (b) that the Irish were so damned disloyal to them at the time. They couldn't believe that actually people like my father would welcome Hitler, because he thought Hitler was going to blow up the British. And they couldn't believe that working-class men would stand in houses in Ireland flashing torches up in the air, hoping that the Germans would come and bomb them.

GRAHAM: While the blackout was on.

MOORE: Of course the silly thing was that when the Germans came and bombed them, they came and bombed them indiscriminately.

GRAHAM: One of the things, now that we've—Lord save the mark—*gotten used to* very high explosives, one of the things that I thought was so well done was the sense of surprise at the power of the bombardment. Whole blocks were gone. This (and I do remember World War II—I was in the service then—very clearly) but this sense of the blockbuster, so new, the horror that a whole block could disappear!

MOORE: We blew up Dresden. And our bombing was heavier than the Germans', but we really—people say, people of our generation and younger people, say that when the atom bomb blew up at Hiroshima that changed the whole pattern of bombing. Now that you've mentioned it, I tend to suspect that that was not so. It was saturation bombing in World War Two that woke people up to the fact that they were going to be killed. My father, who was pro-German, when he saw what the Germans were able to do, when he saw what modern warfare was really like . . . It wasn't like World War One which he'd been in.

GRAHAM: Right, barricades in the streets.

MOORE: When they blew up your home, that was all, things were over. We then realized what modern total war is, and perhaps one of the reasons there hasn't been more bloodthirstiness. In fact, I'm sure of it. Among the older leaders, say, people like Kosygin and Brezhnev in Russia, and people like Wilson and the Tory leaders in Britain, all those people remember the first modern war. Russia suffered terribly in that war, and I think whenever we talk about warmongering and people feeling belligerent, I don't think this generation, this middle-aging generation, will ever be belligerent. They were given their medicine.

GRAHAM: And know more than a little about the depersonalization of that bomber that is up so high and never sees its prey.

MOORE: And the second point that we couldn't cover in the book, because it happened later, was that civilian saturation bombing does not affect military operations—I mean we are finding that out now. Or have found it out in Vietnam.

GRAHAM: Well, back directly to the novel, one of the things I liked was, in spite of the experience that you and I are both talking about, which is behind us and fully a part of our consciousness, I think you were able to bring out in the populace this sense of surprise, confusion, at this very new thing. And I think you were able to make it new again, which is a bit of a triumph, really. I was terribly teased, of course, by this young man growing up, trying to find himself, in Ireland, his confusion, really, about the meaning of morality as he withdraws more and more clearly from the Church. He doesn't attack the Church directly but, he sees . . . well, if only in terms of the young student nurse that he may be in love with, Sally Shannon, he sees this dreadful constriction of the Church. Did you want that to be more in the novel? Is this young man really trying to find a whole new morality, a whole new consciousness? I'm thinking, suddenly, of Joyce's *Portrait of the Artist as a Young Man.*

MOORE: Yes, I think that every Irish writer who writes a book about a young man—most of them, anyway, and I certainly for one—has been influenced by the experience of the *Portrait.* I read it, and I said to myself, this is my autobiography written before I was born, in a sense.

GRAHAM: You know, I went at that book I know three or four times. (I was educated by the Jesuits.) And I'd get, oh, maybe twenty percent into it, and I'd quit, because I couldn't tell where Joyce was and where I was. I was feeding so much into the book. As an American, I was feeding so much into the book myself.

MOORE: So, to answer your question in a sense, it was a big influence on me, and no writer with a Catholic background as I have, in Ireland, I felt, could write a novel about—*for* a young person or an old person who'd been brought up in the Catholic Church and confronting what was happening to most people. Now, to digress on that slightly, my first novel, *The Lonely Passion of Judith Hearne,* was a novel about an alcoholic spinster, very devout, who loses her faith because she has prayed . . . all her life she's done novenas to get a man. And a man appears on the scene, she believes. And about halfway through the book the reader and everyone knows this man isn't going to work out. He is not in love with her, and he's not even interested in her. He thinks she has some money and might invest it in a— he's an American—an American failure. But halfway through the book, the book becomes a book about a person's loss of faith, and that was more influenced, by the way, by *Portrait of the Artist*. But what I said was, every young intellectual has a crisis of faith, but what happens to the lady who goes to church all of her life and is a devout Catholic, the bulwark of the Catholic Church, what happens to the ordinary person when they lose their faith? And her confrontation with her faith becomes very shattering. It no longer is the story of a romance, it becomes the story of a woman who feels that God has deserted her.

GRAHAM: Do you, with now *The Emperor of Ice Cream* and *The Lonely Passion of Judith Hearne,* do you read much Graham Greene?

MOORE: Well, I think I've read all his books. Certainly any writer I like in that way I do read all his books.

GRAHAM: I think of this sweat that so many of Greene's characters are in over their faith, some of them having much more than they realize at the time.

MOORE: Greene in a sense is my opposite, or was at one time, in his handling of faith, because he was a convert to Catholicism, and he was usually dealing with a question of a person who had faith, but was a sinner. Now, I was brought up a Catholic and am not a practicing Catholic and do not consider myself a Catholic anymore even though I've written about Catholicism a great deal. But I am always dealing with the opposite thing, the person who was brought up in the Catholic faith, and loses it, and does not really consider themselves a sinner but feels God's the sinner.

GRAHAM: There's a line in *The Emperor of Ice Cream* where lack of faith was the one deadly sin. It's very late in the book, where I read faith then to mean, oh, human fidelity, rather than theological. . . .

MOORE: It is historical in that sense, too. What happened was, at that period of history, the time of the 1939 war, people of my father's generation, who had all their lives been anti-British, and were vaguely startled by being pro-Mussolini in the early days. Then they became rather pro-Franco because he was keeping the Communists at bay. They woke up overnight to find that they'd been wrong, and that they were on the wrong side, and that the values by which they had lived were shot in a sense. And I think all of England woke up—never mind the Irish—all the English woke up to the fact that they were living in the past, that Chamberlain's "We have dismantled danger, we have plucked this flower, peace," Munich had been a sellout. And that was a terrible blow for that generation to take.

II. *I try to make fiction as open-ended as life is.*

GRAHAM: Brian, I had shoved at me not too long ago a book, *I Am Mary Dunne,* which is now two or three years old, isn't it?

MOORE: Yes, three years.

GRAHAM: It was given to me by a young woman who said it's not really fair that a man can write a book like this, and I don't see how he could possibly understand a woman's psychology, especially the rather particular nervousness of the pre-menstrual time when everything seems to get, some way or another, out of proportion. But it's a good bit more than that, isn't it? That is not just a gimmick, is it, just to get her high, so to speak?

MOORE: I suppose you could call it a gimmick in one sense, in that I wanted to make a paradigm of madness, as we all seem a little bit mad today. But I've discovered when you write novels, if you say to the reader that a person is mad, they immediately think they are clinically mad. We can't relate to people who are clinically mad.

GRAHAM: I've found this—this black and white reading of people.

MOORE: Yes, yes, people tend to say, That person's mad, I can't discuss things with him. People still think of lunacy in eighteenth-century terms. This woman is not mad, but all women go through varying degrees in a period of each month when they are more or less upset, some women very little. The pre-menstrual tension is in a way the symptom of the madness we all feel, the tension of normal life. However, because the woman is only pre-menstrually tense, you think of her as normal.

GRAHAM: A normal human being with almost the kind of problem we have when we read the evening newspaper and find some new horrors to intensify life.

MOORE: You're on a bus, and you're too close to other people and you feel nervous.

GRAHAM: You brought up a point that I was tremendously teased by. Through the novel you don't make the inanimate world alive, but it does in some way wind up being an aggressor. Restaurant tables are a little too close to the chair; the seat on the bus is too narrow; the bus starts and someway Mary Dunne hits herself on a post or something; so that you keep the tension there with these interferences with her life. One thing I was wondering with the novel, does it make any difference whether some of these events are real or not? I'm thinking of some of the public . . . well, accostments, really, of Mary Dunne, where one man comes up and makes a vulgar proposition and another man blows a kiss at her. Do you conceive of these in her mind or simply as accidents of life that did happen?

MOORE: They're accidents of life that did happen, and do happen, to women on the street in New York every day in the year. And the tension of New York, the city I was writing about, the tension of a very big city—London, New York, any big city—is that there are too many people in it. So if you write about people living in these cities, the city becomes a character in the novel. New York is a character in this novel. It's an aggressive character in the novel.

GRAHAM: Let me ask you, as a grossly ignorant American reader, are you manipulating Toronto and Montreal in a way that I, not knowing Canada at all, am not getting? Are they characters also, as New York is?

MOORE: No, not really, except I'm still a Canadian citizen. I was originally an Irishman, and I took citizenship in Canada and lived there for some years. And then I moved to New York on a fellowship, actually. And I was always intrigued by the fact that I'd lived twelve years in a country which has a relationship to America much as the relationship Ireland has to England. A smaller country living in the shadow of a big country.

GRAHAM: I hope we don't cast quite the shadow over Canada that England has many centuries cast over my forebears.

MOORE: Not in the sense of cruelty, but in the sense of economic dominance.

GRAHAM: I see. Well, in the novel, *I Am Mary Dunne,* we have one day in the life of a woman. She expands out through these flashbacks into her childhood, the two marriages, and she is now in her third marriage—and this third marriage, is she going to win on this one? I was sometimes confused almost by Terence's—oh, *solicitousness* about her, hovering too much. Was he going to some way encapsulate her as neither of the other husbands did? The poor young boy, Jimmy Phelan, who . . . well, they were just too young, just too many pressures . . . and then the second one, the newspaperman. . . . Terence seems to be talented—is he genuinely talented?

Moore: Well, that was one of the things that I tried to do in the book, and it's always risky. If you discuss in any novel whether the person is talented or not talented, you make a flat statement. And I once wrote a novel called *An Answer from Limbo,* in which a writer was the main character, and you might wonder if he's really talented, then all these things he's doing are worthwhile even if he's not worthwhile. But, you can't. Talent is a matter of opinion. Mary Dunne is in love with this man; he's a playwright who, she feels, might be possibly a little too commercial. But, she's in this state of love, and when you're in a state of love with another person, you are blind to their real merits or not. And the state that she is in at the moment is a state of love. Terence is the husband she does not know, because she has not left him. If you notice, when you've left a wife or husband, it's a closed incident. Then they *do* become a person you can make a judgment on.

Graham: Sort of like the way we view Latin and Greek literature. It's a closed matter now, and we can stand way back and see this unchanging thing.

Moore: But don't you think that's true, though, of any marriage? When you're married to a person, you have to be blind to several of their faults.

Graham: Oh, you may see them, but you better swallow them. (laughs)

Moore: Yes, better swallow them.

Graham: Well, the reason I asked the question, really, is that I'm terribly interested in the way a writer takes a single day and makes it so rich through memory and so often through the suggestion of the future. We're not really dealing here at all with *I Am Mary Dunne.* We're not simply dealing with a single day. We're dealing with this little girl, all the way back to when she was in fact . . . what's the wonderful thing? You switch, in the opening pages, you switch the famous Cartesian *Cogito ergo sum* to *Memento ergo sum.* And she is trying, of course, throughout the novel, through memory, to find out who she is, really.

MOORE: The sense of that theory in the book is stated at the beginning: Descartes said, I think, therefore I am; and I was trying to say, I remember, therefore I am. And what we remember is really the only part of our lives which we retain. And how she remembers her former husbands is how they exist in this book. And perhaps she's not telling the truth about the first. But the drunken newspaperman she was married to, perhaps he did commit suicide at the end, perhaps he didn't. Actually he did, but was she responsible or wasn't she? I was trying to bring up all these things that worry us, how guilty are we, or how responsible are we for other people's lives, for the lives of the people we are mixed up with.

GRAHAM: Yes, precisely how much commitment, in certain ways, can we afford to give, or must give? A major question. The thing that I was attracted to in the novel was your capacity with the— I think particularly, with the newspaper husband, though it happens with the third husband also. . . . You are able to make these men, oh, people you are able to believe she would marry. They are men of considerable charm, really, and their characters are formed, although we don't see that much of them really, and they are always filtered through her eyes. I'm not quite sure, what was going on in a way, when Janice Sloane comes down, Mary Dunne's old friend from Canada, and visits Mary Dunne in New York. And Janice is in a swivet. She's angry with her husband. She's convinced he's having an affair, and she wants to retaliate. Now, that's not the kind of thing Mary Dunne would have done.

MOORE: She's the exact opposite to Mary Dunne.

GRAHAM: She's much more honest than Janice Sloane.

MOORE: What I tried to do with that incident was . . . It's what writers call a set piece in the novel. It's a thing which you could understand on its own, an incident which is almost like a short story, could almost stand on its own. I wanted to show the peculiar relationships that also exist between well-educated, fairly well-to-do women today who do meet over lunch, discuss things extremely frankly, and there are all kinds of hidden barbs behind it. Also what I wanted to do in that is say something about psychoanalysis. I discovered when I lived in New York that a lot of people have been psychoanalyzed and the analysis had not taken. They had reached the point in the analysis where they had transferred, let's say, their guilt from feeling guilty about their behavior to their parents. But then they had moved into the second stage where they merely blamed their parents for everything. Then they reached the third stage where they absolved their parents. So Janice Sloane is a perfect example of the kind of person who has been unsuccessfully analyzed. She blames everybody else for everything, and that makes her a comic character in a sense.

GRAHAM: Yes, she's a gross character, really.

MOORE: Graham Greene wrote me a nice letter about the book, picked on that one incident, and said that in a sense was his favorite incident in the book, because he recognized it was technically interesting to do and get away with it.

GRAHAM: Well, the thing that I was left with from the novel *I Am Mary Dunne* was the continuing, not blame at all, but almost fear that she has of her father. Is she not, does she not remain so afraid that she might be promiscuous, as her father seemingly was, that she almost can't think about him at all? She's not freed of him by any means at the end, is she?

MOORE: No, not at all, and as you said earlier, the thing I tried to set up in this book . . . I try to make fiction as open-ended as life. In other words, I do not try to write nineteenth-century novels where at the end Dickens says, Right, and Tiny Tim went off and he became a greengrocer or whatever. I like to leave it open. I like to leave the reader saying at this point, Well, I dunno if this woman is going to make it. I dunno if she really is clinically mad. I mean, she may be gonna get worse because he's too solicitous, for instance. He must be worried. I want to leave it the way we would worry about a friend. And I find . . . I've written seven novels, and I found that if you have a good, a real character in a novel they are open-ended.

GRAHAM: They do move into the future.

MOORE: So you hear people say afterwards: "Well, I don't think that character would have done that." And then you have succeeded because they're like real people.

III. *I am sitting in this room talking to you. You may remind me of somebody else. The shadow of that person may stand behind you or be flitting around in my brain at that moment I'm talking to you, or vice versa.*

GRAHAM: Brian, I've just finished *The Emperor of Ice Cream,* which was 1965, and *I Am Mary Dunne,* which was 1968. Now, bluntly, I liked both of them. You're probably going to tell me I should read *all* of your works. But what sequence might I go at them in? What do you suggest I go to next?

MOORE: I think if you go to any writer asking what book you should read next, he'll always say the book he hasn't published yet, and I have a new book coming out called *Fergus.* So, of course, that's the one I would like people to read. However, there is a sequence in my work. I was born and brought up in Ireland, and my first two novels are novels written in Ireland with Irish backgrounds. My first novel, *The Lonely Passion of Judith Hearne,* was published in 1956. It, in a way, has always been my best-known novel, slightly irritating for a writer when his first novel is probably the one that people come up to you at a party and say, "You wrote that book." And for many people I never wrote another book. It was peculiar because it was a book about an alcoholic Irish spinster and it doesn't sound a very hopeful subject. In fact when I wrote the book I was turned down by thirteen American publishers.

GRAHAM: Oh, really? That's an encouraging note, then, for the rest of us who might think we can write.

MOORE: Yes, it was my first novel, and it was finally published in Britain. And it got great reviews in Britain whereupon it was immediately published in America and it got great reviews in America. But they had published very few copies of it so that it took a long time to get off the ground, but it did, and stayed in print. It was a book about loneliness. My second book, *The Feast of Lupercal,* was a story about a thirty-seven-year-old Irish schoolmaster, a Catholic who falls in love with a Protestant girl and gets involved in a scandal in the school because he's believed to have had relations with her.

GRAHAM: Is the Catholic-Protestant tension as widespread as the newspapers seem to indicate?

MOORE: I see what you're getting at. Sad to say, it is. I was back in Ireland last year and, to my horror, after twenty-five years, things were as bad as ever they were.

GRAHAM: The tension is still that strong?

MOORE: It's come up again. However, those were two Irish books. And then I went to Canada, and I wrote a book, in which the main character again is Irish, called *The Luck of Ginger Coffey*. That is my sort of second-best book, I guess. Mainly I think, because it was made into a film. And there's no doubt about it, if a book's made into even an arthouse movie, people are going to be interested in it. Many people think that the best book I wrote was a book about New York, which is again conflict of generations between Irish people. It's called *An Answer from Limbo*. And so, to answer your earlier question in a very roundabout way, if I wanted you to read one of my books now—which I have published—I would probably like you to read *An Answer from Limbo,* because in a way it was my most complicated book technically and my most ambitious technically.

GRAHAM: Then I'm interested. One of the reasons I think I like your *I Am Mary Dunne* better than *The Emperor of Ice Cream* —it's a curious reason because with *The Emperor of Ice Cream* I lived with the characters, I think it was a very successful novel —but technically I think *I Am Mary Dunne* was a more interesting book with the flashbacks, with the insets, with the particular complicated human relations there. So I'll take a shot with *An Answer from Limbo*. What about *Fergus,* the brand-new one?

MOORE: I think you always like the book you just finished, but I think *Fergus* is a very interesting book in the sense that it's more original in idea than any other of my books so far. It is a book about a man, rather like myself but younger, who wakes up one morning in a house in California, where he's living with a girl, to the apparent presences of his dead parents in the house. Now, he's not mad.

GRAHAM: All your books have ghosts in them, haven't they?

MOORE: In this book we have the ghosts right in the living room and he has conversations with his father and his mother, both of whom are dead. And he has these conversations with these ghost figures who are very real to him. In fact they even eat food. When they're there, they go and raid the refrigerator.

GRAHAM: That's not a traditional ghost.

MOORE: No, of course not, but how do we know what a real ghost would do? He also meets real people during the day, so he's got a mixture of his past and his present. I am sitting in this room talking to you. You may remind me of somebody else. The shadow of that person may stand behind you or be flitting around in my brain at the moment I'm talking to you, or vice versa. With me, the fact that you said earlier that you were Irish immediately sets up our Irish-American origin, sets up a chain reaction, so I think of Jesuits I have known. Actually, in this book, the priests who educated him as a boy return, too, and they want to hear his confession. And I have that. I don't want to give away the ending of the book, but the book is a mysterious experience. He feels that something's happening. There's some reason why these people have come back from his past. He feels threatened by them. I hope the book is moving—because if there is any real character in it it is probably my own father, so it contains something of my relationship with my parents.

GRAHAM: You writers are absolutely enmeshed in the problems of "memory" and "time," with "memory" seemingly being so strong, whether it's an absolute recording memory or a transformed memory; while "time" almost doesn't mean anything, as if everything is happening now and is some way affecting everything else.

MOORE: For novelists that don't write journalistic novels or people that don't write satire, for people like myself who deal in the real world in novels but at the same time are metaphysically inclined, there is a metaphysical quality in my novels which is started quietly and is now coming forward. These figures from the past . . . one of the reasons for this being, I think, I've been a novelist for fifteen years which means now I've spent fifteen years, most of my working days, sitting alone in a room.

GRAHAM: It's long hard work, isn't it?

MOORE: It's a hard and lonely life in that sense. One of the things that happened to people in concentration camps in the last war was that they found that people could remember whole books they'd read because they were alone all the time, and they would tell them to other inmates. And I think that is one of the reasons to answer you, in a very practical way, why memory begins to play such an important part in my work. Because I'm sitting alone and I'm a lot of the time remembering.

GRAHAM: Not only trying to imagine experience, but trying to dredge from your own experience.

MOORE: Use my own experience, yes. I've always used my own life as the canvas on which I write about these other people.

GRAHAM: What do you find in the act of writing? Or let's go directly to the last novel, *Fergus*. What were your major problems really? Total structure, or the movement of scenes, or the large conception of the book?

MOORE: The great problem of the book was to make the—I hate to use the words "ghost figures"—make the ghost figures as real as the other people, to describe their clothes intimately, to describe their manners intimately, to make you feel that they were just as much in the room as the other people, the real ordinary people you meet every day. And secondly, to make two totally different worlds, contemporary life in southern California and life in Ireland, middle-class Ireland of say twenty-five years ago, totally believable, so that you believed as much in the dead father being in the room as you believed in the repairman being in the room at the same moment. That was technically difficult. But technically—you can tell when you're writing a thing whether it's succeeding or not. And I had moments in all of my books—I know of times when they haven't succeeded—I suspect at times they haven't succeeded. But technically in *Fergus*, for some extraordinary reason, it began to succeed almost from the beginning moment I wrote it; because the man is in the room— I'll just give you a little scene—the man is in the room. Fergus is in the room in the morning, his girl has left, and he's feeling quite sorry for himself, and he finds himself weeping. And he turns and looks at the Pacific Ocean, and he's staring at the Pacific Ocean and looks back and sees his father, who's dead twenty-five years, sitting in the chair wearing a suit and wearing his eyeglasses just as he used to. And Fergus says "Aah, Jesus Christ!" He's terrified at seeing his father. And his father, then, as a very devout Catholic, immediately takes his hand and makes the sign of the cross. Well, in some way, you can see it yourself, you believe in his father.

GRAHAM: The father is doing what that father should have done.

MOORE: And then another thing that emerges in the book. As the book continues, Fergus finds out that, whatever these appearances are, the ghosts can tell him nothing that he did not know about his parents. That's the metaphysical thing. They cannot tell you anything that you didn't know.

GRAHAM: They can prompt memory by their presence?

MOORE: They can prompt the memory you have, and they can prompt the misconceptions you have. But they cannot tell the real truth. He discovers that he is hearing them played back someway through himself.

GRAHAM: May I ask you this now—you've tempted me toward this—do you have to resist temptations, as novelist, to spell things out, almost, in a sense, to write an essay?

MOORE: No, the most spelling out I think I've done has been this interview by far. I am surprised to hear myself spell it out so clearly to you, and if the book were in the bookstores, which it won't be for a few months, I would be much more leery of saying all this to you. I started trying to explain it to you, as a friend, and yet when you say "metaphysics" or when you find yourself spelling it out, that is a little deadening, isn't it?

IV. *One of the things, I think, about getting older is you forgive a writer anything if he's funny.*

GRAHAM: Every writer lives in a world of writers. We're here at the Hollins Conference, and the writers are obviously enthusiastic about talking with each other. They read each other's works. What world do you live in, Brian, in terms of literary work? What books are you reading now or have read that you think I'd like to read? What ones have meant most to you?

MOORE: I live in California, on the beach, quite far away from Los Angeles and can't even get television where I am. So I do read quite a lot.

GRAHAM: Is it a danger for a writer to read a great deal?

MOORE: I don't think so. There's a moment when you're writing fiction yourself when it's dangerous to be reading a lot of other fiction, or perhaps it bores you to read at that point. The writer I've come across recently, in the sense of the last seven or eight years, who really does interest me and I sort of rush out to buy everything he writes, but he writes very little, is an Argentinian writer called Jorge Luis Borges. He is nearly blind now and is in his seventies. And he's director of the National Library of Buenos Aires. He's a man who's written a very small amount. In fact all of his collected writings are about the size of two of my books here. But his stuff is fantastic. It's not realistic, and they are very short pieces. But when you are reading them, you suddenly feel—it's a very strange feeling for me—you feel you're in the presence of a great man, a great mind. And he's a great man because he's a very simple man. He was interviewed by an American called Richard Bergen, who wasn't a very good interviewer—you could see it right away. But Borges talked with this terrific candor and simplicity and pleasure over the fact that he was being interviewed. He speaks perfect English apparently. I suddenly thought, "It's extraordinary, just his conversation is an interesting as everything he writes," and that's the mark of a great man.

GRAHAM: He's absolutely full of what he is, then?

MOORE: Absolutely full of what he is. He writes sharp tales about metaphysical subjects. He wrote a thing which is one page long called "Borges and I," which unfortunately I couldn't quote from memory, because it sums up so completely the difference between one's public *persona* and one's private *persona*.

GRAHAM: You're telling me a man can get you absolutely involved with himself in a single page?

MOORE: A short single page. It's a page when you've read it you say—it's like a picture. You want to put it on the wall and look at it again and again. And this is in translation.

GRAHAM: I think I know Henry Fielding, the man, having read *Tom Jones*. But that runs eight hundred pages; so the thought that a man could hit you strongly in a single page. . . ! Obviously it's a poetic compression. Would you call it a poetic language?

MOORE: No, it's a very simple plain prose, and that's why it translates well. One of the things that Borges does is, if he had to tell the story of—let me see—if he had to tell the story of John Kennedy's assassination, he would tell it, his life and assassination, in about four pages. Because he doesn't bother with character. He just tells what happened, and in the way he tells it, and the way this fantastic mind works, you would have a completely new insight about the Kennedy assassination.

GRAHAM: Brian, I'm sorry but I'm going to take this on an act of faith until I can get Borges, because I can't believe a man can operate this efficiently. I'll certainly go after Borges and see this. Anyone else you have been reading recently?

MOORE: One of the things, I think, about getting older is you forgive a writer anything if he's funny. If someone can make me laugh, I really love that book. I remember when I read *Lucky Jim* years ago. Do you remember *Lucky Jim?*

GRAHAM: God, yes!

MOORE: I sat up 'til about two in the morning, laughing and saying, "Here, read this, read this—wait'll I finish." I've found— like a lot of other people apparently—I found that *Portnoy's Complaint* was a book like this for me. I thought it was hilarious. And I sat up reading this. It was even more surprising. I knew Philip Roth and I'd always thought he was an amusing raconteur fellow to talk with, but I didn't know he was this hilariously funny.

GRAHAM: There are some tremendously funny scenes in his *Letting Go,* that novel about those grim graduate students. One involving a very stuffy chairman of the department and some of these intense young instructors who come to a party and they are introduced to the daughters as "people who work for Daddy." This is one of the great lines in literature. Do you know, you must know, Joyce Cary's work, if you like a funny novelist.

MOORE: I thought *Mr. Johnson* was a marvelous book about Africa, and it was probably the best book on the strange relationship between the British and their African subjects.

GRAHAM: I've heard political scientists assign that book for understanding colonialism.

MOORE: I like his book, but I thought it was uneven. Here's a man whose ambition was greater than his talents in many ways, because he attempted some very difficult things and did not always succeed, for me, technically, as a writer. When he went into the mind of a woman, it didn't work for me, it just didn't work. I was sorry that it hadn't come off. But fiction is suspension of disbelief, and the minute you can suspend it, and that did happen to me occasionally with Joyce Cary.

GRAHAM: Have you read Elizabeth Bowen's things much? I'm thinking particularly of *The Death of the Heart?*

MOORE: Yes, I've read Elizabeth Bowen, but it's a fairly long time ago, to be honest, since I did read her. Like most Irish people, I did read her when I was quite young because she was quite prominent. We are gifted, or cursed, with a great number of very good writers in Ireland. And Joyce was a much bigger influence on me than these other people.

GRAHAM: With your move from Ireland to Canada, do you feel there are major adjustments, or is the back and forth flow strong? Are there major adjustments for your moving from predominantly Irish and English literature into American?

MOORE: I'm living in America now and have been for several years. But the thing which I think, sociologically or historically, I have tried to do—and I'm not taking any pride in this, it's just an accident of Fate—I think I am the first Irish-born Irish writer who came to America and has made the transition to writing about American people: Americans who are Irish, and Americans who are not Irish, and Canadians who are not Irish. But I have never been faulted by anyone in that I wrote bad American idiom, or that my Americans don't seem real. Maybe that might be my little niche in history because the Irish writer and the English writer have a curious inability to leave home fictionally. Even take a good writer like Graham Greene. People have said his American is wrong, Greene once said, "I gave it to everybody to check, my sister-in-law is an American. I listened to her, but the American was still tin." He had something wrong with his diction, and he had something wrong with his psyche. Actually it's because Greene doesn't *like* Americans, and you cannot write about a country without loving it. I know that sounds awfully corny to say, and I didn't think of it until right now.

GRAHAM: It is a matter of commitment to get inside.

MOORE: And to *see* Americans. Americans are very mysterious to Europeans, they're like Russians. They seem to be different. They seem to have a different way of operating, and I am constantly amazed, because I keep going back between the two countries, at how un-understanding most of the English friends I have are about Americans.

GRAHAM: It's so incredibly easy, of course. to live with the caricature that we all have and bluntly, to re-prove the caricature. I've found curious things somewhat in line with this. Having always lived on the East Coast myself, when I lived in the Middle West I wound up almost letting myself use Sinclair Lewis' satires as my handbook for observing—not for understanding, but literally for observing. And I'm sure I did a gross injustice.

MOORE: Perhaps that's something that we all do, and the British particularly do. They see Americans through a fictional glass.

GRAHAM: I know I've upset Englishmen and Germans because I like music. They were really quite surprised that I could handle a subtle distinction musically, because I was nothing but a boneheaded American. They could not believe that I did not lust for a great big car. This was something that they "demanded" of me.

MOORE: We were talking to some people in California recently— English professors who'd come out to teach at Berkeley and UCLA—and they said, "But there's so much protest here." They had not realized that Americans could be disgruntled with America. That's the perfect example of looking at the caricature. In fact, they couldn't even read the papers.

Richard Wilbur

BIOGRAPHICAL

Born: 1 March 1921.

Education: B.A. Amherst 1942, M.A. Harvard 1947.

Occupational: Service in 36th Division ("The Texas Infantry") in World War II; has taught at Harvard and Wellesley, and since 1957 has been Professor of English at Wesleyan University.

Books: Poetry—*The Beautiful Changes* (1947), *Ceremony* (1950), *Things of This World* (1956), *Poems 1943–1956* (1957), *Advice to a Prophet* (1961), *Poems of Richard Wilbur* (1963), *Complaint* (1968), and *Walking to Sleep* (1969); translations—*The Misanthrope* (1955), *Tartuffe* (1963); other—*A Bestiary* (with Alexander Calder, 1955) and *Candide* (with Lillian Hellman, 1957). Has edited a number of collections and is author of some fine children's books including *Loudmouse* (1968) and *Digging for China* (1970).

Honors, prizes, fellowships, and awards are many and various. Among these, the National Book Award and the Pulitzer Prize in 1957 for *Things of This World* and the Bollingen Translation Award in 1968. He is a member of both the American Academy of Arts and Sciences and the National Institute of Arts and Letters.

SNAPSHOT

Dick Wilbur is tall, youthfully handsome, graceful, and slow-moving, almost stately, except when he's on the tennis court, climbing trees or flying kites. He is sturdier than photographs allow him to be, and his voice is always deeper and richer than you expect it to be. Chiefly, moving or in repose, there is an easy, natural, animal elegance about him. Like an eight-point buck. And nothing contrived about it, unless the deer's poise and grace and control is also to be named so. No, it comes with the breath, the rhythm of his breathing. But there is also a sudden childish brightness, a bright and undisguised glint of inner energy that can even mean mischief.

All of which might—and shouldn't—divert attention from the enormous power of his self-control, the lithe but coiled fury of his chosen reticence.

With a wide-brim hat, jeans and boots he could pass for a cowboy if you ever saw one. And it's true, he made the walk in the sun with the Texas infantry.

I. *I think it's an unanswerable question how much knowledge of nature one can presume people to possess nowadays.*

GRAHAM: Professor Wilbur and I are talking about his latest book of poetry, *Walking to Sleep.* When was that actually published, Dick? That's very recent, isn't it?

WILBUR: It was March, 1969.

GRAHAM: It reflects clearly to me some enduring attitudes, concerns, and methods of yours. Your first book came out, oh, twenty-three years ago, wasn't it?

WILBUR: I think it was 1947. I can't subtract.

GRAHAM: That's going back a bit. One of the things that fascinates me, since I've been living in the country and I've always done a lot of hiking, and that involved nature study, what I would call close observation—a great number of your poems find their footing in a very solid sense of sight, touch, a sense of natural growth, often as "action." I don't think these poems are ever static pictures, but it's raw observation we first see. And I was wondering—to bring in another piece, given our urban society—I can remember so clearly a graduate student with me from Manhattan, in reading Emily Dickinson with that wonderful little line of a snake wrinkling through the grass . . .

WILBUR: . . . "a narrow fellow in the grass . . ."

GRAHAM: This really just didn't mean anything to this man, who was one of the most intelligent, sensitive readers I've ever known. The basic question I'm asking is, How are you going to find your common ground, what do you expect the reader to do with the details of something like this? Are you trying to *recall* for me what a little seed growth looks like? Or are you hazarding that maybe I don't know, maybe I've lived in Manhattan and don't know what happens when that little lima bean comes punching through?

WILBUR: I find when I read the poem you're referring to, which is about cotyledons, that it's best—when I say "read," I mean "read to an audience"—I find that it's best to say a few reminding words about what happens when a bean seedling comes up out of the ground. Many urban people, of course, keep backyard gardens and do know what a bean looks like, and I guess there are people in the country who have forgotten. I think it's an unanswerable question how much knowledge of nature one can presume people to possess nowadays. Writers of the last century presumed a great deal and probably pretty safely. At present I don't know what one can do, given the fact that poetry has got to be economical and not too explanatory, but just hope that one will describe clearly enough so that the person somewhat ignorant of natural things will divine what must be the case, what it must be like.

GRAHAM: In one of the poems I like particularly you reverse the process. This little thing called "Riddle"—it's on page thirty-seven. Would you mind reading it? It's so short. This is a sort of reverse temptation in a way, since we've got no title and we don't know what we're dealing with, and the question is, "Do we know?" at the end, of course.

WILBUR: The riddle is a fascinating form. It got degraded considerably, in the last century, into a sort of parlor game for children—charades and anagrams. The sort of riddle that interests me is the riddle which describes a concept or a thing without naming it. It's a serious form of poetry, as the Greeks and the early Anglo-Saxon poets knew. I think one thing that comes out of the riddle, deriving from the period of hesitation you undergo before deciding to name the thing, is a sense of how many properties in the world are shared. If your riddle is full of something about legs—you know, there's a riddle that begins "Two legs sat on three legs, and in came four legs"— well, it takes you a little while to guess that. Before you have guessed it, you spend a moment in wonder at the infinite "legged-ness" of things.

GRAHAM: All the envelopes, all the skins that you find in the world. . . .

WILBUR: Right. And this kind of momentary wonder before you get the answer is not false to the spirit of poetry; because it seems to me that the general drift of poetry is through simile and the bolder form of metaphor to compare things to each other, to liken things to each other, even to say that things are the same. To get everything connected. Well, let me read the riddle that you suggested. It goes:

> Where far in forest I am laid,
> In a place ringed around by stones,

Look for no melancholy shade,
And have no thoughts of buried bones;
For I am bodiless and bright,
And fill this glade with sudden glow;
The leaves are washed in under-light;
Shade lies upon the boughs like snow.

GRAHAM: It seems so obvious to me, after I looked in the back of the book and got the answer, that I'm depressed, really. The word "laid," there. One lays a fire when one is camping and . . .

WILBUR: Yes, that's playing fair.

GRAHAM: I don't think you cheated me at all, that's what's depressing.

WILBUR: Of course, it also suggests being buried, doesn't it? It can go. . . .

GRAHAM: But then you warn against that very thing.

WILBUR: But the warnings operate as red herrings.

GRAHAM: Oh really? I'm not familiar enough with the form then.

WILBUR: If I say to you, Don't think of such and such a thing, you find yourself thinking of it. And it seems to me when I say, "Look for no melancholy shade" and "have no thoughts of buried bones," there your thoughts are all filled up with ghosts and bones. And perhaps you don't pay attention to the real clues, which are the "leaves are washed in under-light; Shade lies upon the boughs like snow." How are you going to get the shade on top of the boughs unless there's a fire underneath?

GRAHAM: I'm afraid maybe I am trying to make an "either-or" of this, but having experienced a campfire, one has through this little poem—a campfire. And yet I don't know, I don't know how much "putting together" a reader can do. You know that awful business with Sir Walter Scott, those interminable descriptions of costumes that someone had on. And then Lessing's argument, in fact, can you really reconstruct this picture? He says "no." Scott obviously said "yes." And I think you're saying "yes" here. Rather than *recalling* the painting, the picture *à la* that "Playboy" poem of yours, you are constructing it.

WILBUR: I suppose people who never had seen a fire under woods before they approach that little riddle may have trouble.

GRAHAM: I'm really very interested in this whole problem of the common ground. What I find in so many of your poems—for instance your interest in astronomy—I have a hard time, having never dealt with astronomy at all, of knowing quite how much is my burden and how much is yours. I guess what you already have said is, You have to do the best you can, throw it down, and hope it can be picked up.

WILBUR: I think so, because if you include in such a poem as my poem "In the Field," if you include a full statement of the big bang theory of the creation of the universe, you lose all impetus, and the poem loses its dramatic quality. It's not intended to be informational, really; it's intended to dwell on two opposing feelings one may have living on the surface of the earth.

GRAHAM: You would cut yourself off from your own experience. You couldn't write a little couplet on Berkeley and Dr. Johnson kicking that stone, even though that was very much a part of your knowledge, if you had to sort of back-check with every screaming reader.

WILBUR: I suppose, really, the things I refer to in my poems are things that on the whole can quickly be got in a dictionary if they're not already in the reader's head. Most people, I think, have heard about Dr. Johnson kicking the stone and most people have in mind what is essential about Berkeley's philosophy, and that's all that's needed for the grasping of that poem.

GRAHAM: With your students, do they seem to see nature as important, or are you getting more "urban" poetry? You, clearly, are drawn toward the country.

WILBUR: I do actually use quite a lot of urban imagery. I describe, I concern myself with urban things. I have a poem about the new railway station in the city of Rome in which I try to describe it pretty thoroughly and to get away with using technical and architectural words in the process. And I describe city fountains, things of that sort. I should hate to get the reputation of favoring nature and contending that the urban—indeed, I'd like to think of the city as a part of nature.

II. *I don't trust anybody who isn't capable of nonsense and of moments of collapse into ridiculousness.*

GRAHAM: Dick, there are a number of things I am fixed on, almost, in your poetry. I'm excited about your powers of observation and the variety of metrics that I find. I should think, in that little "Aubade" you have "well-chilled wine." That's a beautifully put-together little gathering of consonants. But today, rather than the direct observation, I'd like it if you'd talk with me a little bit about the whole idea of wit and humor, mockery, in poetry. I'm afraid of the word irony. I know that I am trapped somewhat in—was it Matthew Arnold who felt that poetry should be of "high seriousness," even though I know better. I've read too much of Pope, so I know that there can be breathtakingly high seriousness in the joke. We're used to black humor now, especially in our novelists, so that I should not have this bind. Can you tell—what's wrong with me at this point? Because I know I enjoy these very witty poems of yours.

WILBUR: I suppose that it isn't a new discovery that wit is not the reverse of seriousness, but a part of seriousness, a means of being serious. But I think, indeed, it was forgotten by a number of people during the earnest last century. Especially as so many poets in England and America gave themselves the responsibility to reassure and uplift a new, expanded literate audience. I do think that Newton Arvin, in his book on Longfellow, was right in explaining so many phenomena in nineteenth-century English-language poetry in terms of "the new literacy." You're given a new audience, toward which you feel a kind of social responsibility.

GRAHAM: There's that whole nineteenth-century passion for education, which has continued certainly into this century.

WILBUR: Yes, education and Longfellow are related phenomena, I think. But now we have quite a different sense of the audience, I think, and I suppose a greater focus on the work itself and are less constrained by the expectations of any possible reader. So we can return to the truth that a serious poem is stronger if it allows itself to be wild and absurd and potentially ridiculous at times.

GRAHAM: All of these terms suddenly call up, I think, that wonderful poem of yours called "Playboy." Would you mind reading that, it's—I think page thirty-eight—it is a serious poem.

WILBUR: It's finally a serious poem. It's a satirical poem, but not satirical in a grim sense. I'm not trying to wipe anything out, you know.

GRAHAM: The wonderful little image of the boy eating, the sidelong swipe at the sandwich that he takes, right there is a kind of sympathetic . . .

WILBUR: Yes . . . I don't mean to be too superior to him, but it is, finally, meant to be a gently satiric poem. Well, let me read it:

PLAYBOY

High on his stockroom ladder like a dunce
The stock-boy sits, and studies like a sage
The subject matter of one glossy page,
As lost in curves as Archimedes once.

Sometimes, without a glance, he feeds himself.
The left hand, like a mother-bird in flight,
Brings him a sandwich for a sidelong bite,
And then returns it to a dusty shelf.

What so engrosses him? The wild décor
Of this pink-papered alcove into which
A naked girl has stumbled, with its rich
Welter of pelts and pillows on the floor,

Amidst which, kneeling in a supple pose,
She lifts a goblet in her farther hand,
As if about to toast a flower-stand
Above which hovers an exploding rose

Fired from a long-necked crystal vase that rests
Upon a tasseled and vermilion cloth
One taste of which would shrivel up a moth?
Or is he pondering her perfect breasts?

Nothing escapes him of her body's grace
Or of her floodlit skin, so sleek and warm
And yet so strangely like a uniform,
But what now grips his fancy is her face,

And how the cunning picture holds her still
At just that smiling instant when her soul,
Grown sweetly faint, and swept beyond control,
Consents to his inexorable will.

GRAHAM: I think that long, long line, that takes the burden of
the description of the *Playboy* fold-out and collapses it of its
own weight, is an absolute delight.

WILBUR: It's fun, for various purposes, to try to write long sentences in verse. In this case, of course, the trick is to make the sentence so complex as to suggest the mad clutter of that kind of photography.

GRAHAM: The sort of pseudo-Eastern richness of the decor. With this poem you give us so many leads that no one could help but join you at once. But your title poem in *Walking to Sleep* was one that excited me. I've read it and reread it now, and I find shifts of tone in the poem. I think some of the shifts involve a warning almost, through wit or humor. Would you read a bit of it, Dick, and say something about—maybe eight or ten lines—what I'm talking about. It happens very soon.

WILBUR: I think something of what you talk about happens in the first few lines.

GRAHAM: Yes, there's that mechanistic analogy, almost, in the first two analogies in the first two lines.

WILBUR: Well, here goes—"Walking to Sleep." This is—I ought to say, parenthetically, that this is a poem about someone advising someone else on how to get off to sleep.

> As a queen sits down, knowing that a chair will be there,
> Or a general raises his hand and is given the field-glasses,
> Step off assuredly into the blank of your mind.
> Something will come to you. Although at first
> You nod through nothing like a fogbound prow,
> Gravel will breed in the margins of your gaze,
> Perhaps with tussocks or a dusty flower,
> And, humped like dolphins playing in the bow-wave,
> Hills will suggest themselves. All such suggestions
> Are yours to take or leave, but hear this warning:

And so on. . . . Yes, I think there are a couple of moments of the kind you're pointing to. For instance, the first line, "As a queen sits down, knowing that a chair will be there," is an encouragement to the sleeper to step off into dreams with confidence, as a queen sits down with confidence. Nevertheless you think of the possibility of the queen sitting down on the floor. And a phrase like "Something will come to you" is very seriously intended, at the same time reflects a very trivial, colloquial—

GRAHAM: —almost vacuous, in a way, possibility. No matter who you are, something happens to anyone's mind. And then the prow, the ship into sleep—and what, gravel grows?

WILBUR: Yes, you shift rather quickly from a sort of marine progress into dreams to a progress along a road.

GRAHAM: And organic, there's the growth of plants, even the growth of gravel, almost, as these things spring up.

WILBUR: The point I was trying to demonstrate, really, what it started off by saying, that as soon as you start to think about something, you furnish it with things, and your furnish any landscape as soon as you start walking along a road, and as soon as you think of a room you start to furnish it.

GRAHAM: As you go on in this poem, you warn, really, that one must not open doors, or must open them with foreknowledge. And then, at some point, you say something like, "What, are you still awake?"

WILBUR: Yes. When I read this long poem aloud to an audience, generally they giggle a little when I say, "What, are you still awake?" because it clearly seems to apply to them, and how well they're taking this hundred-and-forty-line poem.

GRAHAM: Oh, that's bad.

WILBUR: No, I don't mind that at all. I don't mind at all the risk that that line will seem quite simply a gag-line, because by the time we reach it, if my poem is successful, they know that it's serious. And they know that any joke I make will just be a guarantee that there's a whole person talking to them, a whole person who has the sense of balance that's implied in a sense of humor.

GRAHAM: Now this is very interesting. Because another thing I suspect I'm locked in on is admitting or recognizing that there are a number of different kinds of lyrics, not the least being dramatic turns even in lyrics. But this, what you say is very helpful. It is not a single consistent tone like a block of cement, really, but you are revealing the full voice behind this self-aware poet.

WILBUR: I don't trust anybody who isn't capable of nonsense and of moments of collapse into ridiculousness. It seems to be a necessary thing for the serious man or the serious poem, to make these darts, not only into the witty, but into the absurd, into the comic. We don't want art really to be something that's good for us because it's so inexorably disagreeable, you know, like Filboid Studge or rhubarb soda.

III. *My sensibility is attracted to the sculpture kind of thing, in which you bang at something that resists you and try to arrive, with its opposition, at something in the nature of an attractive compromise.*

GRAHAM: I thought that we might talk a bit about your work in translation. The contribution, Dick, frankly, that you've made to my pleasure—my French is best not talked about—lies in your translations of Molière—*Tartuffe* and—what else?

WILBUR: *The Misanthrope* and I'm working now on *L'École des Femmes, The School for Wives,* and expect to be finished this summer.

GRAHAM: This is good news for me, because I've found the language exciting. Unfortunately, I've seen only amateur productions, but with very good leads who could spring with the language really, and you've given me enormous pleasure. This must be a very curious world for you in a way. Is it confining, or exciting, or puzzling? Do any of these words means anything?

WILBUR: It's a lot of things both good and bad to be a translator. If you take on a thing so long as Molière's rhymed plays and are trying to get seventeen or eighteen hundred lines out into rhymed couplets, obviously there are going to be periods of drudgery and frustration. I've spent whole days in which I ended by failing to do one couplet, and that can be very, very distressing. After all, there are only so many rhyming possibilities in English. And there are certain lines, in any French play, for which there is no ready equivalent. You have to think a long time before you get it. Almost always, if you are patient enough, you will find something that will allow you to be faithful, if not to every word, to the thought. I think the important thing is to translate thought by thought.

GRAHAM: Do you, in handling a very long project, such as one of Molière's plays, do you try to go through, almost all the way through, if not quickly, exactly, but to try to get an overall structure, with some finished couplets, perhaps?

WILBUR: I wish I could do that. I've never been good at skipping along, either in my own work, or in translations. There are people who are great, who are quick mockers-up of things, but I can't do it. I have to slog along from couplet to couplet, building it very slowly, and hoping that I won't, in the process, lose a full overview of the work.

GRAHAM: With your *School for Wives* that you're working on

now, do you read a lot of other Molière at the same time you're working on a specific play, to work tonally with him?

WILBUR: I read some Molière criticism. I may read a play or so in French or in English, just to broaden my sense of what he's up to. But mostly I just settle down to it as a bricklayer settles down to building his wall before he starts.

GRAHAM: Is the French particularly difficult?

WILBUR: It's pretty easy. It's a small vocabulary, with certain key words, which are used again and again, for multiple purposes. One does have to learn the flexibility of the key words in playwrights like Molière or Racine. And, of course, you can't ever find, in English, equally flexible key words; so that for a French word of central importance in a Molière play there are going to be seven or eight equivalents in the English. You just don't aspire to reproduce Molière in the sense that you use his limited language.

GRAHAM: Your work in French is obviously your major commitment toward translation, but what other languages do you find most interesting to work with?

WILBUR: Well, I have a kind of a kitchen knowledge of Italian. And so I've done a few translations from Italian, and mean to do a few more. And I've studied a little bit of Russian, but when I try to translate Russian poets, as I've done in the case of Andrei Voznesensky and Anna Akhmatova, and shall do shortly with Yevtushenko, I need help. I need some kind of a linguistic adviser. Indeed, I need someone to sit down with me, go through the whole poem, read it to me in the Russian, translate it into rough English, and then answer all sorts of questions for me as to what the rhythm's doing and what the overtones of particular words are. Then I can settle down and write it as if it were my own poem.

GRAHAM: Then, with this, it is a form, almost, of forced experiment for you as a poet in English, to exercise your skills—I almost want to say against a foreign object?

WILBUR: Well, I like resistance in art. I think there are some artists who think of art as purely expression, as a kind of explosion of the self. My sensibility is attracted to the sculpture kind of thing, in which you bang at something that resists you and try to arrive, with its opposition, at something in the nature of an attractive compromise.

GRAHAM: Dick, would you mind reading the little "Dead Still" here on page seventy?

WILBUR: Yes, this is a poem of Andrei Voznesensky, a youngish Russian poet who's been over here a couple of times and has made quite a hit in America. The translation is called "Dead Still" and it's a poem about a period, oh, I think about 1963 or 1964, when he was being more or less persecuted by the conservatives, or neo-Stalinists, if you will, in the Russian literary establishment. The poem takes place on the shores of the Black Sea, in the midst of a love affair.

DEAD STILL

Now, with your palms on the blades of my shoulders,
Let us embrace:
Let there be only your lips' breath on my face,
Only, behind our backs, the plunge of rollers.

Our backs, which like two shells in moonlight shine,
Are shut behind us now;
We lie here huddled, listening brow to brow,
Like life's twin formula or double sign.

In folly's world-wide wind
Our shoulders shield from the weather
The calm we now beget together,
Like a flame held between hand and hand.

Does each cell have a soul within it?

If so, fling open all your little doors,
And all your souls shall flutter like the linnet
In the cages of my pores.

Nothing is hidden that shall not be known.
Yet by no storm of scorn shall we
Be pried from this embrace, and left alone
Like muted shells forgetful of the sea.

Meanwhile, O load of stress and bother,
Lie on the shells of our backs in a great heap!
It will but press us closer, one to the other.

We are asleep.

GRAHAM: The things that fascinate me in here, and in terms of
the challenge, the difficulty for you as translator—are such
things as the very short lines. It seems to me in here, "Our
shoulders shield from the weather"—it seems to me that the
vowel play, alliteration, and so forth, makes that a fine line. Are
these rather precise—I'm picking on meter and vowel—are these
fairly close to the original?

WILBUR: Oh, they are, they're as close as I can get. I like to try
to have the illusion of perfect fidelity. Of course, that's not to
be accomplished, possibly, but I've pretty well maintained here
Voznesensky's capricious line lengths and his rhyme system,
which is a varying one. And wherever I could find a precise
equivalent to his language, I've done so. There was in this poem
—let's see if I can remember the word for it—darn it, I can't!
There's a word, a Russian word which means small ventilation
window, and the fact is that we don't have in America the
kind of small ventilation windows they have in Russia, and so
we don't have a word for it. Well, what did I say? I said, "Fling
open all your little doors," whereas the Russian of it would
have been "Fling open all your little small ventilation windows." But that's close enough, I think.

GRAHAM: And it gives, actually—"all your souls shall flutter like the linnet"—it seems to me that the flinging open of the doors, in my experience as an American, gives one the sense of out-going, of the potential joining of all these little cells that the lovers could possibly have. So you've got to worry about everything and more, in these translations.

WILBUR: The fact is that no translator can do it all, no translator can simply take any poem that comes his way and do it justice. I think that the translation I just read you comes off fairly well and is one of my better efforts. And—well, the reason it is, is that I feel a considerable sympathy with the attitudes of it, and Max Hayward, the Russian expert, who suggested this poem to me, knew darn well before he suggested it that it was suitable for me.

GRAHAM: This is an interesting terminology—"suitable." It would be madness then, for you simply to take on, let's say in French where you're most easy, simply to take on an "anthology."

WILBUR: That would be very dreary, because I like to do everything I do in the way of translation, for love. And there is, of course, a large puzzle-solving element in any job of translation, but if it's merely puzzle-solving, then it's terribly chilly, and one probably will not convey whatever the emotional content of the original is.

Shelby Foote

BIOGRAPHICAL

Born: 17 November 1916 in Greenville, Mississippi.
Education: Student at Chapel Hill 1935–1937.
Occupational: Long service during World War II, first in U.S. Army in combat in Europe, then in the Marines in the Pacific; since very shortly after World War II he has been a full-time, free-lance, self-supporting writer, except for brief and irregular academic jobs; has taught at Memphis State, Virginia, and he was Writer-in-Residence and remains as Annual Lecturer at Hollins College.
Books: Novels—*Tournament* (1949), *Follow Me Down* (1950), *Love in a Dry Season* (1951), *Shiloh* (1952), *Jordan County* 1954). History—*The Civil War: A Narrative* (Vol. 1, 1958; Vol. 2, 1963). Anthology—*The Night before Chancellorsville* (1957).

Foot has received a number of distinguished grants and awards, including fellowships from both Guggenheim and the Ford Foundation. During the year 1963–64 he was Playwright-in-Residence at the Arena Stage in Washington, D. C.

SNAPSHOT

Women will say, or anyway agree with each other, that Shelby "looks like a Mississippi river boat gambler." They are being more literary than historical, conjuring up *Show Boat* and maybe *Saratoga Trunk*. You can believe it. An easy elegance, unstudied, matter-of-fact, about him. Bearded or not (it changes as he pleases), and even now with a light touch of gray, he is darkly handsome, dark- and soft-voiced. The calm ease of the man who doesn't need cards up his sleeve or a marked deck because he can make a brand-new deck do everything for him. The cool, sometimes icy control of the man with the gun who knows that he can hit anything he shoots at. And, in fact, Shelby is a marvelous shot with a target pistol. And, as artist (novel, story, narrative history) he *does* gamble like that, plays for the biggest stakes with patience, knowledge of the odds, the confidence of earned skill, and no fear of losing. Which adds up to an almost Aristotelian courage. Knows violence well, inside and out, and is therefore not quick to anger or angry action. Once committed (you believe), it is final, no quarter given or asked. It is not difficult to put him in imaginary Confederate gray and on a horse, close by the best, Stuart or Forrest. But, and his history proves it, he could have ridden as hard, far, and as well in Union Blue.

I have heard his wife call him "Bunky." I've never heard anyone else do that, old friend or enemy.

I. *But my point was that when you get looking at the ordinary, it's probably more unbearable than anybody knows.*

GRAHAM: Shelby, all of the novels that you've done are rather on the short side, are they not, sort of a novella?

FOOTE: About one hundred thousand words, except for *Shiloh,* which is about half that.

GRAHAM: That's a distance I'm particularly fond of. It does seem to me that I read too many novels and, for that matter, too many short stories where maybe a full third could be pulled. I'm not talking about *War and Peace* now, I know that needs its breadth. But I am very keen on—I don't want to damn with the wrong kind of praise, Shelby—but a kind of poetic compression that it seems to me you are after.

FOOTE: I like for the middle of a novel to occur in the middle of a book. I like this distribution of space to keep the balance. I think it has its effects. I think you ought to come out of a story just as you came into a story. I think all these things balance.

GRAHAM: The particular novel that I'm interested in right now is *Follow Me Down,* which may be a rather distant item in your memory, but one that I've almost finished and am enjoying immensely. I am very keen on the multiple points of view where you have an incident, a major incident, a murder, and a small packet of people, but nevertheless a varied packet —all looking at the same incident. It seems to me that I can hear the voices of the murdered girl, of the murderer, of the "dummy" who observes, and I'm afraid, I can hear the voice of that cheap-shot reporter with a clarity that I'd rather not pick up. He's got that murder in front of him and what he's interested in is whether he can make a thousand words out of it or not, and, really, whether he can make a few bucks, a very few bucks. He's not even a very highly temptable person.

FOOTE: That's right.

GRAHAM: How do you feel about point of view? Does it frighten you when you write a novel like that when you have to make leaps into very different types of characters?

FOOTE: It didn't then. Whether it would now, if I did it, I don't know. But this novel was an experiment on my part: to examine a crime of passion by moving into it and then out of it, which is what I mentioned a moment ago about the middle being in the center. This is in three parts. The second part, the middle of the novel, is devoted to monologues by the murderer and the "murderee." The first part has three speakers who are increasingly involved. The first one to speak is a minor official connected with it because he happens to be the turnkey of the jail. The next one is the reporter who is professionally involved, so he has to find out the facts to write them for his paper. The third one is not professionally involved, and he is interested, indeed, because he's the "dummy," and he is involved in the crime itself. He was at the scene of the crime so he's an eyewitness. Then, having gone from a person slightly professionally involved, heavily professionally involved, and then as a minor character who was present at the crime, we are into the crime. Then, we deal with the crime, told by the man who committed it and the girl who was killed. And then, we come out of it again, by having a minor character who was slightly involved, an eyewitness, the murderer's wife. We move from there to the lawyer, who is deeply professionally involved in somewhat the way the reporter was, and, then, finally we're out again with the turnkey . . . the person I call the "turnkey" . . . it was really the circuit clerk, but it's the same kind of involvement. We get deeper and deeper involved by people who are more and more aware of what happened, where the very heart of it was, the girl who was murdered. And then, as you come out of it, you get less and less involved until you're back out in "the world" again.

GRAHAM: The interesting thing for me about this was that even with the characters that are not attractive—and again, I find the reporter a rather repellent insensitive man, he has no sense of character or life, all he can see is that it's an incident that will make copy.

FOOTE: And he has a mean nature. He plays bad tricks on people, I think.

GRAHAM: That's right, cheap little shots of typographical errors.

You get a funny sense that he might cheat a little bit at poker, if he stays sober enough to do it.

FOOTE: Right.

GRAHAM: But the thing I like about the use of this multiple point of view, the people speaking in their own voices, is first of all, the change of pace to hear these voices come through. You give not only credibility to the characters through the change of voices, but they can kind of justify themselves. And your—I find that I'm rather willing to accept their justifications —I'm talking about *sympathy*, I think.

FOOTE: I think it's only fair to accept a man when he . . . you should give him a hearing when he talks. It's true. And, then, discount him after he's through. Give him a sympathetic hearing while he's talking. The whole problem of writing, whether you're going to write in the first or third person, is an interesting choice, anyhow, because you make very large sacrifices in both directions. I'm inclined to think that your largest sacrifice is when you write in the first person because your point of view is so restricted that you cannot walk around a subject and look at it the way you can in the third person. But it does lend immediacy to the thing.

GRAHAM: While you were talking, it suddenly struck me that narrator of *All the King's Men,* Jack Burden, who is a kind of coarse man in a way—

FOOTE: Yes, Burden is interesting.

GRAHAM: The novel is very exciting, but there are these limitations of sensibility, I'm tempted to say, because of the nature of the narrator.

FOOTE: Warren, it seems to me, was thoroughly aware of this problem we're talking about, so he injects it into the novel and drops into it somebody's Master's thesis, if you remember.

GRAHAM: Oh, that's right. It had that superb shift.

FOOTE: He had to relieve this thing. And that was his way of doing it.

GRAHAM: I never thought of that as part of the purpose. I remember the section very clearly with the stylistic change. And it took things back into the history and it was splendidly done.

FOOTE: He claimed that he had to do something at that point to stop the novel, do something, and then start it again. And you would start again, refreshed by this change of pace.

GRAHAM: Is there a danger—I can remember again, Graham Greene in *The End of the Affair*—it seems to me that's told from a number of points of view—is there a danger of a novel becoming a non-novel, turning into a collection of short stories? Is this something that could happen?

FOOTE: No. I don't think so. If you have these people concerned about the same thing, the different points of view on that same thing, I think it will carry the validity, the drive of a single unity on through even though there are different speakers. Browning, of course, did it first in *The Ring and the Book*— one of my favorite things and always has been.

GRAHAM: This is an item like Wordsworth's *The Prelude*. These are great books that for some curious reason—and *The Dynasts* by Hardy—these are things that must be brought back into the mainstream.

FOOTE: They go largely unread nowadays because people are unwilling to get down and bite on a nail with regard to reading anymore. If they would bite on a nail, they'd find it tasted pretty good, but they won't do that anymore. They won't really read *The Ring and the Book*. It's not true they won't read it; there are probably a lot more people reading it than we know about. But generally speaking, it's not too easy to find a person now who likes *The Ring and the Book* and has read it two or three times. I've read it three or four.

GRAHAM: I hadn't thought of Browning. I was thinking of this multiple point of view as a discovery of you twentieth-century novelists. And yet, there Browning was doing it.

FOOTE: Browning did it—Browning, incidentally, is one of my very favorite poets, lyric as well as dramatic—was a master of technique anyhow. He's got a great deal to teach any writer, and not just poets either. He's got a lot to teach any writer. However, the influence on me in this book is by no means limited to Browning. There was Faulkner, for instance, *The Sound and the Fury* and *As I Lay Dying,* both of which used this technique. I think it's a valid one. There's a trick to it. It's very easy to do, easy to fill many pages, anyhow. If you want to, you can stop and have your character muse awhile. You can do almost anything you want to and that, of course, is very dangerous. I don't think that any person should undertake to tell a story this way unless he is prepared to bring to it the discipline that Faulkner brought to it. I think it requires more discipline than the third person, because of the dangers of just letting your pencil wander.

GRAHAM: This is a minor point now, Shelby, but with *Follow Me Down* what kind of a judgment were you making when you used as your witness a deaf-mute and, as an extension of that, the rather strange mother that he has? Her tale of real woe does do things to one of your major characters, Eustis, the murderer, and yet I don't think I understand the necessity, shall we say, even dramatic . . .

FOOTE: I think I was, in the course of that book, which deals with a violent and messy crime—drowning a girl, tying weights to her so she would sink in the Mississippi River, and then later she comes floating up having been eaten on by shrimp and gars—I think I was trying to show that this is indeed a sad world in which people live under nearly unbearable pressures.

So many of the people in that book are people who have lived very unhappy lives, way beyond the ordinary, it's probably more unbearable than anybody knows. So that, it's the terrible sadness of life, the tragedy of it, that I was trying to get in touch with in that novel. And I hope that I did because it interested me enormously at the time. I began to find tragedies everywhere I looked.

GRAHAM: Then a very minor figure—you may even have forgotten him, he's so minor—but there's a poor, florid photographer on the newspaper.

FOOTE: Right.

GRAHAM: And the poor devil has to go out assisting the coroner.

FOOTE: And take these dreadful pictures.

GRAHAM: And take these photographs that make him physically ill.

FOOTE: He nearly throws up in the camera, that's right.

GRAHAM: Shatters the poor man. And that particular scene I admired enormously because the horror there was real, but the horror was transformed because you focused your camera on the photographer's disturbance, and everyone else started reacting to the photographer. I thought they treated him very kindly and considerately.

FOOTE: They did, that's right.

GRAHAM: So the scene developed by reactions rather than some . . . grossly detailed . . .

FOOTE: That's what I wanted.

GRAHAM: Focus on this poor, dead girl . . .

FOOTE: That's right. That's very much what I wanted. Somewhere in Hemingway's *The Sun Also Rises,* one of the characters says, "What they are big for back home now [meaning back in the States] is irony and pity. You got to have a little irony and pity." That is what I was after in this book, irony and pity, the irony of these grotesques, trying to lead beautiful lives. The man who murdered the girl took her off to an island to live an idyll. And it turns out to be this horrible crime. That's the irony.

II. *I think that if you're in the entertainment business, they do get hold of you and turn you upside down.*

GRAHAM: I'd like to ask you about a novel of yours that I've *not* read, about this black trumpet player, since I've been hearing about this novel for so long. *Ride Out* is the title. What does this term mean?

FOOTE: "Ride out" is a jazz term. When a song has a "ride-out" finish, it means they ride it hard at the end. In the story, the main character, whose name is Duff Conway, dies in the electric chair, and the executioner says he's going to ride him right out of this earth. The term "ride out" is a jazz term and also applies to the end of his life.

GRAHAM: One thing that troubles me, and it's one of the big problems now that I'm going to spring on you—I can remember so clearly the writing of *The Red Badge of Courage* by a very young man who had not, in fact, experienced the Civil War. And yet we usually say that that is our best Civil War novel.

It may be our best war novel, an act of the imagination. But he did, I understand, talk a great deal with the veterans of the battles. Now my real question here is, believing, in memory, believing that a writer must work out of his own experience, how could you, as a white man, as a non-trumpet player—at least in low dives—how did you strike on this particular story? How did your imagination serve you here? How did your experience serve you?

FOOTE: It came directly out of my background, out of the country I grew up in. Negro musicians were very much part of the scene where I grew up. There was a section of town very much like the section of town described in this story. There was a place called the Mansion House where musicians did play. It was a house of prostitution with orchestras coming and going. The music itself was my first fascination for all this . . . all my life I've heard this music and loved it very much. Most of it was guitar music, but sometimes there were trumpets, clarinets, and always pianos in these places. So that, the music drew me first, and then, as I got older, I was interested by the people who make the music. What kind of life was it that drew a person into the world of music with all its limitations?

GRAHAM: It's an upside down world, I mean, you're working while other people are playing.

FOOTE: That's right. The thing that interested me and I didn't understand it until I'd written about it. . . . Incidentally, a lot of people think that writers are wise men who have some answers to questions to give people. Nothing could be further from the truth. They are looking for answers while they write, and when they find them, they are no longer interested in writing about that problem. But jazz music means a great deal to me.

GRAHAM: We really are of the generation that grabbed the New Orleans, Chicago and New York styles.

FOOTE: That's right, and what I knew about jazz was that it was an attempt to communicate with the listener. The trouble was, and it was a large trouble, the jazz musician himself was not equipped technically to do this communicating. Often even his instrument wasn't. He was playing an instrument, say a trumpet, with valves that would stick on it. He could not read music. His technique was marvelous, but it was by nature an inferior technique. He could not play that instrument the way a man in a symphony orchestra can play it. He knew nothing about music the way a musicologist knows music. But he was doing his best to communicate with you in an absolutely direct way, loaded with feeling. All his feelings he was putting directly into that music. Now that's what characterized good jazz. You can see why cheap bad jazz is so bad. If a man, if he's not giving it all, it's bad music . . . very bad music; but when he's giving it all he's got, his technique becomes relatively unimportant because there's something about the very basic beat of jazz, something about the blues, that communicates from one person to another. Bessie Smith, to my mind, is as great a singer as ever lived. Nobody could sing better than Bessie does, because she does this thing. She has a tremendous hurdle to get over from not knowing music, in the sense that a musicologist knows it. But, her humanity is so large and the song in her soul is so strong that she leaps all these hurdles and she communicates to you directly as well as Flagstad or anyone you care to name could ever communicate to you.

GRAHAM: I'm fascinated by your saying this because as a reader of your work, I see you as something of a precisionist.

FOOTE: I would never say this in a story or a novel. I don't believe in talking to people in books.

GRAHAM: Well, I mean your own style is one of a very careful craftsman. You're not a flamboyant, bursting writer.

FOOTE: No, no!

GRAHAM: And yet, you have this obvious, deep warmth and love for Bessie Smith's art.

FOOTE: I hope that it would come through in the story *Ride Out*, for example. I would never launch into telling you how soulful this music is in the course of writing a story about it. It would have to speak for itself. But my feelings in back of it are strong indeed and my love for that music is very great.

GRAHAM: Can we find any live jazz now, if you can bring us up to date on it?

FOOTE: I've been looking into it. Every now and then, I hear somebody who I think has got it again. I thought Elvis Presley had it at the start, before he ever made a record or was heard of. I heard him in Memphis and I thought he had it. I thought he was going to be one of the great Blues Shouters, anyhow. Before him, there was a man, Johnny Ray, that I thought was going to be good. He was not good, he was terrible. But, just the beginning of it sounded good. I think maybe the record people get ahold of folks and keep them from developing. They don't stay hungry long enough. Somebody said what you need to write the blues is "no money in the bank and nobody loving you." Then you can write the blues. Elvis had a great deal of money in the bank and a lot of little girls loving him almost from the day he stepped out.

GRAHAM: I guess part of this problem of development is that you do get trapped in the commercial world which wants you to repeat the winning formula that you scored with.

FOOTE: I used to not think that that really mattered, if a man had it. But I was talking about writers. I think that if you're in the entertainment business, they do get hold of you and turn you upside down. For instance, the most admired blues singer of our time, now that Jimmy Rushing doesn't sing anymore, is B. B. King. Well, B. B. King plays an electric guitar, and when I contrast him with, say, Leadbelly, or Jimmy Rushing, he just doesn't sound anything like as good as them. He's as earnest as they were, maybe more earnest. But, something has gotten in the way. Maybe it's the electric guitar, I don't know. But something has happened, and it may be something simpler than that. It may be prosperity, I don't know.

GRAHAM: In writing *Ride Out,* it clearly was generated, then, by your experience with the music. Now let me switch you just a little bit and put you in the guise of an historian, or a novelist in the act of both researching and imagining. Did you talk with a lot of musicians? Did you step into their world?

FOOTE: Yes, I did, and some of my inspiration, if you want to call it that, was literary in a sense. For instance, I was familiar with the story of Louis Armstrong's life. I'm sure that's why the jazz musician in my story spent some time in a reform school. I knew that Louis learned to play the trumpet in the reform school. So my man learned to play the cornet in a reform school, and I'm sure that that's where that came from. But, what came of it, the way he speaks, and the life he lives, is out of having listened to many people like him speak and having studied at first hand the life he lived. His relationship with his mother is one of the most important things in the story and I had plenty of opportunity to see that, from growing up down in the Mississippi Delta where this music was important and these people were the way he was.

GRAHAM: I can't remember whether I've heard this about a half dozen jazz musicians or just one, but they started off as very young boys. Didn't one, a great leader, or a great singer, trumpeter, lead a blind trumpeter, and then he learned his . . . ?

FOOTE: Yes, that was Josh White with Blind Lemon Jefferson. That's right, that's what he did, and Leadbelly himself was with Lemon. He was with him down in Texas in Blind Lemon's earlier days. He was blind then. Yes, there was nearly always that. All the singers and guitar players served an apprenticeship. They worked with an older man and he often was blind . . . from syphilis, usually.

GRAHAM: And this, then, is nearly always a part of society, isn't it? It's not some institutionalized thing. The apprenticeship is a nice idea, really.

FOOTE: He served an apprenticeship and he chose his master. He went looking for him, hoping he would take him, because he had heard of him, and finally heard him and attached himself to him like a pilot fish.

GRAHAM: So it's something for a young boy to do, not just to accidentally come into.

FOOTE: I heard Sugar Ray Robinson one time on the radio or television, telling how when he was a boy he used to beg Joe Louis to let him carry his trunks for him from the hotel to the boxing ring. And, he used to carry his trunks. It struck an immediate response in me. Isn't that amazing that Sugar Robinson as a boy should have carried Joe Louis's trunks? But, it's not amazing at all. It happens in the music world from start to finish. Josh White led Blind Lemon Jefferson around by the hand.

GRAHAM: Is there this indigenous sense of an apprenticeship still in the deep South?

FOOTE: It's all gone because the Negroes are gone. There's no sharecropper life anymore, there's no Saturday night anymore. Saturday night is gone. Saturday night's no different than any other night down home now. We got the forty-hour week, which is a good thing, but the price you pay for it is higher than a lot of people know about.

GRAHAM: So our total sociology now is, in effect, making your story *Ride Out* no longer possible, really. The traditions are being lost.

FOOTE: That's right, it's impossible, and I am talking from a point of view that's not with it. I don't like electric guitars. That doesn't mean there's anything wrong with electric guitars, it's just I like unelectric guitars.

III. *I don't know of anything I learned about the writing of novels in the course of practicing my craft that's not applicable to the writing of history. And I quite literally mean that.*

GRAHAM: I heard Mr. Foote give a lecture not too long ago in which, Shelby, you pretty much decided that you really can't make a fiction writer or poet. Would you like to hazard what goes into the making of an historian? It would seem to me, a little bit of fiction, a little bit of poetry, and a lot of other things.

FOOTE: I think that, ideally, those things go into the making of him. The truth of the matter is that they seldom do. There's not enough poet in most historians, not as much as there should be. But I ought to make myself clear. I do not want to give historians any license to distort the truth—nothing but harm could come from that, but I do think that historians need to learn many of the writing techniques which poets and novelists know they need to be familiar with before they can function.

GRAHAM: I don't want to get, right now, into that muddy

ground of the historical novel, but surely any historian, unless he's going to be nothing more than a statistician and a date keeper, certainly has to give us some sense of place, some sense of person, to go to the schoolboy terms that you and I learned, of "plot, character, action, and place." And it would seem that he would have to exercise himself on novelists. Point of fact, many historians do turn to the novel of the period they are writing on, do they not, to get tone and attitudes?

FOOTE: If they don't they should. I have difficulty in speaking about historians. I am not a professional historian. I am writing what I hope is authentic history, but I do not know any professional historians. I have never had much conversation with professional historians.

GRAHAM: And yet, not to be vulgar now, but this three-volume history of the Civil War you are doing is recognized by professional historians as an important work, is it not?

FOOTE: I hope so. I hope my dedication to the truth is as sound as any historian's could be. But, I think of myself as a novelist. What you said a moment ago seems to me to apply eminently well to what we're talking about. An historian would do very well indeed to go to the novels of the period to learn about the period. I have said—and said in the lecture awhile back—that I thought historical fiction was not really of much account. That's bad historical fiction. I consider George Eliot's *Middlemarch* an historical novel, an examination of England on the eve of the Reform Bill. If someone wants to know what England was like on the eve of the Reform Bill, I do not know of anyplace he could go to find it out better than *Middlemarch*. I think she's done a superb job in *Middlemarch* as an historical novel. Now there are no historical characters in it. William Pitt doesn't walk through her pages. But, it's a very fine historical novel because of its accuracy as to place and mood.

GRAHAM: Your basic strong feeling is that when a novelist turns to William Pitt, but instead of going to the documents, going to the contemporary reports, he dreams up a "William Pitt" with his idiosyncracies, his vocabulary, strictly out of the novelist's mind.

FOOTE: I don't give him the license to do that. Almost since Shakespeare's time, the license to take a historical character as Styron did Nat Turner—I disagree with that. I think it's always a mistake.

GRAHAM: Can you get enough distance, really, on Nat Turner? But suppose it had been *The Confessions of Bill Weaver,* a fictional revolutionary?

FOOTE: Then I would have been all for it. That's the trouble.

GRAHAM: You're talking then about the purity of history, are you not?

FOOTE: I am, indeed. I'm talking about the purity of the need for accuracy with regard to dealing with men who once did actually live.

GRAHAM: And our data on Nat Turner is extraordinarily limited.

FOOTE: If I write a story about a very tough little western badman, that is very different from pretending to write a story that I made up out of my head and call him "Billy the Kid." I have no right to do that to Billy. No one has.

GRAHAM: The stream is muddy enough when we're trying hard, without throwing more dirt into the water. In what ways could you hazard that your experience as a very finely crafting novelist —how do you feel that experience has both helped or hindered— maybe hindered is a bad word—maybe set you up with problems as an historian?

FOOTE: I consider that it was all a gain, no hindrance. I don't know of anything I learned about the writing of novels in the course of practicing my craft that's not applicable to the writing of history. And, I quite literally mean that. The historian gets his facts out of documents. The novelist gets his facts out of his head. But they both are, or certainly should be, true to those facts. The novelist is true to his facts. He does not distort them for the sake of selling books or something, the good one doesn't. Therefore, it's not really different from an historian distorting documents; so that is not the problem. Many people think that a novelist, trying to write history, would distort the facts. He is not accustomed to distorting facts, if you understand what I mean by that. So that what we're really talking about is the technique he learned as a novelist. I claim that all his techniques are applicable. Plotting of his novel, if he did learn how to plot a novel, it is of enormous value to him. Now, he does not make up the events that happen, but the making up of the story is not the plotting of the novel, either. It's what he does with the story. In one case, he has made the story up out of his head, in the other he has gotten it out of documents. In both cases, plotting is necessary. Point of view, chronology, the release of information at a time, these things are the things I'm talking about with regard to the technique of the novel carrying over to history.

GRAHAM: I would think that tonally your experience would be fantastically helpful in the sense that you have learned enough through your novels not to let some minor character become so brilliant that he or she would obscure the major thrust of your history.

FOOTE: That's right. There's a use for flat characters as well as round characters. People have often pointed this out and it's quite true. And it works well in history. Your characters who come round become rounded because of the presence of flat characters along beside them. This, too, is a novelist's technique that carries over into history. Now, in history, for the most part, you're so glad to get bright, jumpy, colorful material, that you are very much inclined to include that material for value as color. I've found that it does have its place, but you have to be careful in persuading yourself that it's right to do something that you want to do. I have found that these spots of color, and, mind you, valid color, are of great use to the historian to bring his story alive—in other words, to bring it closer to the truth. I'm not talking about making it livelier than it was, I'm just talking about some attempt to make it as lively as it was.

GRAHAM: Certainly in the fact of history your great man may be comparatively colorless while all around him in life again you have brilliant stars.

FOOTE: An example of what I'm talking about. If you're writing a story of the Civil War and one of your main characters (and he certainly will be) is Robert E. Lee, you have a certain amount of biographical information about Lee. Instead of releasing it all the first time Lee comes on the scene, you can withhold parts of it. When you get to the battle of Fredericksburg, you can have Lee look through his binoculars across the Rappahannock and see the house, that has a tree in its yard with a seat under it, where he was when he proposed to his wife. These things are very real. They are not false,. They are not hoking it up—unless it's bad writing, which will hoke anything up. But if this information is released over the pages instead of in a clump—

GRAHAM: As Lee would naturally absorb it.

FOOTE: Just so, just so . . .

GRAHAM: He is experiencing as we are going through history. It's not a matter of wrapping him up and then moving on to other things.

FOOTE: That's right. And it is not a distraction at that point with the battle of Fredericksburg thundering all around you, Pelham with his two guns holding back the whole Yankee army and so forth. It is not a distraction to say that Lee could see across the river there, this house. It makes Pelham's fight realer, if you see what I mean by that. That's what I'm talking about, about a historian learning from a novelist.

GRAHAM: The temptation that I would imagine that you must have to fight and stay conscious of is the one we touched on briefly at another meeting. Some characters, not the documents or the facts, must grab your imagination, but your imagination is triggered by some man and there must be some tendency here for the historian Shelby Foote to become the novelist Shelby Foote.

FOOTE: Yes, you have to fight it down if it's going to lead you to think you can take any such liberties as a novelist is free to take. I'm not giving the historian license to invent facts, or use facts really in any twisted sort of way. Neither does a novelist do that, if you follow what I mean. He gets this thing straight in his mind and wants to tell the truth; and he knows that nothing worse can happen to his novel than for him to distort these things that he recognizes as true. It is not dissimilar, as I was saying earlier, from the historian's problem.

GRAHAM: You are really saying that the novelist's imagination puts certain perimeters around a character, which are very sharply defined, to work in the totality of the novel as well as for psychological credibility and so forth.

FOOTE: Compression is as important as expansion. It is to be used with wisdom, in both these mediums.

GRAHAM: And with the compression, I would think this is right where your work in poetry and short fiction would be of enormous value to you.

FOOTE: That's right. I don't know, personally, of any writer who didn't start out trying to be a poet, and I think this is right and exactly as it should be. I haven't known any good prose writers who didn't give up poetry. They gave it up.

GRAHAM: I remember Faulkner saying that he gave it up because he wasn't good enough.

FOOTE: Called himself a failed poet.

IV. *The whole notion of this terrific compression that Tacitus brings off—and the way he deals with scoundrels is very interesting. It teaches me how to write about Edwin Stanton and all kinds of people who are pretty scoundrelish.*

GRAHAM: Not to be annoyingly facetious, but after I read your novels and your history, is there anything in particular that you're reading now that I might enjoy?

FOOTE: I've come back to the books I liked best when I was young. When I was about seventeen, I got crazy about books. I have a great fondness for the memory of those summers on the swing on my front porch and reading all these books. I was in a little Mississippi town that didn't have a bookstore, so I ordered them all directly from the publisher. I'd get their catalogs and order their books, and I used to wait for the mailman every morning to get me a new book. But the books I read then with the most pleasure are the books I read now with the most pleasure. The writers who influenced me most were writers that I like best now.

GRAHAM: I picked up Stevenson's *Treasure Island* not very long ago when I was so busy, Shelby, I should not have looked at the newspaper headlines. And I quit about two in the morning.

The story line grabbed me and I remembered an old swing and the park bench.

FOOTE: Well, you're having a Proustian experience, there. You're not only reading *Treasure Island,* you're the boy who read *Treasure Island,* and it is a fascinating business. And, incidentally, you see a great many things that you didn't see as a boy. One summer—it's a big summer in my life—someone told me, I think Will Percy told me, that the three big novels of our century were *Remembrance of Things Past, Ulysses,* and *The Magic Mountain.*

GRAHAM: That's a summer's reading right there.

FOOTE: So I ordered those three books and sat down and read them, you see. In the summertime, it's sixteen hours' reading, I guess. And I went through them like a colt in clover. They were an absolute delight to me all the way. And I have reread those three books, especially Proust, the rest of my life, I've reread them and reread them and reread them. I've read Proust six or seven times.

GRAHAM: I cannot imagine any firmer stones in twentieth-century literature.

FOOTE: That's right. They were the best books. I had another experience, and you have to understand that this is operating out of an unliterary family in an unliterary region, in a little town in the middle of that region. So I had to have some kind of help for this thing. I was enjoying it enormously, reading, but I wanted to read what I *ought* to read. So I got a book, I found it in a junk shop or somewhere, by a man whose name I couldn't even pronounce . . . his name was John Cowper Powys or something like that.

GRAHAM: That's right.

FOOTE: I can't even remember.

GRAHAM: There were brothers, on the edge of the arts.

FOOTE: That's right. I didn't even know how to pronounce his name—and I thought "Proust" was "Prowst," I never heard anybody say it. This book was called *The Hundred Best Books.* And, it began with the Bible and the *Iliad* and the *Odyssey* and went all the way up to, I think, Arnold Bennett, or somebody like that. So, I read those hundred best books, which is kind of a strange thing for a kid to do.

GRAHAM: How old were you then, Shelby?

FOOTE: Seventeen.

GRAHAM: Glorious! I read an awful lot of junk at that age, you know? It was a shame.

FOOTE: I read a lot of junk before that—Tom Swift. I was a great Tom Swift fan, and Tarzan and all that. I had read those things, but this I enjoyed reading so much. The first book I had ever read—I know the first piece of music I ever heard that hit me between the eyes was *Eine Kleine Nachtmusik,* which is a splendid piece of music, to introduce you to classical music—but the first book I ever read that made me understand that reading was going to be worth a grown man's time was *David Copperfield,* which looked to me like the longest book ever written in the world, and it is a long book; but my delight with *David Copperfield* was from the first page to the last. And that was when I was about twelve years old, you see, so then I went on reading a lot of junk. And then finally the pleasure I was getting out of good books made me realize that that was the best way in the world and the most exciting way to spend your time and so I read good books.

GRAHAM: What happened to you when you hit college? Did you just keep bobbing your head at reading lists, indicating that you'd read all of them before?

FOOTE: Yes, I had read them. I had a funny experience in college, though. I ran across a lot of things I did not like that were supposed to be good. Walter Scott was one of them.

GRAHAM: I cannot get through him.

FOOTE: I took a course from a man named McMillan at Chapel Hill who was a very good teacher. And he had ten novels for us to read and one of them was *Quentin Durward*. When we got to *Quentin Durward*, I started it, and I went to him and said, "Dr. McMillan, I'm having real trouble with this book. I honestly don't like it and don't want to read it. Do you take that into consideration at all?" And he said, "Well, if I were you, I wouldn't read it." And I said, "That's mighty nice of you." And he said, "No, if that's the way you feel about it, do that." So, I said, "Fine." We were having a book a week, and when it came time for the test on *Quentin Durward*, I wrote on my paper, "I have not read this book and it was with your permission I didn't read it, if you remember." And I turned the paper in. When the papers were handed back to us, the following Monday, I had an *F* on the paper. So, I went back to Dr. McMillan and said, "What have you done to me? You told me I didn't have to read it." And he said, "That's right, you didn't have to read it."

GRAHAM: But a simple matter of cause and effect . . .

FOOTE: He said, "I admired your attitude and I think you were right not to read it, but, of course, as you know, I had to fail you. You couldn't get a passing grade without reading the book." He was a nice man.

GRAHAM: You've been talking about a lot of novels, would you introduce me to some historians, perhaps?

FOOTE: My favorite historian and the one I read to get the flavor of history, to get a real notion of what history is all about—I have to read in translation because my Latin is nearly nonexistent and my Greek is totally nonexistent—but Tacitus is my favorite historian. The whole notion of this terrific compression that Tacitus brings off—and the way he deals with scoundrels is very interesting. It teaches me how to write about Edwin Stanton and all kinds of people who are pretty scoundrelish. So that Tacitus is my favorite historian. There are others I like. I like Gibbon a lot. The Gibbon periods roll out and give me a lot of pleasure.

GRAHAM: I was about to say the styles there are so radically different.

FOOTE: That's right. Style is what matters. Tacitus's silver Latin, or at least translations I read; and the Latin I try to stumble through is stupid. I do nothing but translate when I try to read it, so I might as well read a good translator. But the tone of Tacitus comes through in a good translation.

GRAHAM: Offhand, do you have a favorite translation of Tacitus you can think of? Didn't Penguin have a good translation of it?

FOOTE: Penguin has a good translation of it. I'm ashamed to say that I can't remember the man's name. A good translation, very good. Somebody really ought to translate—I wish Robert Graves would translate Tacitus. It would be a great service, I wish he would do it.

GRAHAM: I read a C. Day Lewis *Iliad* or *Odyssey* that was knocking me down. I had no idea someone could pull that off so well.

FOOTE: I so much like the Shaw *Odyssey*. The T. E. Lawrence *Odyssey* is one of my favorite books in that translation. And the Richmond Lattimore translation of the *Iliad* is good. I have not read Lattimore's translation of the *Odyssey* which came out two years ago, but I don't need it because I think so highly of the Shaw.

GRAHAM: Well, you go to Tacitus and Gibbon. Any contemporary historians? Do you enjoy Churchill's histories?

FOOTE: I'm a little too conscious of Churchill being a sort of imitator of Gibbon that it bothers me some. I like Bruce Catton's work, I like it very much. I like Douglas Southall Freeman's work. He's a good chance for me to tell you about what I meant about good writing. Freeman is about as far from a good writer as you can get. He likes a sort of jog trot prose—here I am in Virginia talking badly about their leading man—but it fits, perfectly, his subject matter. I like the way Freeman writes. I would not like it out of context. But when he's writing about Robert E. Lee, or Lee's lieutenants, or the American Revolution, this sort of jog trot prose fits very well, gives the book a good tone. I like it. It's dry, unskillful, and there's something I like about that in connection with his subject.

GRAHAM: Is it because of the quick-paced movement of things?

FOOTE: No, they don't really move that fast. It's the awkwardness of the sentences themselves. It's hard to say exactly how that can be good, but it fits. The style fits. Style is not the way somebody puts in flourishes. Style is the way a man is able to communicate to you the quality of his mind. And this does communicate to me the quality of Freeman's mind when he turns it on Robert E. Lee, and it's a very satisfactory kind of thing to be in touch with.

GRAHAM: Maybe by analogy, someone like Theodore Dreiser who, as a stylist, will drive you up the wall, and yet, given his rather grimy subject matter, this heavy-handed style functions.

FOOTE: There's a certain ponderousness that has validity about it. I don't read Dreiser with much pleasure. I don't read some good writers because I don't like their writing. I find Stendhal to be pretty hard reading; although it's always interesting, I find it pretty hard reading. Balzac . . . I'm crazy about Balzac, but I . . .

GRAHAM: I'm just the reverse.

FOOTE: I have a pretty hard time with some of his writing. Nobody could not like Flaubert, I don't see how they couldn't like Flaubert, but some of the great writers make pretty rough reading for me since I have no respect for them as stylists.

GRAHAM: What about the Second World War? You were an artillery captain, were you not? Have you any book on the Second World War that seems to . . . ?

FOOTE: No, and they never will write one. I'd just as soon be done with that. I don't want any part of it. In fact, I don't want any part of any war. When I finish the Civil War, that's it.

GRAHAM: Do you read any poetry at all? Any contemporary writers that you are interested in?

FOOTE: I read a great deal of poetry. It's very interesting to me. There are rhythms to reading. Now that I'm older, I'm able to see that there are whole decades of no poetry reading, and then I'll go in for three years of reading a great deal of poetry. I've been reading a lot of Browning lately and I've gone back to Shakespeare, with enormous pleasure, great pleasure because my appreciation of their technical facility is coming forward to me in a way it didn't before.

GRAHAM: One thing I've barked at students about, when they say some work is terribly difficult, such as a play of Shakespeare's —I've gotten a little snappish, almost, trying to point out that he didn't write for boys. You've got to grow up to Shakespeare, you've got to grow up to Mann, Proust, Joyce. They were not setting themselves up to present a college textbook for nineteen-year-olds.

FOOTE: Shakespeare must be a very great writer if for no other reason than that he survives being taught the way he is taught in high schools today.

GRAHAM: You know, one thing suddenly occurred to me when you were in midstream. How do you feel about Stephen Vincent Benét's *John Brown's Body?*

FOOTE: I find it overblown. It's too much striving to be really American with the bark on "really." I don't know what it is with me. I don't like, it, though.

GRAHAM: He reaches awfully hard for the metaphor, and even when he finds it there, the stretching is distracting, wouldn't you say?

FOOTE: I do, I feel that about him.

Henry Taylor

BIOGRAPHICAL

Born: 21 June 1942 in Leesburg, Virginia.

Education: B.A. the University of Virginia 1964, M.A. Hollins College 1965.

Occupational: Besides farming and training show horses, he has been teaching, at Roanoke College, at the University of Utah and currently at American University where he is Associate Professor of Literature. He also is Director of the Summer Writers Conference for the University of Utah.

Books: Poems—*The Horse Show at Midnight* (1966), *Breakings* (1971).

Taylor has written and published a number of distinguished critical articles and short stories. He is presently editing at least one textbook anthology of poetry and is one of the translators, working under the general editorship of William Arrowsmith, of the great Greek dramas, to be published by Oxford. He has also published translations from French and Italian.

SNAPSHOT

Henry has one talent, a large if special one, which he is at once too young and too shy to make full use of. To begin he is a born parodist and can find, all too quickly, the parodic weakness, the idiosyncratic essence of any poet, living or dead, who writes in English. That, in itself, is a remarkable, if dangerous gift. But *also* Henry can imitate, even *impersonate* the voice and mannerisms of any poet he has seen and heard. Indeed, he *can* do it by voice alone. It's a wild skill and, one imagines, could keep him busy all the time and far away from his own distinctive work. Just as well he saves it for small groups at late gatherings.

Pale, with blond, wheat-colored hair, and lightly built, he seems more fragile than he is. He's a first-rate horseman. As a schoolboy he was a good man on the track and, short and long, can still outrun some strong runners. A bit of a dandy in dress, a very witty and charming young man, he will fool you again unless you look deeper, that is, into the poems. There, without losing a certain elegance and an irrepressible sense of humor, of the ridiculous, he becomes also what he is—a serious Quaker, from a very long line of Virginia Quakers, and, as such, strong in the inner certainty of his faith. And the farm boy is there, too, not out of place in his new suit, but loving the land, the animals and growing things like old friends.

I. *What I was trying to do was to get at my past. And when I say my past I mean as far back as 1874 which is when my grandfather was born.*

GRAHAM: *The Horse Show at Midnight*, Henry, has got one of the nicest dust jackets that I've ever seen on a book.

TAYLOR: The guy who did it was the book designer for the Louisiana State University Press, Robert Nance. He's not there now; he's gone to the University of South Carolina. But *he* has won two prizes for *my* book—which gives me a really funny feeling.

GRAHAM: It must be a kind of fascinating thing to put together, and I almost mean this in a physical sense, a book of poems, because, with *The Horse Show at Midnight,* you've got three sections—they're very different from each other. Quite candidly, if the poems had been shuffled in manuscript with no names, I am almost certain I would have pulled poems close to the way you have set them up—and claim they were by three different authors, which I think is an interesting problem, maybe. The first group I see as essentially rather simple memory poems, almost—I might add that the first group is focused almost entirely on the language of the vignettes—I'm thinking now maybe very specifically of the little group, "Three Snapshots for George Garrett." They're all built on a line of language remembered as much as the incident that pulled it out?

TAYLOR: Yes, they're punchline poems, and what made those— those are all true stories; they come from my rural background —I adjusted 'em a little bit to make it somehow closer to me— but what made them stick with me, as you say, is the quality of the language of the punchlines. There's something very memorable for instance about the ending of, say, "Blackberries."

GRAHAM: Right. Look, would you mind reading the "Mule Trader"?

TAYLOR: Sure, I'd be glad to.

GRAHAM: Because that's short, and the thing I'm basically interested in is you as poet trapped, almost, in a world of language, that—you're bouncing around in a cage practically speaking.

TAYLOR: Always have been. My whole upbringing trapped me that way.

MULE TRADER

Not long after the mule we'd had
For years had died, my father
Saw the man we'd bought it from.
He had a face so brown and hard
It would crack to pieces if he smiled.

"How's the finest mule I ever sold?"
My father told him the mule was dead.
"You, sir, are a God damn liar!
I been selling mules for forty years,
And I ain't *never* heard of one dying!"

GRAHAM: (laughs)

TAYLOR: Now, that's a true story. It didn't happen to my father, it happened to some other fellow around our neighborhood, probably more contemporary with my grandfathers. But I'd heard my father tell the story, and it's interesting—one of the local-color type. Artemus Ward, or somebody in the last century, also used this same gag, and in the thing about mules he said something like "I have never heard anyone use the phrase 'dead mule.' "

GRAHAM: So it's part of . . .

TAYLOR: It's a folk poem.

GRAHAM: Right, it's part of an American tradition. Now this leads to another thing about language I constantly want to return to with you. This whole business of memory. With this little simple incident that hung in your head for twenty years, before you wrote the poem, there are many things: it's mixed up with your father, and his telling of it, which came from a friend, acquaintance, local character, who is like your grandfather in some way. Now, the thing that fascinates me is, with a number of your poems, you are not directly looking at the object. It is not now before you, but you step into yourself and examine your memory.

TAYLOR: Yes, and leave the fact that it is memory in the poem.

GRAHAM: The fact that it is memory is very, very important. Now, at the same time, mind you, I think because of the language in that silly little "Mule Trader"—I think what we do *get,* however, is a mule. We've also got a man whose face may break if he smiles; we've got the sun, the weathering; we *have* a chestnut rail fence in mind, and a stubble field. So it's all—the physical is there in front of me. And yet it's memory. It's not there.

TAYLOR: What I was trying to do was to get at my past. And when I say my past I mean as far back as 1874 which is when my grandfather was born. I knew my grandfather very well—my father's side of the family has been in the same house since 1828 or something.

GRAHAM: So there are plenty of ghosts, then?

TAYLOR: Right, and they're very important.

GRAHAM: Well, I know one poem—and I'm not sure of the name, the visit to your grandmother—what's the name of that?

TAYLOR: "Over the River and Through the Woods."

GRAHAM: Something very funny happened to me with that poem because I. . . . This poor sick woman is dying of leukemia, I gather, but you go to visit—or the speaker goes to visit—and she's afraid to shake your hand. And there's a whole lot of funny guilt involved because your parents say, "Now, Henry, you must go and visit your grandmother . . ." But what happened to me, Henry, I think I probably read it three or four or five years ago, but I can remember the old lady being an old lady, being unwilling to shake hands with a young boy, but loving the young and therefore in effect shaking hands with herself over her head. But I didn't know where I'd read it or whether it had happened to me or not. It got way inside of me, that particular poem. Which—now that I'm talking with—bluntly—with genuine enthusiasm about it—must be a testimony that that's a good poem, then. I don't know whether it's yours or mine, see?

TAYLOR: That's a weird poem. I can make a confession here I think—that poem is really about my mother's father.

GRAHAM: Memory and the transforming imagination.

TAYLOR: I changed the grandfather into a grandmother simply for the reason that I like better the sound of the feminine pronouns that show up in there.

GRAHAM: Form is almost dictating content here?

TAYLOR: It may have been. It's been a long time since I wrote that poem, and I may have at some time had some feeling of guilt at treating it directly—although there are other poems in the book that treat family background matters much more directly that that.

GRAHAM: Well, "Over the River and Through the Woods" sets up a bit of a war already with the less than joyous subject matter and the other thing—the line length and some of the reducing images—this old lady marches in place for exercise in one line, and, then, when the meeting is over, "I'm lowered down through the house." I'm not going to say these are comical, and yet they . . .

TAYLOR: Somehow or another the speaker is trying to hold the experience at arm's length in some way.

GRAHAM: This is the way the title functions for me and it's a kind of terror of a poem, it's a scary poem.

TAYLOR: And the speaker is scared, more scared than he wants to say, you notice. But I couldn't have him say, "All this is terrifying to me."

GRAHAM: Because that doesn't mean anything to me?

TAYLOR: Right.

GRAHAM: This comes to a point where you as poet, and you as teacher of the writing of poetry, the life of poetry—I mean, you've got to find out who Henry Taylor is before you can write *The Horse Show at Midnight*.

TAYLOR: Right.

GRAHAM: And that's hard.

TAYLOR: Well, not before you can write the whole book. I mean you find . . .

GRAHAM: Maybe in the process of writing you find out.

TAYLOR: You find out who you are in the process of writing and that's why you do it. Frost said something like this—"If you know what the poem's going to do, if you know every line in it before you write it down, or even start to think about it"— I think what he said was, "If you write a poem for the sake of a last line that has come to you, it is no poem at all but a trick poem." You're writing the poem in order to explore something, some part of your past, some aspect of who you are, trying to come to grips with some experience to find out why it stays in your mind and says "write" a poem. And when you've written the poem you find out—sometimes.

GRAHAM: And of course the writing of the poem in itself is a major experience for you. I guess this is why poets often write poems on writing poems—the film, *8½*.

TAYLOR: Making a movie about making a movie.

GRAHAM: Right, this kind of introspection. As close an observer of objective reality as a poet has to be, maybe his major task is introspection into his life and his art. He can't distinguish the two, can he?

TAYLOR: I myself don't write poems that seem to be about writing poetry; I'm not interested in that kind of thing very much because it leaves me in a dry kind of abstraction which I find very dull. But, in another sense, every poem I write, and every poem anybody writes, is about poetry as well as about whatever else it may be about.

GRAHAM: Well, one thing that's interested me in your poetry—and maybe this "Over the River and Through the Woods" is a nice simple example—you write very serious poetry, but you're very quick to use poetry to mock—yourself rather often as well as others. How do you feel about that use of language?

TAYLOR: I think it's certainly important. I think somebody that sets out to write a poem which he sees as serious, and I often do—I write a lot of gags, of course, like the snapshots, the parodies, that take off some other poets that are in the middle section of the book—but even in a serious poem I feel that if you leave out the element of humor that can come in even in the most desperate of circumstances—you know, at a funeral, say somebody knocks a prop out from under the casket and it almost falls and an alert pallbearer catches it and everybody has a feeling of nervous humor—if you leave that kind of thing out of a serious situation, you are not seeing all of what is there.

II. *If you don't keep moving out, if you don't keep trying something that's a little bit harder than the last
thing you did.* . . .

GRAHAM: Henry Taylor is with us to talk about his first book
of poetry, *The Horse Show at Midnight.* We're at the Hollins
Conference on Creative Writing and Cinema and, Henry, we've
been talking about poetry for about a week, the writing of poetry, and I'd like you to sort of turn on yourself a little bit, and
talk some more about *The Horse Show at Midnight.* I almost
hope this is true for you; it must seem like a strange book to
you.

TAYLOR: It does.

GRAHAM: It's been out four, five or six years. What kind of
distance or perspective do you have on it now?

TAYLOR: Well, there are some poems that, if I had it to do over
again, would not be in there. But on the whole, you know, I
knew the author of those poems only briefly, and that was sometime back. He was a good enough kid, but I don't remember
him too well.

GRAHAM: I know that you have a new book that we might talk
about in preparation, and we might get to some of those poems
. . . but with *The Horse Show at Midnight,* one of the things
that remains of interest to me is the middle section.

TAYLOR: The parodies, you're talking about.

GRAHAM: The parodies, yes, of various poets. Let me put my cards very hard on the table now. I may take poetry almost too seriously.

TAYLOR: You think I was too irreverent in that?

GRAHAM: No, I'm worried about you, really, in the sense of are they not simple exercises?

TAYLOR: That's the way they turned out. I think really that good parody as done by a . . .

GRAHAM: Now, it's fun, mind you.

TAYLOR: Sure it's fun and it's also useful. I think it's a kind of criticism.

GRAHAM: This is helping. Frankly, I think your poem on "James Dickey in Orbit" helped me to read "Firebombing." Is that what elicited the poem?

TAYLOR: Actually, no. Dickey had only published two volumes when I did that. He had only published his first two—*Into the Stone* and *Drowning with Others*. That's what I was working on. That's odd. I feel something like a prophet, you know, having done a poem there in which I made the speaker into an astronaut. Now, four or five years later, Dickey is publishing poems in *Life* magazine about the astronauts, which amuses me.

GRAHAM: Does it amuse Mr. Dickey, by the way?

TAYLOR: I don't know. He'll be along here to the Hollins Conference in a few days, and I'll just have to see.

GRAHAM: I take it, then, that what you're basically saying is that at least part of you as poet, thinker, remains glad that you did do the parodies—that you did to exercise, in effect, both your critical and creative faculties.

TAYLOR: Yes. Now, all of these poems were at least begun and mostly finished before I graduated from the University of Virginia in 1964. And, at that time, I was trying to find my own voice. In order to find out what voice is . . . I mean, you can sit around and talk about what a poet's voice is for a long time in critical classes. But unless you do imitations, you don't really find out what it is. Now, I fell under the spell of James Dickey.

GRAHAM: Well, this is really exciting. What you're saying in effect is that you're using a very, very old exercise that goes all the way back to your classical rhetoricians, the use of imitations.

TAYLOR: Sure. It's kind of funny. I wrote a number of poems that are very much influenced by James Dickey, the title poem, for example. I let it stand because I know that James Dickey is afraid of horses and couldn't have written it. But I wrote this astronaut poem. The first time I wrote "Mr. James Dickey in Orbit" it wasn't called that. I forget what it was called. But it was to be a serious poem. And I suddenly realized that it was too much like James Dickey, so I went back and tried to make it funny, which I think I did, and more or less purged myself of that problem, that influence. And I sent it to Robert Bly, a man who published parodies in his magazine and he wrote back and said, Do me parodies of the following people, enclosing a long list of people who at that time I really had not heard of. And it was a very educational experience.

GRAHAM: This is rather fascinating, the way the accidents of life wind up leading you to do things and learn.

TAYLOR: I'd go to the library and read Galway Kinnell or someone like that, you know, and then I'd go home and do a parody, and send it off to Bly. It was a very useful thing. I can't do it very well anymore.

GRAHAM: It may be a young man's delight.

TAYLOR: I think so.

GRAHAM: You may really have your finger on it as part of a necessary maturing process for understanding another man's craft, and also, from what you said of Dickey—not to get too simplistic now, Henry—to triumph over the master, to get rid of him, to exorcise him.

TAYLOR: That's right, to purge an influence that has become too heavy-handed. George Garrett influenced me greatly. In the "Snapshots" you can see his influence, and I did a parody of George Garrett, which I'm rather fond of.

GRAHAM: And done with love, clearly.

TAYLOR: Absolutely, absolutely.

GRAHAM: This is very intricate and interesting, this is dangerously put now, but where in a sense the artist has to "use" other artists . . . or at least their craft.

TAYLOR: Yes, one thing I'd like to say about the young man going after his elders and betters, in a smart alecky kind of way. My most successful parodies are those of poets whose work I admire. The French say something like "One makes fun of that which one loves." I could not do, for example, a successful parody of Rod McKuen, whose work I don't like at all.

GRAHAM: I'm afraid he parodies himself, Henry, so where do you start?

TAYLOR: Just quote a few lines and that's enough. But it was a lot of fun. I can't, as I say, do it much anymore because I'm more sure of my own voice. And I find it harder to get into somebody else's way of doing things.

GRAHAM: Are you not working on some translations in the

new book? There is a very close analogy, a translation and a parody. . . .

TAYLOR: Yes, there is, because the translator has to subordinate his own voice. Not always, not all translators do this. Robert Lowell did what I think is an excellent book called *Imitations* in which he took remarkable liberties. They are not to be seen as translations. You should not take him to task for lack of faithfulness in that book. But if you want to translate, then the translations will of necessity, unless you're very lucky in your choices, sound different from your own work. And that's useful. That's a way of continuing to grow, I guess.

GRAHAM: This is a matter, then, of the broadening of your experience really, both as a man and as a craftsman.

TAYLOR: Sure, if you don't keep moving out, if you don't keep trying to do something that's a little bit harder than the last thing that you did, then you'll never get to the point where I am now, where I can look back at *The Horse Show at Midnight* and say, "Gee, I wish I hadn't put such and such in there," or "I wish I could do that line over again."

GRAHAM: With the translation, what do you like to translate most . . . or is this accidental?

TAYLOR: French—I like the French symbolists best. Baudelaire, right now. And for the last couple of years, I've been deeply involved in the translation of a Greek tragedy, which is kind of odd. I don't know any Greek, and I worked with a classicist on it. That hasn't been as much fun as it should have been, because I'm not comfortable with it. If I know the language then I can have fun. It's a game—a game again. Like any poetic composition, you have little counters that you move around as in a game. But somehow, the game with the Greek was not as much fun because I can't tell quite who my antagonist is.

GRAHAM: It would seem to me that you'd get spooked up too

often with this awareness of this lack of knowledge, where, with the French, you can live with this much more easily and go at it.

TAYLOR: It's still impossible, finally. Translation is impossible. You know, the people who criticize translation keep giving us that ancient and absolutely impossible dictum, "Give us the original." Well, that doesn't make any sense. We already have that. The original exists.

GRAHAM: People who think this can happen simply don't understand language at all, and, above all, they don't understand poetry. This gets me a little angry, by the way. We're into a funny world, because I respect the translator so much. In part because my language abilities are so limited, I need the translator. Do you have anything in current process that you're translating that you like in particular?

TAYLOR: Yes, I have a very strange little poem by an Italian poet name Vittorio Sereni, who is still alive.

GRAHAM: Can you dig it out of that batch of manuscripts? Would you read it?

TAYLOR: Yes, it's called "The Terrace," and it's an odd little low-keyed poem.

> Sudden nightfall around us.
>   You no longer know
> where the edge of the lake is;
> only a whisper
> moves over our life
> under a hanging terrace.
>
> We are completely suspended
> from the silent event of this evening
> caught in the light from a torpedo boat
> which peers at us, then turns and vanishes.

GRAHAM: Sounds like you're under water almost.

TAYLOR: Yes, it's a weird poem. I see it as two people trying to confront the center of a thing which is between them, that is, a set of feelings which is between them; and, suddenly, this torpedo boat which stands for heaven knows what, appears and then is gone. It peers at them and then it disappears and they are left with some vague understanding of where they are that they didn't have before. Sereni likes it, incidentally, I'm happy to report.

GRAHAM: Now that's an interesting point. Are you able to contact the translated poets?

TAYLOR: If they are alive. That's one other problem with Euripides.

GRAHAM: Are they helpful or are they resisting almost?

TAYLOR: They are helpful, they are not resistant. They like the thought that they'll be translated. So would I, I'd love to be translated.

GRAHAM: I was just thinking, in terms again of the difficulty of translation, I could see a poet—I wouldn't call him being precious about it—I could see him feeling that "no, it can't be done, so why should we talk with each other?"

TAYLOR: There are some who do.

III. *I sometimes wonder how I did that poem at the age of nineteen.*

GRAHAM: Talking about *The Horse Show at Midnight*, I know that I like the third group of poems the best. They are longer poems, more intricate, one is very intricate . . . Henry, what's your distance on it? It's like somebody else's book now, isn't it? It's been five years.

TAYLOR: Yes, it is. I look back at it with some affection. It's a book that I like to read from time to time, but I don't know very much about the guy who wrote it. But, you're right, the last section is a group of poems which at the time I thought was the strongest in the book, which is why I put it at the end. I was just beginning, in most of those poems, to find out some things that I've been exploring since. You mention the intricate poem, I presume you're talking about "A Blind Man Locking His House" which is very formally complex, a very difficult stanza. I hadn't done much of that before and I've been doing a lot of it since.

GRAHAM: I remember the poem very much. It's interesting, it's not by any means my favorite. There's one line in it that upset me enormously, as this blind man locks his house—"because some thing stalks me and will not speak." That line popped right out. It's two-thirds through the poem and I was ready for it, but I think the word "stalks" pivoted the whole business. I think the finest poem in the book is "Things Not Solved Through Tomorrow Came." It's a couple of pages . . .

TAYLOR: It's two hundred and fifty lines.

GRAHAM: Well, I cheated a little bit here, Henry, and counted. You've got the speaker as both man and boy. Let's call it two characters. You've got the daughter, wife, father, grandfather, a waitress, and a counterman. There are a lot of people in the drama of this man's life. I've got an idea that what happened to me with the poem may be keyed by those first three stanzas where the man drives his daughter to boarding school.

TAYLOR: He sets the stage. Shall I read that and say what happens very quickly?

GRAHAM: A major reason I'd like you to read them, really, is I think—and this is foolish perhaps to extract a virtue from a complexity of poetry—but I think the pacing is there, in terms of rhythms, the shifting of tonal attitudes. In just the first three stanzas where you set the stage, I think the first stanza is comparatively flat. You've got a long line in there, and that gets us in with the tactility of the steering wheel. And then we can meet these people. I'm sorry to talk so much but this is a splendid poem, Henry, so if you would read some, it would be good.

TAYLOR: "Things Not Solved Though Tomorrow Came" is the title. . . .

> There is silence in this blue car now.
> My daughter and I have driven for hours
> Through early morning, where we started,
> High noon on the turnpike, where we stopped
> To eat in a pink brick restaurant,
> On through to afternoon, the hour when
> The sun shines on the sides of golden things,
> Until we are struck dumb by nearness to the end,
> The long green shadows of her boarding school
> Where we are bound, where we arrive at last.
>
> We unload the car in several trips,
> Carrying up the stairs to the third floor

Her clothes, her blankets, pennants, lamps,
Stuffed animals. The job at last is done.
She stands before me, smiling, as I lean
Against the car, my hand on my thick middle,
Trying not to sweat or gasp for breath.
It is time for me to leave. She kisses me
On the forehead
              "Goodbye, sweetheart," I say.
"We'll miss you. Hit the books. Write home some time."

She kisses me once more, then walks away.
I think of last year at this time,
Her first year here, when neither she
Nor I could keep tears back for long.
She walks across the dying, dark green grass,
Her brown hair, her mother's hair, shining
As it comes between my eyes and the sun.
Some friends of hers are waiting on the porch—
A tall boy smiles, and she begins
To line up love in the nick of time.

GRAHAM: I could listen to you read it again, Henry, because I think that's a grand opening. I think it's quick, it's efficient, unhurried, and it sets up this man with his muddied . . .

TAYLOR: That guy is sick. What happens in the course of the poem . . . there's something wrong with that fellow. He's not a freak. He's not a special case, really.

GRAHAM: He's a survivor?

TAYLOR: What I'm concentrating on here is what happens to all of us. He goes on away from the school, stops at a motel, picks up a waitress, goes to bed with her, and has a hideous attack of guilt, and drives on. Not really understanding what he's done, of course. In some way, the waitress stands for his daughter, it's a proxy sort of thing. He begins to see that and that terrifies him. I sometimes wonder how I did that poem at the age of nineteen.

GRAHAM: Why don't we talk about that a little bit? You have not, in fact, delivered a daughter to a boarding school.

TAYLOR: No, I haven't.

GRAHAM: You don't have a long-legged fifteen-year-old to deposit on the porch.

TAYLOR: Right. Well, but I know my father very very well. We're very close friends, and have been since I was a rational being, really. I happen to know that this poem scares the hell out of him, but a lot of the way that poem talks is the way he talks. I took some experiences of my own, with other people, driving with a girl friend here and there, that sort of thing.

GRAHAM: Well, here at Hollins, you can see someone depositing his daughter at the beginning of the year. I don't see this as a kind of terrifying poem, but as an agonizing poem, though.

TAYLOR: No, to go back to the part that I read. There are games all the way through it. When the guy says here we are coming to "the long green shadows of her boarding school," he knows that he's got to spend money and to "line up love in the nick of time." He backs off there and he says, "by george it's about time, or it's too late, or it's too early. . . ."

GRAHAM: Here's the cycle of the world. His observation of that expands the poem out over the ten- or twelve-hour period that these things seemingly take place in. It gives this distance of memory.

TAYLOR: There are humorous shots all the way through. When he stops at the motel, he notices that it advertises "rest for weary bones," he says.

GRAHAM: The one scene there, as he remembers a pet lamb and the rabbits he tried to keep when he was a boy, even there, in that stanza where you pity this little fellow who feels that life and death is his responsibility, really, and yet, the tone in there is so gentle in observing the boy's guilt that it almost absolves him of the guilt. I'm not going to say now, it makes light of it, that's not true at all. I can hardly believe that you did that when you were nineteen.

TAYLOR: I don't know how, really.

GRAHAM: I don't mean to put you in an impossible situation, but is that one of the poems that you can still turn to and see as a real piece of work?

TAYLOR: Yes, I'm still pleased with that, and I guess I always will be. For a long time, it was a problem for me because I went through a long period after I wrote it, when I thought it would be centuries before I would ever write anything as good as that again. It doesn't scare me in that way anymore, because I've been able to go back and make a few changes in it. You know, I can see spots in it that weren't quite right and that made me feel good.

GRAHAM: What about the title poem in *The Horse Show at Midnight?* I may as well be perfectly candid with you, the poem keeps evading me. I went at it and went at it, and I can understand the first half but not the second half. The section where the horse speaks throws everything I concluded about the first half out.

TAYLOR: Exactly.

GRAHAM: Okay. What do you mean by "exactly," Henry?

TAYLOR: Well, just to say very briefly what happens in the poem. It's in two sections. The rider speaks the first section, and he says he has a dream vision in which everything goes absolutely right for him until the very end when he feels a distance between himself and the horse. And the horse goes out of the ring, back into his stable in a kind of dreamlike way. Then the story is retold from the point of view of the horse.

GRAHAM: There's no sound. There are no hoofprints. Inanimate objects move into place. This is all real.

TAYLOR: And then the horse starts back at the beginning, hearing the calls. As he's lying in the stable, he hears the rider's call, and the heart, and the heartbeat, you know, the two heartbeats, the rider's and the horse's, join together. He goes to the ring, he goes through these motions, and what happens is that we see somehow that the rider's vision carries over. In some way, really, the horse section is not really the horse, it's the rider's version of what he wishes the horse *would* say, if the horse could speak. And what it's about is that you can't be a super rider, which is what this guy wants to be, without a super horse. And the horse is superior because he knows more about it than the rider does in the poem. This is never really the case, of course; horses are stupid. That's what it's driving at, that the rider has missed the partnership aspect of the thing and the horse, for the purposes of the poem, knows it. He sees it. At the end of the poem, he goes back to the stable and he lies down

> Wide-eyed, breathless and shining,
> Still hearing within me the call
> That brought me over the jumps.
> This time I cannot obey:
> This man is only partly a rider
> And the rider in him is within me.

GRAHAM: Why did you use that as your title poem?

TAYLOR: Well, I liked the title.

GRAHAM: I don't mean to go and lock in so, but I do think that "Things Not Solved Though Tomorrow Came" . . .

TAYLOR: That's a better poem.

GRAHAM: Not that this makes any final difference, but that's an interesting problem.

Michael Mewshaw

BIOGRAPHICAL

Born: 19 February 1943 in Washington, D.C.
Education: B.A. University of Maryland 1963, M.A. University of Virginia 1965, Ph.D. Virginia 1969.
Occupational: a variety of jobs; after receiving his Ph.D., he taught, as Assistant Professor of English, at the University of Massachusetts. Plans to resume teaching in the future.
Books: Novels—*Man in Motion* (1970), *Waking Slow* (1972).
He has held a Fulbright Fellowship.

SNAPSHOT

Mike has a wild Irish handsomeness, all the more distinguished now that his dark hair is threaded with premature gray. He has the build and physical style of a certain kind of athlete, a good quarterback, say, or maybe a pitcher, or a good-dribbling guard with a hot hand for outside shooting. Something of the swagger (and loneliness) of any of those. Which is true, but not the whole truth, and could fool you. Because Mike is a hard, steady worker, patient, tireless, and a "quick study," quick to learn from the example of others and from his own hard knocks. Has a quick Irish temper and, equally sudden, an uninhibited expense of his laughter. He seems, at times, so much *younger* than other "young writers." Covers this with a mask (also youthful) of high seriousness. Most of all, he's a creature of delight in discoveries. Earns his luck, but wears it with bravado like a fresh flower in his buttonhole.

I. *What can a romantic breakout do for you once you've come back? There's no real life out there.*

GRAHAM: Mr. Mewshaw has agreed to talk a little about his first published novel, *Man in Motion*. As a professor, Mike, you'll be giving courses in creative writing, and you've just been through the long and dangerous process of actually finishing a novel. How did the novel get started? Can you pinpoint things, the genesis of *Man in Motion?*

MEWSHAW: Well, this is not the first novel that I've written. It's the first to be published. Like many novels by young people, it's an attempt to deal partially with my own experiences and partially with experiences I've observed and stories I've been told. It's an attempt to deal with youth itself. Its genesis came—I can date it pretty much—about four years ago. The process was long, as you say. I think I did six or seven versions of it; so, it's difficult to say when things started to develop as they are presently seen in the novel itself.

GRAHAM: This is petty now, but just the raw physical act of getting those versions down—forgetting about the problem of finding the words and the rhythms—this is what intimidates me. But what's the novel about?

MEWSHAW: It is a *Bildungsroman* of sorts about a man growing up. He's already a man, I guess—he's twenty-six when the story begins. But in many ways he's still a boy. He's attempting to come to grips with his own past and, I guess, with his own character, attempting to understand what he is in relation to his own family. I deal here with a subject that is becoming more and more important and more and more apparent to many people. There is a class of people in this country which is emerging, first generation or second generation children, but the first generation to go to college. This immediately opens up a chasm between them, their past, and their parents. This is all lumped together under the cliché of this year, last year: "the Generation Gap." I didn't want to deal with something that was, in the parlance of the day, meaningful and relevant. All I wanted was to examine what I saw as a truth, that there is a gap between people and their parents.

GRAHAM: Just as one generation, for instance, had a gap created through World War One. Another through the Great Depression and World War Two. This is a gap that's genuine. I get very angry when we slide, when the catch phrases like "Generation Gap" are used for cheap cover-terms for normal human problems. But from what you're saying, I think this college-trained group, the first in the family to go through this very heady and changing experience of college, this does create a gap. It's real.

MEWSHAW: It does, but probably not any more so than the gaps you mentioned. I agree with you the terms like "Generation Gap" constitute a sort of mental shorthand and prevent people from confronting the real situation. What I've tried to do is confront the real situation. This fellow, like so many young people today, feels that he really has very little to do with his parents, has very little to be grateful for, wants only to get away from them.

GRAHAM: What's he doing? How does he make a living?

MEWSHAW: He's doing very little. He's a cashier in a Safeway supermarket, biding his time until his chance comes. He's finished college, but he refuses to get a job because he doesn't want to compromise what he sees as his uniqueness, his opportunity to express himself in some suitable fashion. He's unsure as to what this suitable fashion is, and from the title you can probably guess that he equates motion with progress. He feels that if he's still moving, nobody can pin him down. If he hasn't chosen, he's still free to choose anything or to do anything. He refuses to commit himself for fear that whatever he commits himself to will be what his parents, through one process or another, have been locked into. His father is a construction worker. His mother, at the opening of the story, is in an insane asylum. It sounds pretty grim, and if I say now that I meant it to be humorous, it would probably sound unbelievable. But I meant to approach it in that way. There is a great deal of humor in it.

GRAHAM: I started to jump in when you described the man at the check-out counter. You know most of those jobs are ten-hour-a-day things, about as automatic—if you're pressed at all—as a job could be. So he's already in his box, whether he knows it or not. That's a joke.

MEWSHAW: He feels, as he says a number of times in the book, that what really matters is his mind. It's a burning coal of sensibility and sensitivity, and the mechanical process of checking out groceries doesn't interfere with the free play of his thoughts.

GRAHAM: That's a naive belief.

MEWSHAW: I think it probably is; I've worked at a supermarket before, and I found it a job that was bearable only because you couldn't think for the ten hours you stood on your feet, you could only feel the pain.

GRAHAM: And it does something to you, too. Every mechanistic job that I've had, the very repetitiveness of it kills that incandescence, or at least mutes it, shall we say?

MEWSHAW: I believe that. And it's a strange thing, because I always had a horror of jobs like that, because I felt like . . . they run scientific experiments now where people sleep. They wake them up when they think they're about to have a dream, and they find ultimately that this drives people to states of paranoia, almost psychosis. People have to dream. I feel I have to daydream, I have to think. And if I'm doing something like carrying hods, laying bricks, checking out groceries—I've had a lot of boring jobs in my life—I've found I can't think. Ultimately I become very jumpy and frenetic, and I prefer not to do that. I like to, need to daydream sometimes.

GRAHAM: You've been talking of this man in terms of society, really, in his problem of—I won't even call it a problem—about his lack of commitment, which could be even admirable. Is this failure? I don't want to say that, because, again, that's a judgment. Is this lack of commitment part of his emotional life? You've been talking of him as a mind and as a social being in a sort of broad career sense, but with his relationship with other people, is this fine sensibility able to commit to other people?

MEWSHAW: He's reluctant to commit himself to other people. He has a girl at the start of the story, a girl who is very much in love with him, and he with her. But he's afraid to commit himself irrevocably to her; he's afraid to marry her. What he does, he goes into motion. He decides to leave his home, to leave this girl, and to think things out. He begins a trip. He's driving to the West Coast, where he feels that he'll find what so many American characters . . .

GRAHAM: Riding into the West?

MEWSHAW: Some kind of opportunity out there in the Territories. But on the way he picks up a girl who seems to him to be very much tuned in and turned on to the things he feels he should be. They have an affair, and he wants to prolong the trip. So they go to Mexico together. But the longer they stay together, the more he realizes that the open-ended opportunity that she appears to offer is really a very narrow dead end.

GRAHAM: You know, you might be interested in this—I was talking with Bill Robinson from the University of Florida about film, during the conference here, and this may be old hat to you now, Mike, but he expressed brilliantly that *the* key American experience, and sense of experience, is the breakout. Just as most of us, not too long ago, broke out of Europe, he argues that the theme of most movies will be a breakout of some kind. *Bonnie and Clyde* opens with the girl standing in a hot small room looking out of a window, and, in effect, that opening scene of the movie asks a question of how is she going to break out? And then Clyde drifts by the door. Now you've got a man breaking out, or wanting to break out.

MEWSHAW: Well, I. . . . When I name the authors that I'm going to say in the next breath, I don't mean to equate myself and my work with them, but I think it's an old theme in American literature as well as American cinema. If you go back as far as Melville, the idea of sea voyages, the idea of having a romantic experience which you think will allow you to understand your own life better. The problem has always been what you can bring back from these experiences, and what will help you to live in a different kind of world, in the world where people get up in the morning and go to work, kiss their wife on the cheek and eat dinner and watch TV. What can a romantic breakout do for you once you've come back? There's no real life out there. The breakthrough is an immediate, desperate gesture. You want to get beyond the prison of self, and once you get out there, you very often—at least it's been my experience—once you get out there, there's not much there either. You wind up coming back.

GRAHAM: You've got another scene here that we're both familiar with, of course, of the underground journey that we find in the epic in Western civilization—or for that matter, in our fairy tales—where you and I must try to climb the glass mountain and bring back the treasure. We don't live on the glass mountain, but we've got to find those treasures.

MEWSHAW: So many things are in so many places where we can't live. And so many things we really can't get, but I think all humans are compelled, whether artistically or really, to do just this—live in a constant state of flux and a constant condition of ending. We're always ending something, and our whole life is constructed of endings. You end school years, you end marriages, end youth, and great looking-backs, retrospectives.

GRAHAM: Your protagonist in *Man in Motion,* is he a man who refuses to acknowledge that there are endings? Does he think he can . . . ?

MEWSHAW: He thinks he can attain that state which scientists have despaired of gaining, that of the perpetual motion machine.

II. *Better to read the contemporary writer than to read the newspaper. You get a truer picture, I would think.*

GRAHAM: Mike, one of the things that fascinates me is the reading that an active professional writer does. Does it stimulate you, does it depress you, or do you see it as an exercise looking for techniques? Do you just read? What happens with you?

MEWSHAW: I think it depends a great deal on what you read. The effect of what you read depends on the type of book. I'm probably very naive about this, but I very seldom get depressed by reading great people. Maybe I should, but I feel that they always act as a stimulating force. I like to try and equal what I read. Perhaps it's hopeless, but I think it's worth striving for.

GRAHAM: Of course, the books we read are part of our experience too, so it could be taken in that way. I've often wondered, though, if you've been laboring on a passage and then suddenly you're reading this magnificent novel, say *Gatsby*, so gracefully written. It would just seem to me that it would "bother" you.

MEWSHAW: It can very much. It seems effortless' although we know it took a lot of effort. I think that you have to face that and not let it bother you that much. I still bring to each book a great deal of enthusiasm and I'm thrilled when I read someone good, whether it's F. Scott Fitzgerald or a contemporary writer.

GRAHAM: Well, who are you reading now? What three or five or ten books might I read that you've been reading?

MEWSHAW: Some of these books aren't "new" but they are new to me. I've come at books at different times in my life. Some of them I read when I was too young. Others, which are young man's books, I came at a little later. Last summer I began to read J. P. Donleavy's *The Ginger Man*. There's a great vitality to his prose, a lot of momentum behind his scenes and incidents. Also, he's very, very funny.

GRAHAM: While we were talking about your novel, *Man in Motion,* the Ginger Man is a man in motion too, isn't he?

MEWSHAW: Right, exactly. I think it had a great deal of influence verbally on my book. In a sense there are some correspondences between the two characters. Mine's not quite as raffish as Sebastian Dangerfield.

GRAHAM: I can remember some mad bicycle ride that he took. It's a crazy, turned-upside-down book.

MEWSHAW: There are a lot of Mack Sennett cinemagraphic effects in the novel. He has such vitality and a great deal of energy, and I thought that this was what was lacking in my own prose. The difficult thing for me was to make the words count. To have a crispness to them and a freshness. The only way I could do this was to practice and work at it and read other writers I thought did it well.

GRAHAM: Is Donleavy able to sustain this energy and the crispness of *The Ginger Man* in other books? Are they rather similar books?

MEWSHAW: They are, I think, too similar. After a while, it begins to wear on you. I think it even begins to wear on you in *The Ginger Man*. It's a style that ultimately strikes me as being manic or so frenetic as to wear you down. And it also calls attention to itself to such a degree that behind it, there doesn't seem to be a great deal of content. Pardon me, J. P. Donleavy.

GRAHAM: It's the problem that we all recognize. If we hear the background music in a movie, it's a bad background music, and if we see the man's style too nakedly before us, he has some things to learn.

MEWSHAW: Well, I feel like I'm contradicting myself now. I read him and I liked him and I feel that he helped me. It's the kind of novel that I feel is enjoyable and would be enjoyable to anyone who likes to read. But I feel that I recognize where his deficiencies lie. I hope I recognize my own, as clearly and candidly. But for language, I don't think that Donleavy can be beaten. There are other writers whom I've read and I think that, like a lot of people, I choose the writers consciously. I still read a great many of the classics, of the older books, the great books. But I like to read ones that are contemporary. Eliot himself was asked why we should read contemporary poets, and he answered in what seemed to be a redundant way. He said, "because they are contemporary." And that would be my answer to anyone who would say, Why do you waste your time reading contemporary writers? Simply because they are contemporary.

GRAHAM: I need any window into my own world that I can get, so I want you writers to help me. That is the function of the writer in society—to take the veils off our eyes.

MEWSHAW: Better to read the contemporary writer than to read the newspaper. You get a truer picture, I would think.

GRAHAM: Who else other than Donleavy are you popping around with now?

MEWSHAW: There's a Southern writer by the name of Walker Percy whose book *The Moviegoer* . . .

GRAHAM: I understand it is first-rate.

MEWSHAW: It is, and his second book, *The Last Gentleman,* is also. Percy is dealing with situations and characters which interest me and which I see could influence the way I approach character. He's dealing with the banality of day-to-day life as it's lived. Now, he's dealing with a section of the country that is supposedly rich in lore and rich in anecdotes and rich in tradition. He's dealing with the South. He approaches it in a different way. He says the South has changed. Where before we had magnolia trees and great white houses with columns, we now have gas stations and army camps and Tasty Freezes. And he deals with the conflict between men who have a sense of tradition and a sense of history, who are now living in an essentially nonhistorical, nontraditional age. His man, "the last gentleman," is born into this world and tries to make the best of it, coming to grips with these changing times. I'm making him sound very, very serious. The book is fast-moving. It's probing, poignant, but also very funny. Percy has a wonderful sense of wit; he can poke fun at himself, his characters. He has a great ironic sense. I enjoy his writing for that reason, and I also enjoy his writing because of the light he throws on a section of the country which is going through a change similar to the changes elsewhere. He shows how people are attempting to cope with these changes.

GRAHAM: Are these in paperback? They've been out for a while, haven't they?

MEWSHAW: Every one I've named so far is in paperback. They are all out in paperback, and a funny thing is the thing that everyone notices about other people's books and certainly about their own books—*The Last Gentleman* has a picture of a very voluptuous nude on the front which is a little confusing and troubling. I'm sure Mr. Percy finds it so. I'm sure that some place in there, *someone* was once naked, but I—

GRAHAM: Someone had to take a shower at one time.

MEWSHAW: There is so little of that sort of thing in the book that the mind boggles to understand why they did this on the front of his book.

GRAHAM: One knows only too well why.

MEWSHAW: Yes, one knows, one knows.

GRAHAM: What else, Mike? What other authors?

MEWSHAW: Well, there's another author by the name of Wright Morris whose. . . .

GRAHAM: He's published what—ten or fifteen novels?

MEWSHAW: Nineteen.

GRAHAM: And no one reads them, it seems.

MEWSHAW: Yes, and it's a funny thing. I never heard his name mentioned until I was twenty-five years old. Then, I learned that he was the writer whom writers should read. He was a writer's writer. And now, his collected works, I believe, have been brought out in some "portable" edition. Malcolm Cowley did the same thing for him that he did for Faulkner, trying to raise his reputation in the estimation of critics in the country. I think it should be a lot higher than it is. He's an extremely gifted, skillful writer. He's dealing with a difficult subject and difficult problems. Again, he's trying to deal with the problem of banality. He writes about characters in the Midwest, people driven by strange forces, misunderstanding. And he attempts to deal with it in the only way that I think anyone can deal with that, which is humorously. He tries to understand what motivates these characters. I guess by extension of what motivates himself. He's from Indiana. He's now transplanted in California. But he wrote a book called *Love Among the Cannibals,* which I enjoyed very much, and another one, indirectly about the Kennedy assassination, which was called *One Day.* So far as I know, and this sounds, I guess, sacrilegious, but it's the only *humorous* novel ever written, centered around the assassination.

GRAHAM: It's a little hard to imagine, frankly.

MEWSHAW: It must have been written in a strange mood. I think it's a kind of gallows humor. It certainly is not wildly funny, since it's more a despairing assessment of what he sees as coming unhinged in America.

GRAHAM: While we're talking, I think now I can remember any number of reviews on Wright Morris, all of which opened on practically a despairing note of "why isn't this man read more?" And then would follow a review of very high praise. It's such a phenomenon.

MEWSHAW: Well, I've met him and I know him a bit, and I think there are several reasons, one of which would probably open a whole can of worms which you would not want to get into. And that is "the publishing scene." Wright Morris lives in Mill Valley, California. He's almost inaccessible. He's a very, very private kind of man. He has no patience whatsoever with the kind of machinations of New York publishing.

GRAHAM: He's not going to go to the cocktail party that may help sell the book.

MEWSHAW: No, and he is a very straight-shooting Midwesterner. He said, and I think that this is good advice for anybody who wants to write, "Remember, if you have to deal with an agent, you better call him early in the morning because he'll be drunk by eleven. And you won't be able to contact him later on."

William Manchester

BIOGRAPHICAL

Born: 1 April 1922 in Attleboro, Massachusetts.

Education: B.A. University of Massachusetts 1946, M.A. University of Missouri 1947.

Occupational: From 1945 to 1955 he was a newsman, beginning as a reporter on the *Daily Oklahoman* and finishing up as reporter, correspondent, and associate editor of the *Baltimore Sun.* From 1955 to 1965 he was Managing Editor of Wesleyan University Publications; since 1965 he has been Fellow of the Wesleyan Center for Advanced Studies.

Books: Novels—*City of Anger* (1953), *Shadow of the Monsoon* (1956), *Beard the Lion* (1958), *The Long Gainer* (1961); non-fiction—*Disturber of the Peace: The Life of H. L. Mencken* (1951), *A Rockefeller Family Portrait* (1959), *Portrait of a President* (1962), *The Death of a President* (1967), *The Arms of Krupp* (1968).

Manchester's honors and awards have been various, reflecting his wide interests and different kinds of achievements. He's been a Guggenheim fellow; he's also received such honors as the Dag Hammarskjöld Prize (1966), the Gold Medal in Journalism (University of Missouri, 1969), and the Overseas Press Club recognized *The Arms of Krupp* as "Best Book on Foreign Affairs" (1968).

SNAPSHOT

A little bit of the *Front Page* style, brought up to date of course. Comes on at first that way, casual (it seems), but lean and sharp-eyed, patiently straight-faced. Maybe if he weren't a reporter, you'd take him for a good, big city detective, weary, uncorruptible, a man who has seen it all and heard your story many times, but will keep on looking and listening nonetheless, like Adam on naming day, and missing nothing.

But there's more. Bill is also pure New England. All that discipline and skill as reporter, researcher, writer is real enough, but also a means to an end which is likely transcendental. The newshawk style disguises and preserves a poet, a real one in the great tradition. The purity of Walden Pond, as it was for Thoreau, is a clear memory and prospect for him. He suffers for those who, by hard circumstance, have never known that dream; has righteous rage against those who, knowing better, deny the dream and deprive us of it.

A superb and careful maker, he knows without doubt that in all our art and craft it is the *spirit* which lives and gives life.

When I look at Bill Manchester, I know why we lost the Civil War. And I can't fault the justice of it.

I. *A really first-rate interview with an articulate man can be fascinating for him. And if he is fascinated, then it will go on and you will learn more from him.*

GRAHAM: Mr. Manchester is known for his novels and his five works of nonfiction, the most commonly known being *The Disturber of the Peace,* a biography of H. L. Mencken; *The Death of a President;* and, most recently, *The Arms of Krupp.*

Bill, you talked earlier tonight and you said that in the process of writing contemporary history, what really excites you is—"I write to find out." You don't know where your nose is going to lead you, and, in a way, this is what a novelist does, and you do have your four novels. Now, how do you change your search for discovery from the world of fiction to the world of contemporary and oral history?

MANCHESTER: I think that it's a difficult transition, but a very important one, if you can retain the narrative drive, which is what makes fiction readable and should make nonfiction readable. What you have to stifle is your imagination. And this is why I think it's important to annotate a book, to provide it with a scholarly apparatus, so that you cite sources.

GRAHAM: To nail it right down to the fact, and if nothing else, you've at least presented a workbook then?

MANCHESTER: Precisely. And I have named most of my sources in the Krupp book which are German and they have been checked out by critics in Germany. And I have not heard that any of them are wrong, so that the numbers are right anyhow. I know that when I go into a bookshop and look at a book of nonfiction I look in the back to see if it isn't annotated, indexed, if there is a bibliography. Otherwise I'm not interested, because I don't know whether the fellow is telling me the truth or not.

GRAHAM: We have a sufficient number of rather breezy experts who can paraphrase handily a few newspaper articles and turn out a short book on a particular incident. Now this business of the imagination is an enormous tease to me. At an early age I was just bombed by Pirandello's *Six Characters in Search of an Author*. And my first reaction to you, really, was that you must have a terrible problem when you've got data on the man, and the data starts to tease you into imagination so that you want to—the man's a very attractive character—so you want to "expand."

MANCHESTER: I think there are times when it is not only irresistible, but should not be resisted. When you have just enough facts so that—for a premise, but not enough for proof—then I think at that point that the author should simply say to the reader, "Look here, I don't know, but I can conjecture, and it may be true that it was thus-and-so." And that way you're on the square, you're being honest with the reader.

GRAHAM: You make a very careful distinction between what you have data on, the hard statistic—and "This seems to be the direction the statistics lead." As long as you leave the "seems" in there, or a warning that conjecture now is afoot, you're playing straight.

MANCHESTER: Yes. I think that probably the best illustration of that is in *The Death of a President,* in which I describe the atmosphere in Dallas, which was very hostile to President Kennedy. I went through a year's volume of Dallas newspapers, and I talked with people who worked with Oswald. And it was clear that they had very little use for the President. And we know that Oswald was in this environment. We know he was an unstable figure. Now, I cannot state that there was any link between this, but can suggest that there *may* have been, just as there was between the articles traducing Abraham Lincoln in 1865 and the unstable figure of John Wilkes Booth. But that is conjecture, and the author is free to reject it.

GRAHAM: And yet a reasonable establishment of condition is hardly a leap of the imagination, if the Dallas papers were in fact rather vigorously anti-Kennedy.

MANCHESTER: Of course, I cited examples. That's important.

GRAHAM: With the general process, I know from listening to you earlier, I know you have pursued this business of interviewing. And I found many of your remarks exciting. This whole business of that little thread that the unprepared interviewer simply can't find in a man. You must live out of a suitcase. When you start to try to make appointments with busy people, and as you cited, "Friendlies" and "Unfriendlies," trying to sometimes, I am sure, trying to manipulate around a man just to get an appointment with him, can you figure your time on a project?

MANCHESTER: No. . . . The first time I interviewed President Kennedy I was supposed to see him for ten minutes. The interview lasted three and a half hours. It was exciting and it led to further meetings. I think it is very important for a person to do his homework. I remember once Bernard De Voto came to Hartford, and a Hartford reporter came in, rather disheveled, just at the last minute, and he said "Can I interview you?" Bernard De Voto said "Splendid," and the reporter said, "I'm sorry, I really didn't have time to look this up. Just exactly who are you, Mr. De Voto?" And De Voto said, "Young man, if you don't have the time to look it up in a *Who's Who* or in your own library and find out, I haven't any time for you." And he dismissed him. And so he should. There's nothing more insulting than to ask a man, like a President of the United States, a question that he's answered many times before. Then he's quite likely to dismiss you.

GRAHAM: Or very quickly get bored with you so you're never going to tap his inner resources.

MANCHESTER: So what you want to ask are the questions he's never been asked before, questions that show that you have a great familiarity with his life. And then he's likely to respect you and be interested in the exchange, the colloquy.

GRAHAM: Something of a meeting of peers. That's perhaps too strong, but at least two reasonable minds reasonably well-equipped.

MANCHESTER: Yes. For example, I went through the appointments that President Kennedy had made, his special assistants and his cabinet advisers, and I found that over eighty percent of them were all within two or three years of the President's age. So I asked him if he was a "generation chauvinist." Now, he'd never thought of this, but he liked the idea and he played with it, and it was entertaining for him. A really first-rate interview with an articulate man can be fascinating for him. And if he is fascinated, then it will go on and you will learn more from him. It all depends on how much time you spend in advance.

GRAHAM: One thing I was wondering, now, in the craft of history, with your present schedule, as busy as you are, do you get much chance to both learn and see what the standards are, by reading a lot? Is there any big swatch of time you can ever steal for reading the great historians, the great letter-writers, perhaps, of history?

MANCHESTER: Oh yes, I set aside great blocks of time for reading. I think you have to. In some cases it's important to read as much as two years. As for my current project (which I don't want to discuss) I have just begun interviewing, and I have been reading for over two years and I have read about two thousand books and have taken outlines of them. I think it's impossible to ask intelligent questions or to gain, acquire information unless you know what has already been published on the subject. Otherwise you're just duplicating the past, and you're wasting your own time as well as that of others.

GRAHAM: This may be a false distinction, but would you make a distinction, in the writing of contemporary history, between the *action* and *biography*—the incident, if you will, very specifically with *The Death of a President*, say, versus *Disturber of the Peace*, your book on H. L. Mencken, where you were going so much more directly at character. I want to say "versus," and that's not fair, of course. I'm not trying to get an "either-or."

MANCHESTER: The two may be interwoven, and in fact, in the Mencken book there were specific incidents—he was arrested in Boston Common, he covered the Scopes trial—that were action. But in a biography you include many other things: childhood, associations, the pressures upon him and the pressures within him.

GRAHAM: Of course, I'm probably thinking about letters, in a way, where the letters or the incorporation of, say, journal notes might be much more important in a biography.

MANCHESTER: They are, but then, of course, I think they enter into contemporary history too. The thing that one must never forget is that the contemporary historian, like the fiction writer, must bring his characters to life. Now, I'm an admirer of Gibbon and those great block paragraphs that roll on and on, but he's telling me *about* Rome; he doesn't put me in Rome. You spoke of letters. Now in the case of *The Death of a President,* one of the most valuable, most treasured letters I have is one that President Kennedy wrote to the parents of a Texas boy who died in Vietnam. And he wrote it just before he went to Texas. It's a very moving letter. President Kennedy made it a point to always write the parents of every boy who died in the service, and he invited them to Washington. And if they came he would spend a few minutes with them. That shows a lot about a man's character.

GRAHAM: One very interesting thing you said, brought up in your lecture, was your emphasis on research. That was the backbone, and tremendously interesting to me. But you talked also about the conception, the writing, and the editing of a piece of work. Could you expand on this idea of editing a bit?

MANCHESTER: I think that it's difficult to edit yesterday's work. You can go over it and do some things with it, but after a passage of time, the yeast is there. It ferments. There's a leavening process. And then you can go over it with the pencil and eraser. I count, at the end of a book, on spending one hour on each page in editing, and I try to be as ruthless as possible. I ask myself of each sentence, "Is it clear? Is it true? Does it feel good?" And if it's not, then I rewrite it.

II. *I'm not one of those who believe that you can lie your way to the truth. You present yourself exactly as you are, and you play it dead straight.*

GRAHAM: One of the fascinating things that Mr. Manchester has revealed here is himself as nonfiction writer and yet creative writer. The difference is hard to spot. The fact of the matter is Manchester sees his strength in terms of research. You do your homework, don't you, Bill?

MANCHESTER: Yes, I do. I go into very extensive research, particularly when I'm dealing with a very important figure. I read everything he has published and try to read everything of significance that has been published about him. Then I have about thirty, forty, or fifty, depending upon the figure, interviews with men who have known him throughout his life.

GRAHAM: I should imagine one of your major problems is making sure that in the thirty, forty, or fifty you get people with different world views, very specifically different attitudes towards this man.

MANCHESTER: People come out of different context. Members of his family will have a different view of him than people who have known him as an eminent figure.

GRAHAM: Well, you talked earlier at a lecture about the "Friendlies" and the "Unfriendlies." How do you get through to the "Unfriendlies" and how can you trust the "Friendlies"?

MANCHESTER: Well, you don't trust anybody, not when you're a writer of contemporary history. You weave into your interviews questions that you have asked other people, and you balance them out. When I was writing about the Dallas Motorcade, on November 22nd, 1963, if there were six people in the car, I interviewed all six. If five of them saw something, I concluded that it happened. If only one saw it, I concluded that it did not. Now, with the "Unfriendlies," that's an espionage term, really. With the "Unfriendlies" you get unexpected cooperation, partly because people are compulsive talkers, or because they think they can straighten you out, and mostly because if they realize that you've done your research you are going ahead anyhow. And so they think they may be able to help you, and very often they can, though in ways that are not evident to them.

GRAHAM: I should imagine that on occasion they are trying to prove to you the solidity of their unfriendliness.

MANCHESTER: Sometimes, you get a very hostile person, and this can be a real workout.

GRAHAM: I know I find these simple and very pleasant conversations leave me tired at the end, so when you're fencing and trying to get through the barrier, you must walk away drained.

MANCHESTER: Yes, and it is important to retain the professionalism of the interview. You don't quarrel. You don't introduce color words. You ask questions that are as objective and detached as possible. I'm not one of those who believe that you can lie your way to the truth. You present yourself as exactly what you are, and you play it dead straight.

GRAHAM: Excuse me, but has it gotten easier for you now that it's clear that you are serious, responsible? Is it easier for you to interview now, are people more willing, do you think?

MANCHESTER: People are more willing to be interviewed, a lot more willing. But I have the same problem that Teddy White has, that people realize that they are going plunk into history, and then they are self-conscious, which is not helpful. One of the problems is divesting them of that feeling, so that they forget about history and are able to speak honestly and candidly about themselves.

GRAHAM: The thing that I was fascinated by was your casual remark, when we were walking over to the lecture hall, that you write everything out longhand and then whip it on to the typewriter, revising en route. I write at such a wretchedly slow pace that I can't believe your production over these last years. How do you do it? What happens?

MANCHESTER: You know what Red Smith said? He said, "Writing is very easy. All you do is sit in front of a typewriter keyboard until little drops of blood appear on your forehead." I do write in longhand with a pen. I tried a typewriter. I'm a fast typist and rap out a sentence, and then there is an embarrassing lapse before the next sentence occurs to me. Whereas, if I write, the pace is slower, but steadier. I have to put it on the typewriter later because I can't edit it properly in longhand. I have to get the words okay. That's the second stage really. I have a first draft of *The Death of a President,* the whole book, in longhand. And then I have the second draft in type.

GRAHAM: This leads me to the sequence you talked about— of conception. That would include your research patterns and then the editing. I'm not sure I understand what you do in the editing because it seemed to me you were suggesting it was more than line by line, paragraph by paragraph, but some larger revision, even of your conception.

MANCHESTER: Oh yes, yes. There are parts that are tossed out because they are really irrelevant, or you overprove your point, or something is out of proportion. You've let a character run away with you, and you have to cut him down to size. And he's just not that important.

GRAHAM: You had a lot of interesting phrases that I'd like to spin off on. But, I'm most tempted once again by the statement that you write "to find out." With, let's say, *The Death of a President,* or *The Arms of Krupp,* did your large view of the issue, the large view of the drama, change very much from, let's say, early conception and research, as you progressed along?

MANCHESTER: I think that it is important for the contemporary historian to suspend judgment for a long time. I suspended judgment on the identity of the assassin for over a year. In the writing of that book, I had far more appreciation of Lyndon Johnson's difficulties in Dallas with becoming President in a Texas city, in his home state, where his predecessor had just been brutally murdered. This would have been a terrible strain on any man, and I appreciated that more as I began to put the words on paper. I think that writing ought to make the writer more compassionate, give him a greater understanding of people. You don't become flip, and you don't toss out quick judgments about a man if you're trying to recapture him and his mood in an atmosphere that is also re-created.

GRAHAM: This is fascinating, because just the other day, Shelby Foote, the Civil War historian, suggested much the same thing: that even with a man who you read as a bad man . . . the historian must try to understand, to have compassion and sympathy for the complexities of life that that particular man was caught in. And then perhaps let the reader stand back and make the moral judgment. But you, as truth seeker, need to withhold that moral judgment though the data may dictate rejection of the man.

MANCHESTER: Yes. Well, most conspicuously again, in *The Death of a President,* in describing the plane ride from Dallas to Washington, there was a great deal of tension on that plane. And everyone seems to have been aware of it except President

Johnson, who now says there wasn't any there. Well, members of his family—members of his official family who were there— they all agree that there was great tension. But no two people had the same account of what happened. And it was very hard to unscramble that omelet.

GRAHAM: Well, I recall the sense of paralysis that I experienced, and every one I knew. I was in the Radio-Recording Center at the University of Virginia and everyone was just paralyzed in there. It was a fantasy, or maybe a very, very vulgar joke really. And I don't know . . . I couldn't . . . I know what I was doing when I first heard the news. But what I did for the next twenty-four hours is vague and confusing to me. A sense of impotency, really. . . . Not unlike the deaths of the four Kent State students. A strange sense that something had to be done and yet, not knowing and therefore, I don't know, talking to oneself. . . . I know this is a dangerous question, but with your passion really for research can you spot your cut-off point? Does it come when you start to realize that you are re-finding out data?

MANCHESTER: Of course if you're interviewing a President, it ends when he stands up. When a President of the United States stands up, you leave immediately. But, I usually close an interview with someone by simply asking the person, "Is there anything you think is important which I haven't asked?" And sometimes what they think is important is not important at all. But they should be given that opportunity, and sometimes it is very revealing.

GRAHAM: I should imagine that sometimes very simple questions may tease out from the deep recesses of memory some very telling points. But I'm thinking also of research in a larger sense. When you say you interview thirty, forty, fifty, is there a clear point of no return? When you go to the fifty-first . . . ?

MANCHESTER: Oh yes, I think . . . it depends on how important the figure is, really. If it was a very important public figure, a VIP, you may very well go to fifty. With Kennedy, I certainly did.

GRAHAM: I'm rather interested in the statement "off the record." Do you run into that a great deal? Or, does it vary so much, there's no answer?

MANCHESTER: Most people are pretty intelligent about this, and I let them know the rule in advance. They can put in a remark off the record, if they wish to. If they tell me, I will put it in brackets, in my notes, and so I know it's off the record. It's all very well to say, as some reporters do, that nothing can be off the record. But, I don't think that is fair. Particularly with people who are not accustomed to being interviewed. Because they forget it's an interview, and they let all sorts of personal detail spill out. Then, I think, it becomes an invasion of privacy, and this is something that one must be careful of. One can easily invade privacy.

GRAHAM: And you can poison your own well—simply from a point of self-interest—with future interviews.

MANCHESTER: That's right, that's correct.

James Seay

BIOGRAPHICAL

Born: 1 January 1939 in Panola County, Mississippi.
Education: B.A. University of Mississippi 1964, M.A. University of Virginia 1966.
Occupational: A number of jobs, including construction work and being an Insurance Investigator, to put himself through school; has taught at Virginia Military Institute, University of Alabama; presently Associate Professor of English at Vanderbilt University.
Books: Poetry—*Let Not Your Hart* (1970); forthcoming—a new collection of poems, tentatively titled *Patching Up the Past with Water.*

Together with the late John Berryman, Seay was a winner of the Emily Clark Balch Prize for Poetry in 1968.

SNAPSHOT

Tall, rangy, broad-shouldered and muscular, his muscles once hardened and bulked by heavy physical labor, now well-conditioned by regular workouts at the Cosmo Health Spa in Nashville, Seay cuts a striking figure, the more so because of the black patch he wears to cover a blind eye. Very soft- and slow-talking with his gentle Mississippi accent unchanged, he's an expert public reader of his own work. Hard work and pain are not strangers to him, are in fact the source of an unsenti-

167

mental countryman's delight in the difficult job, well and gracefully done, and a deep compassionate understanding of human suffering, common and uncommon. He has a certain gravity and dignity beyond his age, but all this tempered by a quick vital sense of humor. Which is fortunate, because he is married to the novelist Lee Smith. And she is one of the funniest people alive.

I. *Some readers and listeners have had problems determining the tone of this title poem.* . . .

GRAHAM: I thought we might talk a bit about your first book of poems, *Let Not Your Hart,* that was published in 1970. Jim, I enjoyed the volume very much. I might also add I like the looks of it.

SEAY: Yes, I was real pleased with the cover, the type, the whole physical thing itself.

GRAHAM: I think that these little books of poetry, often issued by university presses (in this case it's Wesleyan), are exercises in superb graphic art as well as in verbal art. One thing, in reading your poetry, that I can observe, is a kind of emerging general principle about your poems, a kind of new thing in poetry for me. It may be quite common, and you might check me on it, but to take the title poem, "Let Not Your Hart Be Truble," I get a very clear sense of some gentleness and the probing of some mystery, maybe even some fear in here, and also, maybe a little self-mockery.

JAMES SEAY | 169

SEAY: That—yes—is in there.

GRAHAM: Now, the thing that I find interesting—I see this in Richard Wilbur's work, this kind of mixture—now, the thing that I'm interested in—I don't want to go automatic as to what a lyric or amusing poem might be—but it's that the poem does not have a "single" tone, by any means. It has a complexity of tones. Is this a conscious part of your operation?

SEAY: It was not at the time I was writing this poem. In fact I can remember very vividly the place where this poem was written—it was in Lexington, Virginia. And I did a lot of the work out on this porch which was glassed-in and screened also, had a lot of light coming in. I can remember getting up early in the mornings. Some readers and listeners have had problems determining the tone of this title poem, which was taken from the back of a bus, a former school bus which had been converted. A church in Memphis, Tennessee, had taken this bus and was using it to go out and pick up their people and even to proselytize.

GRAHAM: I saw a picture of this bus, an old ramshackle, hand-lettered bus—

SEAY: —dilapidated—

GRAHAM: —and I saw the picture before I read the poem. And just the picture grabbed me. So I can see how. Would you mind reading the poem and maybe talking about it? You see— let me say this, I am not troubled by the mixed tonal quality, as I see it. I think it's an enrichment.

SEAY: Well, in fact, that's part of my approach to poetry. You know John Crowe Ransom—well maybe I missed—I think I've quoted Ransom for years and it may be Auden—in any event, one of those fine poets said, "Poetry is the clear expression of mixed emotions." That's very nice, you know, because rarely do we respond to a given stimulus with the same emotion. And so all of that is in here with this complexity of tone. I haven't thought about it. I know people have had trouble, but if we define tone as the writer's, or the speaker's attitude toward his subject matter, tone as, say, distinguished from mood. . . . The person that very crudely lettered or painted this on the rear exit door of this bus—obviously illiterate because this is misspelled here. That man is trying to say, to repeat, the words of Christ to the disciples, or to one of the disciples. "Let not your heart be troubled; ye believe in God, believe also in Me." And what he means is the human heart. Of course, here, unless you have the text before you, you won't see the plays I make—sometimes I'm talking about "hart," and sometimes about "heart," but usually the context will reveal that—I'll read it now. . . . The title is "Let Not Your Hart Be Truble." Usually when I'm reading this to a group, I preface it with a few remarks, since I use some scriptural allusions. The situation is that the speaker of the poem is driving along, and this bus passes him. He sees this legend very crudely lettered on the back of the bus, and it sets his mind to thinking on this thing, this statement of faith—the man trying to tell him to not have a troubled heart. I thought of the conversion of Saul of Tarsus on the road to Damascus, struck blind and converted to Christianity, and how he became Paul, St. Paul. And there's one other little play in here. Paul defined faith as the evidence of things not seen, the substance of things hoped for. And that's a lot of what the poem's about—faith and statements of faith. So here's the poem.

> The horn of your silver bus
> Sounds in the rocks and trees,
> Black Saul of Tarsus turned Paul,
> And you come telling
> Under what tree and with what light
> You were struck blind
> And now see.
>
> On faith and a curve, both blind,
> You double-clutch and pass my car,
> Hoping against the evidence

Of things not seen,
Or, should it appear from around this curve,
You trust the roadside rocks and trees
Will open like the sea.
That failing, you take the rock and wood
For what it gives.

Your pass is good, and made, I guess,
With the same thick hand that lettered
The words on your rear exit door:
LET NOT YOUR HART BE TRUBLE
You exact too much, black Paul,
My lane, my life on your faith,
My troubled hart.
And yet I do not deny you unlettered
The gift of metaphor, or even parable;
The Master himself spoke thus,
Lest the heart of the many be softened.

You talk like you clutch, old black soul,
For you know the troubled hart
Takes the hunt
Into a deeper wood.

GRAHAM: You know one thing that came through very strongly. There's a kind of conflict of language in here. I'm looking right now, especially in the second stanza where we've got "On faith and a curve, both blind, You double-clutch and pass my car." Now, we're already way into the Biblical language—the echoes of Saul of Tarsus turned Paul. We're about to come into hoping against the evidence of things not seen. And I'm tremendously teased by—again I call it a "conflict." Do you still use the word "tension" in poetry? Because there's a verbal tension in here. What I would call the almost trashily mechanical language of "double-clutching."

SEAY: Yes, an idiomatic expression, and then I move from that and play on the scriptural allusion, that definition of faith by Paul.

GRAHAM: And then we get that reinforced—"Will open like the sea." So you're pulling our twentieth century and two thousand years almost all together at once. Do you read the Bible much? I mean, is this part of your reading? Your experience?

SEAY: In the past. I think most of us can draw on these more familiar scriptural allusions, and we'll take something like the sea opening, you know, and connect it with a kind of blind faith that would expect the woods and the rocks to open up and make way for the bus if it left the road.

GRAHAM: How have you found this poem working with younger students? Quite candidly, I'm finding more and more one can't make quick allusions to the Old or the New Testaments. Do young students now seem to be able to bring these Biblical things that were part of my childhood . . .

SEAY: And of my own . . .

GRAHAM: And perhaps particularly in the South. . . . But can they bring this equipment with them to read a poem such as your "Let Not Your Hart Be Truble"?

SEAY: I'm perhaps not qualified to answer because I've never really had them come up and ask me. I usually get a good response at a reading, and this poem caught the attention of the judges for the Emily Clark Balch Prize in poetry in 1968, and was the first one they printed of the nine poems that they selected. And so I figure that's some indication it's understood. But I don't really know about the younger people. They respond very favorably. Whether they get the "Master himself spoke thus" and the talk about parables, I don't know. Or with the conversion of Paul—Saul.

GRAHAM: Basically, I think, what my question is, and is generated by the initial business of the "double-clutch" and "evidence of things not seen" conflict.

SEAY: What that is, would be another car coming round, another vehicle coming around a blind curve.

GRAHAM: Now, your audience of the young can get "the double-clutch" and "the blind curve," but what I'm interested in is the problem for you in general as poet, you who can, because of your reading, draw on a long tradition, so that what is your sense of a common ground between you and, let's say, a young audience? I mean, they haven't read *Moby Dick*. They haven't read maybe even *The Sun Also Rises*. And yet that's part of your life and part of my life, and so we can talk about it. But you can't talk with—write for—an audience with a very limited literary experience.

II. *It's something that's lain there and it haunts you and continues to haunt you 'til you finally put it down on the page and see what you can make out of it.*

GRAHAM: Jim, the poems in *Let Not Your Hart* were fun. Some of them, well, I guess you could say the majority, are rather what I would call "easy" poems. They do not have the much-maligned complexity of modern poetry. One thing you do that I enjoy a great deal is you give me a very keen sense that you observe physical things closely, and not just through sight, but through all of your senses. I get a kind of roundedness. Do you go bird-shooting, do you hike a lot, or did you as a kid? I get a sense of this.

SEAY: I did then more than I do now, and a lot of these poems do take rise from personal experiences. That's not to say they're history. I mean, I think, if you're bound by the experience itself as it literally happened, you're going to cripple yourself as a writer because often you make discoveries along the way, take leaps into the fantastic—trying to talk about your actual experiences.

GRAHAM: I've read in the past very few days, really, probably, say, six or eight books of poetry by young poets. And as a kind of consistent pattern, in contrast to an older and more experienced poet such as Richard Wilbur, many of the younger poets have a sense of *memory*. There's almost a musing quality, which is very attractive. What I get from some of your poems, certainly, is a search of experience, a search of memory would be better, with, I think, a concurrent attempt to understand what happened to you, where you at one time had been.

SEAY: These things, say, if you're dealing with a situation, a mood, whatever, that is out of the past, it's something that's lain there and it haunts you, and continues to haunt you 'til you finally want to put it down on the page and see what you can make out of it.

GRAHAM: Am I making this too analytical? It "haunts" you. You must get it down on the paper—in a sense so that you can understand it yourself?

SEAY: Partly that. . . .

GRAHAM: Is it a kind of exorcism, almost, do you think?

SEAY: Certainly that. To say that it "haunts" you is to say also that you're trying to get it down, and in doing this, perhaps to understand it better, and also to get it out of you. It's a coming to terms with experience, trying to fit it together, in some meaningful pattern.

GRAHAM: We're going to memory, at least in some of your poems here, and yet, I do think one of the virtues of your poetry is your capacity not to make memory immediate, but the experience remembered immediate. I think of the poem—one of the poems I like very much in *Let Not Your Hart*—as I mentioned to you at supper—is "The Dove." I get a sense of immediacy there, and you yourself indicated that this was your aim. And then you immediately fed me another example which I am looking at right now. Would you mind reading "Grabbling in Yokna Bottom"?

SEAY: Yokna is actually a river in Mississippi, and this is something that is an image more than anything, from the past. I just retained it and one day it came to me, this image of rural Mississippians engaging in what a spectator might call "sport." I'm sure the participants didn't look on it as a "sport" because most of them were down there trying to get food, you know. It's called "grabbling"—the poem explains it. It's simply that in a drought season when the water's down and on a river or creek or even a lake you can muddy the water and some of the fish will come to the top and can be taken off very easily, but others will go back into the stumps and roots and you have to "grabble" for them with bare hands. And the water's muddy and you're going down . . .

GRAHAM: Into the darkness. . . .

SEAY: And thrusting into crevices. So I'll read that if you like.

GRAHAM: I've found, by listening to the poet's voice, I can spot certain manipulations of vowels that were much more pleasurable hearing than seeing.

SEAY:
The hungry come in a dry time
To muddy the water of this swamp river
And take in nets that fish or eel
Break surface to suck at this world's air.

But colder blood backs into the water's wood—
Gills the silt rather than rise to light—

And who would eat a cleaner meat
Must grabble in the hollows of underwater stumps and roots,
Must cram his arm and hand beneath the scum
And go by touch where eye cannot reach,
Must seize and bring to light
What scale or slime is touched—

Must in that instant—on touch—
Without question or reckoning
Grab up what wraps itself cold-blooded
Around flesh or flails the water to froth,

Or else feel the fish slip by,
Or learn that the loggerhead's jaw is thunder-deaf,
Or that the cottonmouth's fangs burn like heated needles
Even under water.

The well-fed do not wade this low river.

GRAHAM: You know one curious thing that happened to me, and it was through the reading, and totally unexpected: I didn't realize where the turn of the poem came. And I'm going to tell you—you wrote it, but I'm going to tell you—it came with "cram." That's the word that scares by its sound and the precipitous action.

SEAY: It has a kind of desperation.

GRAHAM: "Underwater stumps and roots" is a little spooky, but then this rough action of "cram" sets up for things like "scale and slime" and, then, "cold-blooded"—which we know fish are —but suddenly "cold-blooded" is a scary word in the context. And then that builds to that snakebite "like heated needles," which makes me hop a little bit. That's what I want to say about your poetry. This is a very strong example of the tactile, obviously, since the eye cannot go there, but this is where I think your stuff will hop off the page, Jim, and one of the things I enjoy.

SEAY: Some listeners may not understand about that, and I had it called to my attention today. I make reference there—"learn that the loggerhead's jaw is thunder-deaf." A "loggerhead" is a snapping turtle, and when the turtle—you're told as a child if a turtle bites you, it won't let go 'til it thunders. Did you know that? Had you ever heard that?

GRAHAM: Like the snake won't die until sundown, if you break its back, kind of thing?

SEAY: All of those bits of lore, folklore. How true that is I don't know. I don't want to have empirical knowledge of that. But in this case, of course, the loggerhead is deaf to any thunder, meaning he's going to hold on, if he bites.

GRAHAM: With your poetry, now—this is a memory. You haven't lived in Mississippi for a good while. Do you find your poetry shifting? You're older and you change. Do you find your poetry shifting to present observation, or are you still exploring your memory a lot? Has this volume, *Let Not Your Hart,* exhausted your pursuit of memory?

SEAY: No, there're still things that I know will work into poems, whether they are simply a remembered image that you want to work around, or a personal experience, in which there's some narrative thread, or a mood associated with place, where you have a strong sense of place. Still, those are there. But like any act of writing, it can come from anywhere. There's a poem in here that takes rise from a personal experience at the Waldorf in New York, and here's a Mississippi plowboy writing about Orientals at the Waldorf. Or there's a poem where the speaker's on a jet airliner, caught up in a crisis, an interior crisis. Just from all over. But, still, I have things that go back to Mississippi, the South, Alabama. There's some poems in here that take their images from experiences in Alabama.

GRAHAM: You have what I feel with the "Grabbling in Yokna

Bottom," the brief action. It's generalized in the sense that it's a repeated thing. Do you find the sense of narrative really a useful way to keep a poem alive, or do you ever work with landscape, the static image?

SEAY: Kind of impressionistic? Visual? That too, yes, but in this first book you'll find a number of narrative poems. I was interested, during the five or ten years in which these were being collected, interested in seeing what I could do with the narrative in poetry.

III. *I want pleasure from my poetry. I want to sit down and have a sense of felicity in the poet's mind.*

GRAHAM: Jim, one thing that has always tempted me when I get around a writer is that I like, first of all, for him to talk with me about his work, his intentions, and what-have-you. But I find it extraordinarily valuable to pick your brains about your own reading. What writing means something to you as a man, but maybe also, particularly, as a poet? Have you got any people you're reading now that you're excited about and feel I'd enjoy reading and maybe don't know? Or if I do happen to know them, we'll just talk about them anyway.

SEAY: A poet is often reluctant to talk publicly about this, or on record, because he's afraid that the order in which he names these people will be some indication of his estimation of their writing ability. But just off the top of my head, I think of James Wright, a relatively young poet, with a book of collected poems coming from Wesleyan University Press. Wright has published his last three books with them.

JAMES SEAY | 179

GRAHAM: He's got a lot of material out then.

SEAY: Yes, and he's much respected, especially among a lot of younger poets that I talk with.

GRAHAM: Is he experimental? Is he doing anything really strange?

SEAY: No, you wouldn't place him out in the *avant-garde*. What he has is tritely known as "a distinctive voice." And I think probably what wins some of the readers to his poetry is a certain simplicity of statement, simplicity of image. But also there is in this a profundity. You sense a depth of experience in this man, and you sense an honesty, and a genuineness about his poetry that engages me and gives me pleasure.

GRAHAM: In a way, you've already defined almost by indirection one of the problems I know that a great many people that I have talked with informally have. For a while poetry was, in fact, so obscure that unless you were prepared to *study* a poem, you might as well not start it. And I think in reading the poetry of a man under, say, thirty, now, I think I'm finding things that, shall we say, offer no real resistance at all. I think poetry is getting simpler and clearer, at least the material I've been seeing.

SEAY: Most of what you read by younger American poets today has a surface simplicity. And there is a strong evidence now of a strong influence from the surrealists, of random images thrown at you, in a seemingly unrelated manner.

GRAHAM: I think if the images are extended enough, one can do something with them. You can, in effect, take on your job as reader and operate with the poet, permit yourself to be caught up in a multiplicity of images and sort of combine them. As rich as allusive poetry can be—all the world's literature may be referred to in ten lines—as rich as that may be, it's got to have a limited audience. I don't think your surrealistic poet, mixing up time and sequence, I don't think he blocks the way the "need to be learned" blocked.

SEAY: The first poet that comes to mind is Eliot, with his copious footnotes to, say, *The Waste Land.*

GRAHAM: And the second poet who comes to mind is Ezra Pound. And I still have so much trouble with Pound, it's not much of a pleasure.

SEAY: You know, I can't read Pound with a great deal of understanding and finally a sense of pleasure. I want pleasure from my poetry. I want to sit down and have a sense of felicity in the poet's mind.

GRAHAM: Now, this young man, James Wright, we can get at rather directly, you tell me.

SEAY: Yes, in my estimation, and it's in contrast to Eliot's poetry, or, more recently, say, Lowell's early poetry.

GRAHAM: *Lord Weary's Castle* still remains a difficulty for me, and I'm a great admirer of Lowell. I've read a lot of him.

SEAY: Same here. I mention that because he's a poet that I respect, and yet I have trouble with some of that earlier poetry. I think it has a surface density that's often almost impenetrable.

GRAHAM: Have you ever read his—I can't remember the name of it, it's a little autobiography, the prose work?

SEAY: That's in *Life Studies.*

GRAHAM: The purity of that man's prose proves once again that poets are often our best prose writers, as Sir Philip Sydney and Shelley showed us.

SEAY: Quite. Quite. That, in my estimate, is where Lowell won me, with that collection, *Life Studies.* That was where he came through and took me.

GRAHAM: And now I am willing to go back and work on something like *Lord Weary's Castle*, which was so highly praised when it came out, but I just couldn't handle it.

SEAY: Something like "The Quaker Graveyard in Nantucket" has that surface density that gives a lot—and complexity, and shifts—that gives a lot of readers trouble.

GRAHAM: Who else are you reading? We've got James Wright. . . .

SEAY: Certainly anything of Wright's will have me as a reader. Richard Wilbur, certainly. You have to mention him in any discussion. I'm talking now about contemporary poets. And as a young poet I watch this, I want to know what's being written in my own time. It is taken as a given, that you know Yeats and Eliot and all of these, and have some sense of the traditions of English poetry. But I'm talking now about contemporary American poets. Or we might talk about some of the foreign poets that are being translated. But, back to the American poets, certainly Richard Wilbur is one of the finest poets that we have writing in America today.

GRAHAM: I just finished reading his *Walking to Sleep*, and there was one pleasure after another there. And one rather good joke after another. The man is, I'm not going to say obsessed with wit, but he has it. I see your poems and his having at least some distant kinship in the sense of a willingness to have some fun, a little wit, a little self-mockery.

SEAY: Yes . . . And again this term, I mean "felicity," you know, a little joy. Certainly that's readily observable in Wilbur's, and especially in the latest one, *Walking to Sleep*. You'll notice in there, still, Wilbur's commitment to form—he's very formal—but there are some shifts of direction in that book. Wilbur moves away from the formal attentions in some of those poems.

GRAHAM: One thing that I think Wilbur's done for us—in terms of your point about foreign poets that you liked. Wilbur's work on translations has got me excited. His work on Molière, of course, is well known, but he's got three or four things in there that he's translated from the Russian, that I'm going to read and reread for the rest of my life.

SEAY: He's doing some good work also in translations from the Spanish. He is very fond of, and respects very highly, Borges. And certainly I have a great admiration for and will read any translation I find of Borges.

GRAHAM: I've been now at this writers' conference for—it seems to me years! I guess ten days. But I guess I've heard Borges' name from more people than any living writer. He is a man who has all types of people from, oh, very analytic writers to what you might almost call very emotional writers, absolutely excited with the brevity of his works and the apparently highly imaginative aspects. I simply have not read him, and he's clearly one I have to get to. Do you read much prose?

SEAY: I don't read as many first novels as I did when I was on that Faulkner Committee to choose a first novel for the 1967 William Faulkner Foundation Award. I was reading a lot of first novels, and a lot of young writers. Since that time I've gotten away from it and I'm ashamed to say it. But I do try to keep up on the prose right along with poetry.

GRAHAM: Is there any novelist that you've run on lately, or is that nearly a pause in your life now?

SEAY: There's a lot of enthusiasm now for Kurt Vonnegut, and I've been reading him.

GRAHAM: He seems to have caught the undergraduates a great deal, especially with *Cat's Cradle*.

SEAY: That, and most recently *Slaughterhouse-Five, or The Children's Crusade*. It's about the Dresden fire-bombings.

GRAHAM: That bombing has become more and more our image of horror.

James Whitehead

BIOGRAPHICAL

Born: 15 March 1936 in St. Louis, Missouri.
Education: B.A. Vanderbilt 1959, M.A. Vanderbilt 1960.
Occupational: Has taught at Iowa, Millsaps, and is presently Associate Professor at the University of Arkansas.
Books: Poetry—*Domains* (1966); novel—*Joiner* (1971).
He has received a Guggenheim Fellowship and is a member of the National Council on the Arts.

SNAPSHOT

Though you should never (and Jim warns you about this in his interview) *confuse* Jim Whitehead with Sonny Joiner, you could do worse than to read *Joiner* for—quite aside from the overwhelming energy and pleasures of it as fiction—a sense of some of Jim's range of passionate interests, physical, intellectual, and spiritual. Jim Whitehead is big enough, strong enough, and quick enough to play professional football. And indeed he would have, was supposed and set to do so until, during his college ball playing career, he received a savage, almost crippling injury. Like Sonny Joiner he knows a lot of history and loves it. Like Sonny he's fascinated by the pomp and circumstance (and the naked, forked truth) of politics. But the one thing never to forget is that Jim's a poet and loves passionately everything about poetry, from its history and traditions and grand designs to the glorious mechanics and the working tools of it.

For which reason (among others) he is an extraordinarily successful teacher of the art and craft of writing poetry.

Turn to the poetry and you'll see more and deeper. A range, from strong aggressive rhythm to the most subtle and delicate of moves.

As a big man, Jim is shy of seeming silly in his natural gracefulness. But at times in his poems he moves and floats like a ballet dancer.

I. *I work in whatever mode happens to give me a poem.*
I'll start writing symbolist poems if I like them.

GRAHAM: James Whitehead's first book of poetry, *Domains,* issued by the Louisiana State University Press, is very exciting, a very powerful book, Jim. The *Domains* are, I guess, the land of your life in both a physical and a mental sense?

WHITEHEAD: As I tried to lay the book out and tried to state in the title poem at the end—to put it bluntly—it's sex and politics, and trying to live in those two worlds.

GRAHAM: The one thing about your *Domains,* relative to sex and politics, is this very particular voice, the modern vocabulary, a kind of rough handling. You mentioned that a friend or translator has been trying to work this into German. It would seem to me that problems of translating slang, localisms which are a part of your voice, and the voices of the people in *Domains,* it would seem to me this would be, practically speaking, impossible.

WHITEHEAD: It *is* difficult. The original translator had a great deal of trouble because he is a rather genteel person and because apparently—I'm not skilled in German—the German poetry has somewhat more difficulty than English poetry in appropriating the vernacular into poetry. But I have another friend who knew several other dialects of German and was able to come up with some figures that approximated.

GRAHAM: I'm trying to think, with my experience in German, what I'd do with "tonk," for instance, and I can't ever remember seeing the equivalent.

WHITEHEAD: *"Gast Haus"* doesn't make it.

GRAHAM: It doesn't touch it, and so, I don't know where you'd go. One of the things in the book that I enjoy is the sense of voices. We have all read Robert Browning, just to grab the most obvious figure, with his dramatic monologues. And we know a lot about voice in poetry. It does seem to me, with younger poets I've read over the last few years, that they are maybe hyperconscious of their particular voices, when they try to step inside a character, see the world through his eyes, and then speak to the world with his particular tongue. I see all through your book many different people talking to me. Is this a way of charging the imagination or a way of commenting on life simply from more perspective than Jim Whitehead has?

WHITEHEAD: That's a very difficult question. To give it the simplest answer, possibly it was a way of working that gave me what I considered to be relatively finished poems. The more traditional or standard lyric voice was not particularly working for me. It wasn't working well at all. And I do like to imitate, and I do like the idea of trying to see if I can get inside of someone else. And so I began to attempt these poems. Now, you mention Browning. I'll admit to influence by Browning. I think that Browning has been a great influence on me and on a great many other contemporary poets. One thing I did want to do, I have an instinct to be a little more economical in my next book. I think

I will. But I am writing longer poems and, if they're good long poems, I'll be delighted. But I work in whatever mode happens to give me a poem. I'll start writing symbolist poems if I like them.

GRAHAM: I've broken the volume of poems, *Domain,* open here and we have this old friend who sometimes comes to talk, and there, this is your voice commenting on this sentimental . . . maybe a loser. But then, on the other page, we've got "The Politician's Pledge." Would you mind reading that, because that's another man's voice that you may approve of or agree with. But that's a big shift.

WHITEHEAD: The background on this character is essentially that I knew some politicians in the South and in Mississippi who had gone through somewhat of a transformation in their lives. They were sick and tired of the violence that was being caused by the social problems around them. And they realized that they were causing these problems themselves by race baiting, or, as it is called in that part of the country, "nigger riding." That's what a politician does when he baits a white crowd. So he decides that he will reject that, he won't do it again, he has seen the light—and some of them have—and he decides rather ironically or comically, I hope, that he will run on a platform that will offer air-conditioning to all of his folk. He says, "if that doesn't work, well, you know, let it happen to them." So, here's your poem. And he's talking about his constituency and how he feels about them. This poem is written in couplets. It rhymes every way I could imagine—full, slant, half, repetition of words, that sort of thing.

THE POLITICIAN'S PLEDGE

You'd think there was heat enough all day,
With the sun the whole white sky—
But in my counties they burn things down
At night. No cool Christ in the tomb
Will do for them. They thrive on fire,
And I'll be damned if I'll feed fire.

Preachers! It's preachers I always blame.
They whine in the dusk for Zion's flames.

Make me an out-of-work mechanic
And bring my whole family down sick
If I ride one nigger again.
When it comes time for me to run
My tongue is ice—
Conditioned air in every house—
And if for that I'm not sent back,
I hope they're resurrected black.

GRAHAM: That's fine, Jim. The thing that interests me about
the poem is the big mixture here of anger, bitterness and much
more, but, also, almost a mockery. We open with the line,
"You'd think there was heat enough all day." And then that sets
us up, for his major campaign pledge of conditioned air in every
house as if he's prepared to pull a colossal joke. So, his air-
conditioning is his first colossal joke. But then, if that doesn't
bring the vote, the joke becomes a very grim joke, but nevertheless, a joke. "I hope they're resurrected black." Which flashes
back through the poem with the preacher.

WHITEHEAD: And the fire.

GRAHAM: My sense of discovery about the poem is that when
I first read it, it seemed of one tone. And yet, I'm learning a
mixture of tones, all of which don't simply survive together, but
live and work very actively together, giving us a fully rounded
character rather than giving us just a relevant manifesto.

WHITEHEAD: I'm not interested at all in mere relevant mani-
festos. I want to create out of a particular situation, in language
I know, a character, a voice, and I think if that voice is rich
enough and if the rhetoric is as complex or suggestive of complexity as I hope it will be, then I think the poem will get
beyond whatever regional habits it has. For example, one of
the things I liked in this poem was rhyming in the sounds of it.
And I almost got into the situation of enjoying playing with

lines like "with the sun the whole white sky," rolling those sounds; and something like "no cool Christ in the tomb will do for them." All that is part of the pleasure of the execution, and you hope that that will surface and, in fact, dominate whatever parsing or thematic dimension the poem has. Which is to say, you hope you write a fairly good poem—no more, no less.

GRAHAM: You used the words "play" and "fiddle with," and it seemed very clear to me that one of your toughest decisions as a poet—I would think this would be general—is knowing when the poem is finished. In getting sounds such as "no cool Christ" you must fret as to whether those alliterations of those explosives of "cool" and "Christ" (with the harsh stop of the "t" there), it must be a major decision to decide whether that's too much.

WHITEHEAD: What you do is, you write it, and then you recite it to yourself, again and again, and you walk around the house saying the poem. You decide whether it is that character's voice. That line came quickly. I listened to it again and again as I read and recited the poem to myself. It wasn't a particular problem with me.

GRAHAM: Do you ever have a friend, for instance, read something you've written? For you to see if your writing dictates a tone of voice?

WHITEHEAD: Absolutely, absolutely, because I want the rhythm in the reading. The way to read the poem must be built into the poem if at all possible.

II. But I decided where I wanted to go. I wanted to work with something both economical and dramatic.

GRAHAM: Jim, one thing I guess I've always been fascinated by is the appearance of a book, as well as the content. And they certainly did you proud, I think, with this particular jacket for *Domains.*

WHITEHEAD: You really like it? There's a tree on the cover. I like the script title, *Domains.* It is written out in script, but I'm not terribly fond of that tree. I like the white jacket and the green script, but it looks like a Walt Disney tree. I had a fearful fight with my editor and I swore if and when we did the next one, I was going to have complete control over it. I'm pleased that you like it, though.

GRAHAM: I think the tree is the tree in the book of poetry, that very grim poem about a fall from a tree.

WHITEHEAD: I'm sure that was the idea.

GRAHAM: I see that this is more of a forbidding tree than one that Ferdinand the Bull sat under, frankly.

WHITEHEAD: Yes, it is.

GRAHAM: How do you feel about *Domains* at this point? You've got some time between you and its publication.

WHITEHEAD: I can live with it, rather comfortably.

GRAHAM: Were they written over a long range of time?

WHITEHEAD: Three or four of those poems, I suppose, I wrote drafts of in college, and then played with them somewhere in between '60 and '63. Most of that poetry was written between '62 and '66, and most of it in the year 1964, actually. I had written a great deal of poetry and published some. And I had been writing essentially lyric poetry. I didn't like it, because it didn't seem to be saying anything that I wanted to come back to and think about later. It didn't seem to be anything I could build on. Some people like to read it. But I decided where I wanted to go. I wanted to work within something both economical and dramatic. And I played with the idea of little stories, sometimes anecdotal material in some fairly traditional forms, to see if I could sort of tell a story in a sonnet, for example.

GRAHAM: One characteristic of the volume seems to me to be a kind of aggressiveness in the poetry. It comes at you, not as reminiscence or lazy memory or comfortable memory.

WHITEHEAD: I found a greater sense of present action, or at least a memory that, when recollected, has the force of an immediate event.

GRAHAM: Well, now, your word "recollected" switches me over to Wordsworth's thing. I don't see these as recollected in tranquillity. These are rather heated poems.

WHITEHEAD: Well, I'm a rather aggressive talker at times. And I like the idea of good talk, and recounting stories to tell your friends. Poems are rather that way. You sit down and you read a book of poems, and you've met a new person and you're going to hear what they have to say about themselves. I guess they are, in a sense . . . well, clearly they are something of a projection of me, although many of them create characters who are not in any way, shape, or form necessarily me. I like the idea of creating character in poems.

GRAHAM: This leads me to one poem which I enjoyed in particular, "Two Voices." Because the voices are there, the characters are very much there, and in a way I think a testing of this particular poem lies in the fact that I'm curious as to what other characters are there. We have Taggart, who speaks first, and Thompson, who speaks second. And these two men are real enough to me, in their reactions to knifings. They're real enough to me to make me know that there are still other people who are reacting to these things. Would you mind reading this, Jim?

WHITEHEAD:

TWO VOICES

Taggart says he gives them what they want—
They come to him in the night blind drunk and broke,
And he sews them up free, without a shot.
With his coarse thread he has the art to raise
Great scars from ear to ear, and he does just that—
It's part of a ritual they've done for years.
"I send them proud to the fields and gins," he says.
"With their heads pulled back that way, those bucks are grand,"
He says. "They brag after all we did it raw."

Thompson says you can hear their cries to the creek,
And he nearly objects, believing the fish in their way
Are offended—or at least that so much yelling
Can make a cat hook-shy, and anyhow
It's always Saturday night and Sunday morning
After the tonk fights and when he fishes.
"And not only that," Thompson says, "it's giving
Sorry dreams to my children." And almost angry:
"You'd think a doctor and all, he'd think of his neighbors."

GRAHAM: I don't like to pick too closely, but in a funny way when Taggart—the use of names here, I think, starts those voices very quickly, the harshness of "Taggart" over "Thompson"—but the thing that turned the poem, the voice of Taggart for me, was the line, "with his coarse thread," as he's sewing up these slashed men. I think the word "coarse" came through and triggered more sharply—well, it's the *tactility* of it. Even more, then he sews them up free without a shot, with "coarse thread." We've got this "without a shot," which should have hit me harder. It didn't happen until the "coarse" came in.

WHITEHEAD: It's also a rhythmically overstressed passage in the line, which is intentional, if I can confess that chicanery.

GRAHAM: No, this is fine. Of course, we've got the accent on "coarse" and on "thread." Then the word "ritual," giving some kind of a distance to this murder.

WHITEHEAD: Oh, of course, this is a small-town doctor who is sewing up the blacks in his town who come to him after they've been working each other over. And, on one level, he's doing the work free, and they do take pride in it—some of them. Just as white, honky-tonk men take pride in some of their wounds, some of the blacks take pride in some of those great scars they receive. Which I guess is analogous to some of those Prussian dueling scars.

GRAHAM: The initiation rite kind of thing. Thompson, though, in a way, upsets me even more than this ritualistic . . . this distance that the doctor has, because he doesn't understand the doctor or the wounded man, really.

WHITEHEAD: Well, I think the point is not that he doesn't understand him. And the point is not that he does understand him. The point of his voice is that he is making a move in the direction of understanding that the doctor, Taggart, has not made. He is aware that he is bothered by the cries of the men and they do yell occasionally when they are being sewed up. He's bothered by that, but he's not sure why he's bothered. He's not sure whether he's bothered because they may scare the

fish away so he can't catch them on his hook and there's . . .
you know . . . a little connection with that . . . goes back to
the sewing there. And he's not sure whether he's bothered because he knows in his guts that this is a bad scene he's hearing.
And then he knows that his children are going to live with the
effects of these rituals. And, they are giving bad dreams to his
children, either really or figuratively. I don't put Taggart down
in any absolute way because . . . so he's a racist, so he's a
little sadistic. But Thompson is the hopeful character. He's the
one, he's, let's say, an intelligent man. Call him an okie farmer,
a redneck, or a glasscat. But he's likely to make it. I trust him.
I think the irony at the end of the poem is . . . you think a
doctor and all, you think he'd think of his neighbors . . . well
who are his neighbors? What does Thompson mean by neighbors? At first level, it would refer to him, the other white man.

GRAHAM: We've got a good samaritan thing going right in here.

WHITEHEAD: Well, the first thing is that he is. I think there's
a suggestion in that line that many people have caught that
he also realizes that the relationship of neighbors, between the
blacks and the doctor, is not going very well.

GRAHAM: To make a circle on this, I can hear a whole lot of
other voices coming up because of the strength.

WHITEHEAD: What do you mean by that?

GRAHAM: Well, there's at least a third voice. There's a woman's
voice. What I think I'm saying is I want more. More poems on
the subject? I want some more points of view. Perhaps a black
voice in there, perhaps a woman's voice, perhaps a child's voice
even. Because I think, in this little exchange between the two
men, there's a kind of radiation out so we've got a play. It is
a drama.

WHITEHEAD: Well, it is a suggestion of a drama, as many of the
modern, the contemporary poems are. The book itself, of course,

doesn't deal with that specific problem, but the general problem of violence, the general problem of the community, in the region I write about is there.

III. *All right, we do fall apart and then we feel terrible guilt because we fall apart, from time to time. Our bodies and our souls are broken. But we mend, we mend.*

GRAHAM: I understand from your talk at the lunch table that we have a novel in press with Knopf. Why do I need to read this novel, *Joiner?*

WHITEHEAD: Well, you really do need to read this novel, John. As a matter of fact, I have been obsessed with a group of characters for years. I did happen to publish a book of poems first, but that's just because I happened to get a book of poems done first.

GRAHAM: In many ways your book of poetry is a book of characters. There are many, many people in dramatic actions there and a great variety of voices; so in a sense, the fact that you are now working on fiction as well as poetry is not a surprise.

WHITEHEAD: I've always tried to write both. I have a novel in my drawer, of course, that I wrote in college and a long one at that. What I set out to do several years ago was to write several short novels with interrelated characters. I thought there would be four, and I've discovered with *Joiner* that I really put two of them together. So I guess what I'm actually doing is writing a trilogy. *Joiner* is the first of them, but it's an autonomous novel, it's a total thing. *Joiner* is essentially about an ex-professional football player. He only plays five games, but much of the action takes place in a time after he's left the NFL and goes home and has too much time off to think about what has happened to him the last few years. And he gets involved in the social problems of the community and, in a sense, starts a minor league revolution in his own town. The book was, at one point, called *Joiner's Revolution*. I didn't like that title because the word "revolution" has gotten to be quite popular these days, and I didn't mean it to be something about the New Left or the Old Left or any of that; but, mainly, about what happens to this man. I know him very, very well, and I have followed through and made discoveries about him, and how a culminating action finally helps him discover himself. Sonny is a very bright lad. He majored in history at a middlin' good school or college in south Mississippi. And he's fascinated by history, especially by things like the Bohemian Revolution. He's interested in their tactics and all of that. And then he gets involved in Leveler tracts, the English Revolution and all those people that helped Cromwell, and then Cromwell knifed them in the back, as so often happens. He's got a little belt of Southern Populism in there, and he's also lived a rather interesting life in trying to adjust to this strange place he's in. People ask me if it's a football novel. Why yes, there are chapters about football games and the sensual response to the game that I don't think has been handled well in fiction before this book. It's there, and I'm pleased with it. But it's the totality of the nature of a man who is both an athlete and something of an intellectual. He's not "degreed"—only has a B.A.—but he's in conflict between himself because he's lived an aggressive, in fact, violent life. And he is, in a sense, looking for a mythology, I guess, one way or another, to account for this violence and reconcile himself to it.

GRAHAM: In effect, his whole college experience, in terms of both football and history major. When he *does* leave the professional game, the seeds start to grow.

WHITEHEAD: He loses his wife in the first place. He's going to tell you why his wife left him, and, in fact, married his best friend; and why he started this little war in his own hometown. But along the way is the life. That's okay, it worked out after three years of, I hope, tender loving care. And it's plotted, and I think has a certain "fearful symmetry." But, on the other hand, I enjoy the details of the book. It's a long novel, I guess, probably about four hundred pages, but I enjoy the sensuality of moving from page to page, of getting to know the people he knew, discovering the way he perceives the world and mainly discovering his language, the way he articulated both his body and his language. "Articulate" is a very funny word to Sonny Joiner, because the word articulation applies to the body and the voice. And he's trying to get these two things together.

GRAHAM: Not to slap labels now, but is this a *Bildungsroman,* but maybe starting later?

WHITEHEAD: Somebody has hit me with that word a couple of times, and I got very angry about it.

GRAHAM: Okay, go ahead.

WHITEHEAD: At first, and I was even joking with my editor, I said, "All right, dammit, if I'm going to be stamped, put *Joiner: A Bildungsroman* on the dust jacket and let 'em have it." I don't think it's a *Bildungsroman* in the sense of the pains and tribulations of growing up. It's not Salingerian at all, and it is, I think, an absolutely unsentimental book. I detest that kind of whining. Sonny, to me, is not a whiner at all, and I think that we can have confused men without being deeply neurotic men.

GRAHAM: They don't all have to be young Goethes leaning against the doorposts with the hand at the forehead.

WHITEHEAD: Absolutely not. Sonny's a successful man, really.

He can do anything he wants to with his life, finally. He has all the options available. He can go to graduate school. He can try to get his wife back, if he wants to. He can go back and play pro ball, but he gets hurt and has to lay out awhile. Starts a little trouble, that's all. He ends up being a policeman for a while, at the end of the book, which he finds very satisfactory. He feels like that is something he can do well. So, it's not a novel about a failure. I think the anti-hero is what everybody has expectations for when they move into this kind of literature. But I don't feel that Sonny Joiner is an anti-hero at all.

GRAHAM: I'm interested in your word "discovery," because discovery, when connected with a man who has all the options, is going to produce a hero unless he can't choose any of the options.

WHITEHEAD: I don't mean in the old-fashioned sense of hero, but a man who's got his head together and has got his mind and body functioning in some basic harmony or another. Who will fall apart from time to time. I think this is one of the shocks that people have when they are growing up. All right, we do fall apart and then we feel terrible guilt because we fall apart, from time to time. Our bodies and our souls are broken. But we mend, we mend. And I think one of the terrible things about so much contemporary literature is that it's in this wretched, Freudian bag, with its negative view. It has no place for grace—this is not religious grace in any sense of traditional metaphysics or Christianity, but there is grace in the world. We all know there is grace. And yet, people have tried to convince us that there isn't.

GRAHAM: The word "a box" or "a bind" or "a trap" or "in a bag" and so forth—these are standard ways of describing many protagonists in modern novels. But they are caged.

WHITEHEAD: That's all right. This is a real problem with us.

Alienation is a big thing. But not everybody is alienated. Sonny's not alienated, he's got too many options. He's got too many roles that he can play fairly well.

GRAHAM: I'm interested in what ultimately happens with *Joiner*. You thought you had three or four short novels?

WHITEHEAD: The next novel is called *Boykin Flying*, which is about the fellow who gets Sonny's wife. It takes place several years later, and Sonny wanders through it here and there. I've got a draft of it written, but it's really about the other guy. Royal Carle Boykin is in *Joiner*, and he's an important figure, of course. But he deserves a book, so I'm going to give him one.

GRAHAM: In the process of writing one book, you get, I'm sure, this enormous sense of creating a world that is very populated. And then you've got to do something with these people, don't you? And then you're thrust into your next novel?

WHITEHEAD: One of the problems that I know people have is that they get upset. It's quite possible that I could get halfway through the next book and say, "Aahhh, I really don't want to write that book." I might not write into the third one. But I think that I will at this point, and I think I will because I may have to think I will. It gets me up in the morning and takes me to my desk. It's as simple as that. But with *Joiner*, somebody's going to say it's "Gothic." I don't believe there is such a thing as Southern Gothicism, really. I think there are situations which people from other parts of the country *think* are bizarre. I think Pennsylvania is the most Gothic place in the world. I don't know why they have to stick literary names on the curious antics that we do in our particular region.

GRAHAM: You talked about what "gets you up in the morning" to live in this world you both have created and are creating. With a long haul like this—I can imagine myself, let's say, writing poems—is writing a novel, especially a novel where you can already anticipate a sequel and more, dependent on habit, Jim? Is some of this just guts and habit?

WHITEHEAD: Writers have to know their craft and they have to be fairly intelligent human beings. But, the main thing they have to have is energy.

Sylvia Wilkinson

BIOGRAPHICAL

Born: 5 April 1940 in Durham, North Carolina.
Education: B.A. University of North Carolina at Greensboro 1962, M.A. Hollins College 1963, Stanford University 1964–1966.
Occupational: Has taught at Asheville-Biltmore College and William and Mary. Presently serves on the writing staff (part-time) under Max Steele at Chapel Hill.
   An accomplished racing car driver, she has driven and worked for Porsche and Ferrari. And she does public relations for the booming North Carolina stock car racing circuits. She is active in statewide educational work.
Books: Novels—*Moss on the North Side* (1966), *A Killing Frost* (1967), *Cale* (1970).
   Her short stories have been anthologized. Among her awards are a Eugene Saxton Memorial Award (1964) and a Wallace Stegner Creative Writing Fellowship (1965). In 1965 she was also chosen, by *Mademoiselle,* as one of a select group of Outstanding Young Women in America.

SNAPSHOT

   Ah, Sylvia! "Li'l Sylvie. . . ."
   She is so pretty. Small, delicately trim, with fine features, large dark eyes and long shining dark hair, she's something to

behold whether she's wearing her blue jeans and sweatshirt, her mechanic's coveralls, or (more rarely, but for the folks) one of her bright, mod, respectably fashionable "creations." You could (I will) even say she's sexy. Which she is.

But all that is the instant star-struck blindness of the typical American male chauvinist pig. There is so much more than the glitter. She has never lost her downhome accent. It surprises, but is right and you listen when she talks. She has, somehow, forgotten nothing she has ever seen or felt. Not burdened with the freight of her past, she writes of it, re-creates it and makes it new again, all the while living brightly here and now, at the *center* of it on the track at Sebring. And, in her steady work for and with public school children and teachers, she's involved in the future. As writer she is a *worker*, rain or shine, in success and disappointment. She has studied from some of the very best, without harm to her own voice and subject. And right now, besides writing better than ever, she is, herself, one of the best teachers of writing in the country.

I. *Now, with "Cale," I have a brother, and I've asked my brother a lot of questions. I've told several people that if my brother is lying to me, I'm in real trouble.*

GRAHAM: Sylvia, I read only one of your novels, *A Killing Frost*, and I enjoyed it very much. I found it a deceptive novel. I thought for a little while I was reading a very low-keyed, lyrical novel, a kind of idyll told by an adolescent girl. But then I kind of grew up in the process of the novel, and saw that it was much more complicated. Now you've also written *Moss on the North Side* . . .

WILKINSON: That was my first novel.

GRAHAM: And anything else, then?

WILKINSON: My current novel, *Cale.*

GRAHAM: Would you want to talk about either one of them?

WILKINSON: I'd like to talk about *Cale,* because in *Cale* I do what I frequently talk about in teaching. It's creative rewriting instead of creative writing. *Cale* was an educational experience for me because in it, I switched points of view. This is something I tell my students they shouldn't do in the early stages, and, in many ways, it may be a transitional book.

GRAHAM: In effect, you're taking chances?

WILKINSON: Right. Big ones, I'm sure. And a lot of people wonder, I suppose, what are all these stupid country people doing in this book? But in *Cale* I took my own lifespan—I was born in 1940—and I gave my character the same birthday, so I would be sure to be able to follow the Nazis and the wars.

GRAHAM: You wouldn't have to have a big chart up on the wall to find out what happened when.

WILKINSON: The almanac would be nicer. In *Cale* I wanted to start out with a boy at eighteen. Then suddenly, I found myself flashbacking through his earlier life and, eventually, I ended up with the first chapter, with Cale being born. His mother was having him. So this has just been a real experience, it's been a writer's education for me.

GRAHAM: Well, all writers want to find out where things come from, don't they?

WILKINSON: Yes, you rarely start a novel with the first chapter. You write a chapter and then you go back, and you write a chapter in front of it and one in front of it. It's funny. You never know where a novel takes off.

GRAHAM: You mean, in a sense, the classical business of the epic, where it begins in the middle? Maybe every novel, in the making of it, begins in the middle.

WILKINSON: That's the way it's worked for me. In the last one, it started with the end, but the others started in the middle. You do all these things that people do. For instance, you are impatient. When you don't have an outline or plan, you don't know how it's all going to end up. Frequently, you leave a lot out of the middle, just trying to get to the end too quickly.

GRAHAM: I should imagine, impatient and just a little anxious?

WILKINSON: Oh yes. Your curiosity just overwhelms you.

GRAHAM: Wait a minute. My curiosity as reader should be there, but *you're* saying—

WILKINSON: That as a writer it's the same thing. It's readers, writers, and people. When you get to know a character in a novel, when a writer gets to know a character, when a reader gets to know a character, or when a person gets to know a character, it's just, bit by bit, what they do every day. You may like them for a while and then dislike them.

GRAHAM: You kind of piece things together and part of them.

WILKINSON: Yes, exactly. Then, when you rewrite a novel, you go back and you eliminate the kind of blind trails and the useless information you went through to get there. You just have to allow yourself this kind of looseness, because I think the best things I write are the things I didn't know I was going to write until I sat down at the typewriter and just let it happen.

GRAHAM: This basically is through the exercise of your memory and imagination, then a cutting. This is a short novel that I just read, of two hundred and a very few pages, *A Killing Frost*. Is this the result of a lot of pruning back, then, writing of lots of false leads perhaps, and then lopping them off so that you will wind up with a formed totality?

WILKINSON: More so my first novel. My first novel took me thirteen years to write. I had, from the age of twelve to the age of twenty-five, a great deal of growing up to do and I unfortunately did a lot of it on the printed page. I ended up with about eight hundred pages which I trimmed down to two hundred and fifty. So the other one is more of an example than the second novel. Now, my new novel was also an extremely long book, probably eight hundred pages. I think I'm down to about six hundred and fifty that are in the final printing.

GRAHAM: You talked a little of the multiple point of view in *Cale*. Is there a major incident that many people look at, respond differently to?

WILKINSON: The major thing is the growing up of Cale. When I grew up in the South, the early years were like Ramie's early years. I had a kind of isolation. I was cushioned from world events. But something with the Civil Rights Act of 1954 meant the outside world had an effect. I felt the war a little. Rationing —I glued the ration stamps to a chair leg and got a whipping. All these little things, you know, I can recall these. But the Civil Rights Act was the big turning point, when the outside world was going to come into the South. It broke two generations in two, parents and children. This is what I think I'm writing about.

GRAHAM: You're dealing with this young man discovering the breaking.

WILKINSON: Yes, and I want to get so close that people don't apply things they already know to him.

GRAHAM: I don't understand you, exactly.

WILKINSON: So that people don't use the canned phrases about Southerners, about partial bigotry, about partial racism. I want them to know Cale so well that they understand his reactions, that they *feel* his reactions instead of having some sort of sociological thing about his reactions.

GRAHAM: I have such a limited imagination that I don't know what a writer's talking about a lot of times. But with both *A Killing Frost* and *Moss on the North Side,* you have a woman as protagonist. Now, as a woman, you go ahead and write, but this is a man's mind you're leaping into. Now, believe me, I think that men and women are more alike than unlike, we'll start with that. But you know Brian Moore's novel *I Am Mary Dunne?* I've had women say to me with indignation, almost, that it's unfair for a man to be able to understand the psychology of women so well and write that novel. How do you feel about the leap?

WILKINSON: That brings out all my anti-fem lib feelings. I feel that men have written so much better about women—of course, James Joyce's Molly Bloom being just the beautiful one—and I see no reason why women can't write about men. Peter Taylor, who was here at the Conference, has just the accuracy of detail, the little things men watch and which women frequently don't watch themselves do. The way they pin pins into skirts, the way they put chickens into ovens. T. S. Eliot watched his mother with horror as she ripped apart a chicken. How could she just hack this poor chicken apart? She thought nothing of it, of course.

GRAHAM: In a sense, you come as the observing stranger? You're the traveler who sees stuff that the natives don't even know is going on?

WILKINSON: Sure. The taking for granted problem. Now, with *Cale,* I have a brother, and I've asked my brother a lot of questions. I've told several people that if my brother is lying to me, I'm in real trouble. But, it's a fascinating kind of thing. It makes the role of writer an interesting one.

GRAHAM: Would you be tempted to turn over your manuscript to me and ask me, "Is this the kind of thing a man would do?" You may or may not accept my comments, mind you, but would you be tempted?

WILKINSON: I would do this. I did this frequently. I have a strong interest in racing, and I wrote a scene where the boy was attending a race. But I still showed this to a driver just to make sure I didn't make any terrible blunders. This sort of thing gives me much more confidence than listening to a critic talk about my work.

GRAHAM: I can appreciate your checking with a pro about what a "pit stop" is, let's say. But what I'm really interested in is checking on whether a driver can think about anything other than driving when he's in that pit stop.

WILKINSON: That comes out when you talk to these guys. What does it feel like to drive a car? Of course, I, being a tomboy, come very close to a lot of these experiences myself.

GRAHAM: I've heard of what I will call an unhealthy rumor around the Hollins Conference that you've done a fair bit of racing yourself.

WILKINSON: I've been very involved in it, and I have a sweet car, a Porsche, that is quite an automobile and one that you don't just go from "point A" to "point B" in. You drive it or it will get the best of you.

GRAHAM: The concern that you've come to very often with *Cale*, a research job into the psychology of the boy, the use of the almanac, the exploration of your memory, do you get hung up in libraries? You're not writing an historical novel, it's a part of your own life. But you were not joking about your ration stamps. Do you feel you've got to hit that library, to check, to find out just how much a bottle of ketchup cost in ration stamps?

WILKINSON: I avoid these when I can, but I write a lot of letters and people are wonderful about answering. I wrote the Carolina Trailways just to find out when they put bathrooms on Trailways for the first time. And they wrote me back immediately with this information; so, I have a wonderful collection of letters.

GRAHAM: You know I have a rough time just getting a Trailways schedule for the day.

WILKINSON: You write the president and he passes it down.

GRAHAM: You've got to know that kind of thing if you're going to have that little touch of the detail that will—lurching back in a bus—that will bring a whole scene to life. But if there's not a bathroom, back there, you're being pretty silly, if you've got him lurching back there.

WILKINSON: And there are people who read novels with just this sort of thing in mind—how can I trip this author up? I had a man once leap up in the back of an auditorium and say, "Miss Wilkinson, tadpoles are not in the water at that time of the year." And I informed him that I had just done some biological research and bullfrog tadpoles are in the water at that time of year. He was a biology teacher at the local high school.

II. *When you create a character like that Miss Liz, you suddenly find out she never does anything that she doesn't want to.*

GRAHAM: Sylvia, over the weekend I read your very fine novel, *A Killing Frost,* and I'm going to jump in rather heavy-footed at this point. It's superficially, and only superficially, a lyrical novel. I found, for instance, that I read it very slowly because I was pausing. I was looking at the landscapes. I was above all— one of the things that was great fun—I was playing with the little seed-pods that the girl finds. I was occasionally holding a frog, or the little bird that tumbles down the chimney. But it's a violent novel, I've decided. It's a novel about a fight. It's about responsibility, about freedom, about art—I want to say, about ecology. The whole business of freedom and growing up is all involved with the planting of things, the catching of things. We have range from very little children dancing in meadows . . . they're like Impressionist paintings, by the way, those kids playing out there. Then we've got a thirteen-year-old girl; we've got a deaf-mute; and then we've got "grown-ups." There's a war here that I find loaded with tension. That's my superficial lyrical rejection. You spoke earlier that the novel in a sense started out to be a novel about the grandmother and it changed some en route.

WILKINSON: When you view the world from the point of view of a child, as I finally chose to in this novel—an adolescent really, not really a child, this child can experience the world with a kind of minuteness, just a quality of detail, and can put things down and in order which an adult cannot. For instance, she can see things that she does not understand, but she can see them in such completeness that the reader will understand. And here the writer's only chore is to put these things in an order in which the reader can understand them. Although some of the critics said I had the terrible handicap of the child narrator, I didn't think so at all. I felt very comfortable, very natural. It was a pleasant sort of regression into my own childhood, at which time my parents, who were quite kind, left me alone a great deal. They didn't try to program my activities. They let me go out in the morning and come home for meals.

GRAHAM: The girl, without being isolated—and there are some problems about being out after dark, and her aunt certainly wants to box her in—kind of roams, when she lives in the country with her grandmother, or in a very small town. We're on paths an awful lot, or cutting through a field, or chasing a mule or not chasing a mule. And you get a—I guess "meandering" is what I'm after. Time is all crazy. She's only got to move a hundred yards, but as with any young person, it might take her one minute or fifty minutes to cover that hundred yards because of the distraction, the freedom, there. The function of the boxes in the novel—am I right in reading it this way, that people are in rooms a lot, looking out of windows?

WILKINSON: One of the big things, to me, was when winter came, the grandmother sealed the house up. My grandmother did this. When she saw the killing frost, which is the title of the novel, it was suddenly time to seal the windows. And she stayed in her house all winter. And when you go into this box, you go into this box with preparation. You have to have enough wood. You have to have enough food canned. She knows that she has these things, but she was always uneasy. It was almost like she didn't believe that spring was ever going to come again. And she always told me, old people, they always die in the spring. She says, they make it through the hard winter, but they die in the spring. And she did, herself, die in the spring, my grandmother.

GRAHAM: The sense of the dangers of life, that death is there. Things are killed. I think this is worked with marvelous indirection, if only in the killing of a harmless spider or a very dangerous spider.

WILKINSON: I had some reviews from different parts of the country, places like out west where they don't even have screens on their windows. . . . But here we always say, you sit down in the grass you get chiggers, you sit on a log you get ticks. There's always a bug to associate with every place you might happen to perch yourself. And it seems that at a very young age you are told about the evil of certain creatures, and this immediately, as you get older, starts being attached to the evil of certain persons.

GRAHAM: With some of this evil and the danger of death, you keep the men way back, except for Papa, the grandfather, and Dummy. I was interested in Uncle June. Did you have any feeling about Aunt Cecie, the one who is rearing this young girl? The young girl has to sort of watch out for the aunt, whether she stays up late at night or not, and so forth. But how did you see the function of the *men* in the novel?

WILKINSON: Miss Liz had a way of—something I discovered as I grew up—a way of canceling out males, and it was a funny thing. When I started writing this novel, I knew Aunty Cecie had to have a husband because this would be a good home for Ramie, and I found myself canceling out this male. I lost interest in him and didn't want to write about him. It's funny, but the effect of a really powerful character—powerful to me, like Miss Liz, she just took hold of that book. When you create a character like that Miss Liz, you suddenly find out she never does anything that she doesn't want to. You, as writer, have no control over her once she is established. And suddenly no man could come into that novel, because of Miss Liz's presence; so I was unable to deal with him.

GRAHAM: This accounts for a number of my basic reactions to Ramie, in the sense of her being almost a household god, with Miss Liz controlling her even when letting her go free. Then— the warnings. How much should I tell you now? The novel does expand, I think wonderfully, with that idiot basketball business, and buying the fish to make the funny little block print. Here Ramie is now reaching out of this small town, she is in a bigger town and there's a young man in the picture.

WILKINSON: And she originates her own activities for a change.

GRAHAM: The defiance of Aunt Cecie when Ramie as a thir-teen-year-old decided that her grandmother must go outside at that family gathering at Christmas, I frankly felt came off very well, because the girl's a little scared. She's got a skinned knee, she's still a kid. She wants to take the hose off and put socks on. So there's all the wonderful ambiguity of trying to learn to con-trol your world and yet you've got all these hazardous battle-scars of childhood. Let me ask one thing, because it's been driving me wild. There's a recurring freeing of things and catching things, everything from bugs and tadpoles to fish. But you make a great deal in the novel of the jar of water catching the light and refracting—we have a rainbow, and at the risk of being petty or tiresome, that you seem to be making important. And I wasn't getting it. Was it meant to be held as a simple observation of— like the screen door banging—that was ringing in the novel, and working for me?

WILKINSON: Well that rainbow thing. . . . No, I didn't really have any strong intentions for it. It's just that that's one of those things about life that absolutely amazes me. How can that jar of water have sunlight shine through it and have all those colors? Although I know—I go to my physics class, I'm told all these things. And in a way that relates to Ramie's whole notion of biology. Suddenly I study plants and I study animals, and it becomes. . . . Teachers call them things, and I don't even know what they are anymore.

GRAHAM: That's right. She had all that wonderful business where she had all the local names for plants and insects.

WILKINSON: "Earthworms" versus "fishing worms." "Fireflies" versus "lightnin' bugs."

GRAHAM: And here's Miss Robinson, whom she clearly must like a good bit, not understanding the language that all of this rich experience that the kid has had brings to bear.

WILKINSON: A terrible comment on education, that you're not able to transfer this natural education into the education of the school.

GRAHAM: It has a murderous effect when you're trying to identify things in books. I can remember people feeding me all sorts of local plant names and bird names, and I'd go to Roger Tory Peterson, that *Field Guide to the Birds,* and I was about to write him letters, at the age of twelve, to tell him what he didn't know.

WILKINSON: When I was being translated into German I had more fun with "doodlebugs" and all these things, trying to find the words for them.

GRAHAM: What on earth could they do with these localisms?

WILKINSON: There's an easy way of doing it, actually—what you do is, you look up the local name, doodlebug, and you can always find the scientific name. Once you find the scientific name, she can find it in German. But she can't transfer the doodlebug—

GRAHAM: In conjunction with the painting, is Ramie trying to control life, in a way, or fix it, through her paintings? I mean the carvings she makes of Miss Liz, of Dummy, of the bird?

WILKINSON: I think she's trying to do, in a way, what I'm trying to do in the novel. Frequently it's the act of writing something, the act of carving or painting. I tried to paint, myself, for a while, instead of writing. You're trying to put your feelings into some other form so you can sit back and look at them. And Ramie wants to do that because her past, her parents, everything in her life, needs to have some shape that she can see.

Jonathan Baumbach

BIOGRAPHICAL

Born: 5 July 1933 in New York City.
Education: B.A. Brooklyn College 1955, M.F.A. Columbia 1956, Ph.D. Stanford 1961.
Occupational: Has taught at Stanford, Ohio State, New York University, Tufts and Queens College.
Books: Novels—*A Man to Conjure With* (1965), *What Comes Next* (1970), and *Dreambook* (1971); critical and texts—*The Landscape of Nightmare: Studies in the Contemporary American Novel* (1965), *Moderns and Contemporaries: Nine Masters of the Short Story* (1968), *Writers as Teachers/Teachers as Writers* (1970).

Baumbach has received a number of awards including the New Republic Young Writers Award (1958) and Yaddo Fellowships for 1963 and 1964. He makes films and teaches film.

SNAPSHOT

I don't know Jon as well as I ought to. Considering I met him long ago; that we met and talked any number of times; that, one time and another, we wrote things for each other's projects; that, in the beginning we both had the same literary agent, the celebrated Candy Donadio, I have to intrude because I don't "know" him well at all. I know his work, his fiction, which always strikes me as very . . . well, more *mysterious* than strange, but always strong, intelligent, skillful, and original in general and in details.

I am forced to recollection rather than impression. Tall, well-made, relaxed, outwardly anyway, with large, moist eyes which seem not so much sad as sadly sympathetic. And which surely, with or without his movie cameras, see everything, many things freshly though not for the first time. A trained, experienced, even sophisticated eye, then. But I neglect his humor, and that's a serious omission. He has it, wit and comedy, often poker-faced like the sad and very funny clowns of silent films. And, *just* like that, it builds by and through scenes and sequences rather than by a ladder of quick quips.

I've *heard* he is or was a good softball player. And I have seen him play, smooth, even, steady (and sweatless it seemed) against good (literary) competition on the tennis court.

He earns respect easily, but I'm beginning to think he's found another more difficult virtue, the ability to be his own man, finally as private as he pleases, in even public situations. I call that a wonder in this age while I look forward to (excuse me, Jon) what comes next.

I. *I'm just trying to find another way of getting at reality. I mean, my sense is that the conventional novel, for me, anyway, is on its way to a dead end.*

GRAHAM: Jonathan Baumbach seems to wear a number of hats. He's involved with the movies, writing for them, and perhaps, Jon, you have a certain amount of eagerness to do some directing at some point. But right now, could we talk about your novels? You've got three of them out—*A Man to*

Conjure With, What Comes Next, and *Dreambook.* I'm in the unfortunate position as a host of not having read any of these. What do you want me to start with? The first one? Read them all now? What kind of a novelist are you? Are you experimenting? Are you fairly traditional?

BAUMBACH: Well, I guess the word "experimental" in some way might apply. I'm trying to do things with the form that I don't think have been done before.

GRAHAM: That was the opening line you were supposed to give me, because I've reached the point, frankly, where I'm rather tired of the straightforward novel. I'm looking on John Hawkes with his *Second Skin, The Lime Twig* and *The Cannibal,* as the great novelist in America. And I like people who are doing "curious" things.

BAUMBACH: I'm a great admirer of John Hawkes, so we are on good ground.

GRAHAM: Fine. What about *A Man to Conjure With?*

BAUMBACH: It is somewhat of a naturalistic novel. It's about a man who's obsessed—it's the only novel I've written that is wholly in the third person—who tries to make sense of his life twenty years after the disintegration of a marriage which was in some ways key to him in terms of his ambition for himself. It's set in New York City, and he returns to New York after wandering around the country having various negligible jobs as a means, essentially, of marking time, of almost earning the right to return to what he left behind.

GRAHAM: Is he avoiding himself essentially when you say "negligible"?

BAUMBACH: Yes, I would think that that is essentially the case. His ambitions for himself are too large for him to come to grips with.

GRAHAM: You start off saying "a man obsessed," and writers are obsessed with memory, aren't they? Both within your own lives and within the lives of the characters? Characters have to look back and search, don't they?

BAUMBACH: Very much so. I guess that one of my haunting themes is memory. One of the obsessions of *A Man to Conjure With* is he begins to keep a diary long after the event. And he becomes obsessed with recalling things exactly as they were and not leaving out details. Sometimes, an event may be twenty years in the past. In a sense, if he can't hold on to the past, he loses himself.

GRAHAM: The definition of self is maybe not necessarily in the understanding of the past, but simply a reconstruction of it?

BAUMBACH: Understanding is the final goal. The first goal is to have seen all there is to be seen.

GRAHAM: In effect, a certain amount of the CPA is going on here. He's got to have the data before he can find out whether or not the man is bankrupt. He needs to look at the books, with the debits and credits?

BAUMBACH: I'm not sure I like that. It's as if all the details will add up to a picture of himself. And then, he can look at himself as he was. He has the idea, perhaps, that the man he was at twenty is still somewhere there, all the potentiality that was there at twenty and forgotten and lost. To look at himself at twenty is to come back there and start again, to recoup what he's lost. An analogy is Gatsby's obsession.

GRAHAM: I'm teased by titles. *A Man to Conjure With* . . . "conjure" is a word that is not in my vocabulary, really, so why the title?

BAUMBACH: It was an idiom that we used as kids in New York. It would be used about anything. I might say, "That's a shirt to conjure with," or, "That's a tie to conjure with."

GRAHAM: *What Comes Next* was your second novel. What kind of plot-theme were you working on there? From what you have already indicated, you started experimenting a bit with style.

BAUMBACH: Yes, *What Comes Next* moves very closely to— *Dreambook* follows on its heels. Though *A Man to Conjure With* deals a great deal with interior experience, I tried to find a *language* for it in *What Comes Next*. There are two questions that don't quite alternate, but, in effect, they do. The book is very much about the contemporary scene experienced internally through a rather seismographic twenty-one-year-old. Though most people have felt that he is mad and he's certainly mad by conventional standards, it seems to me that his madness is relative sanity. Given any number of public madnesses . . . I don't have to enumerate them.

GRAHAM: You know, I haven't read the newsprint for about ten days in this Conference, and Hollins College has become sort of an oasis in time for me. I keep walking away from these "public madnesses." I was talking with Brian Moore and very much along the lines with what you're worried about here. He recognizes the madness of the world. He says, though, it's so difficult to write a novel about someone who might be tapped with the label "mad" because, then, a reader is apt to push the character off, the way animals will drive out the wounded member.

BAUMBACH: You say that's me? I'm not touched in the way he is.

GRAHAM: It has relevance to my life. He's a backward patient someplace that we ignore and pay too little taxes for. Brian was talking almost in terms of a technique of establishing the person as physically, very clearly physically, but temporarily sick. So the irritability, the feistiness, could be justified in the terms that you and I can understand of the painful broken leg or an ulcer or some such thing that is still within the range of permissible human experience.

BAUMBACH: Well, I hope my character isn't beyond the pale.

GRAHAM: How do the characters within *What Comes Next* view your protagonist? Do they find him as mad? Are they isolating him?

BAUMBACH: I would say that everyone in the novel is mad in a certain way. It's really too complicated to talk about, particularly from my vantage point. It's a book I completed now three years ago. There are two characters who are, in a sense, secret sharers. When you read it, you'll see that. Let me make this point. Almost everyone in the book is so atomistic, and so unrelentingly selfish, that what tears the central character, Christopher Steiner, is the small pieces of compassion that he allows himself. I mean his openness, wherever it is, is to accept the wound; so that, in some ways, I like to think of him as the least mad figure in the book; though that's probably a very private reading.

GRAHAM: With the last novel, then, *Dreambook*, what themes, plots, what new things are going on there with you?

BAUMBACH: *Dreambook* is a very hard book to describe. The frame or structure of the book is rational man. A scientist, though he's an editor of books, is separated from his wife, his family. He's living in a residential hotel room, and he finds a manuscript in the bottom drawer—notebooks. The manuscripts are clearly written by someone wholly unlike him—someone with apparently no superego at all. And he presents the book to us rather grudgingly edited; and he is finally taken over by the book as he takes it over. So, the main body of the book, that is, the interior book, "the dreambook," is the life of a man through certain kinds of dream reality. That is, the succession of episodes in his life, as perceived through what might be real dreams or what might be invented dreams.

GRAHAM: I suddenly thought of Fellini's *8½* where dream, memory, actuality—I'm not going to say get all mixed up—but you can't tell the difference. And it doesn't make any difference. The meaning is all there in spite of the mixtures.

BAUMBACH: Yes, the dreams are sometimes fairly realistic and then diverge into dreamlike reality, though they are all of a piece. Apart from the editor's comments on the book, the entire text is, in fact, a dream. Unlike *8½* there's no play between dream and reality. The dream is the reality, and there's no other reality, finally, in that book.

GRAHAM: This may seem terribly naive since Sigmund Freud has been much abroad, as well as Jung, for way over a half century now. Why is it that so many authors go to the dream? I know in the past ten days I've read ten novels, and they all bring the dream in. I can't see, in many instances, where the dream ends up being the ultimate meaning or the symbolic center of the book. Do you think I've just read some bad novels?

BAUMBACH: I hope so.

GRAHAM: Why is the dream in your view terribly important? It must be symbolic.

BAUMBACH: Well, I try to use it without concentrating on the symbolic. I mean, letting the dreams happen in an intuitive way and relying on my own notion of process is a way of not letting consciousness get in my way; knowing within reason what I'm going to do and trying to escape awareness of what I'm doing, and letting it happen and let it be. I'm not using the dream in the traditional sense, in the psychological sense where it's an almost compacted parable, with special symbols. I'm just trying to find another way of getting at reality. I mean, my sense is that the conventional novel, for me, anyway, is on its way to a dead end. And I'm trying to get at the way things are in a way that no one has seen them before.

Ralph Ellison

BIOGRAPHICAL

Born: 1 March 1914 in Oklahoma City, Oklahoma.

Education: B.A. Tuskegee Institute 1936, Ph.D. in Humane Letters, Tuskegee 1963.

Occupational: Ellison did a little of everything to survive in the Depression, including hunting and trapping professionally and playing jazz trumpet. Since the publication of *Invisible Man,* he has been a full-time writer with many part-time and visiting teaching appointments. Among the institutions where he has served on the faculty: N.Y.U., Columbia, Fisk, Antioch, Princeton, Bennington, Bard, Chicago, Rutgers, Yale, and Arkansas.

Books: Novel—*Invisible Man* (1952); essays—*Shadow and Act* (1964).

He has contributed short stories and essays to many anthologies over the years. His list of prizes, honors, and awards, both literary and in public service, is as extraordinary as it is extensive, and includes such distinctions as the National Book Award (1952) and the National Newspaper Publishers Award (1963). In addition to such literary honors as membership in the National Institute of Arts and Letters and the American Academy of Arts and Sciences, he is a member of the Institute for Jazz Studies, a trustee of the J.F.K. Center for the Performing Arts, and a member of the National Council of the Arts.

SNAPSHOT

He's graying now, looking, each year it seems, more distinguished. The lean vigor and quickness are still there, but a little age has given a certain gravity. He always had the same relaxed dignity. Ralph has unassertive but impeccably good manners. Which, beyond the amenities of politeness, permit him to give every man his due; rough or smooth, each (it seems) is worth hearing out. Deeply reasonable, his mind ever alive and working in consort with his feelings, he can persuade and be persuaded. But he cannot be conned or shaken by anyone. He is a patient, hard-working optimist. The intellectually sloppy offends him, he is dismayed by the slovenly habits of those who shy away from the tough and true and settle for the comforts of clichés and borrowed, easy feelings. An exemplary artist, he is a Socratic teacher (in life, in classroom) who keeps after his pupils until they are moved to teach themselves.

We have all learned from Ralph's example.

I. *The real point is somehow, if you're a novelist, to put it into some sort of human perspective, and a perspective which can be communicated to other people who cannot have the immediacy of what is now called "the Black Experience."*

GRAHAM: My guest today is Ralph Ellison, well-known novelist whose fine, fine work won the—what prize now was it in 1952, for *Invisible Man?*

ELLISON: Well, it was the National Book Award.

GRAHAM: They don't come any better than that. We've learned to shrug our shoulders at the Pulitzer, but the National Book Award for *Invisible Man* is something to be proud of. Ralph, one thing I'm interested in was your seemingly rather early turning to the authors that the college professor is going to insist that young writers—or non-writing types—read: Joyce, Dostoievsky, Stein, and Hemingway. I can remember the line quite clearly in that earlier response of yours, in *The Paris Review,* that you "studied" Hemingway. You didn't "read" him, you "studied" him.

ELLISON: I studied them and taught them in college. I was a music major and so much of the reading that I did, official reading as a student, was in the area of music. Although I must say that the first novel that suggested to me the power of fiction, the ability to really wrench me out of myself, was not modern at all. It was the Brontë sisters, Emily, who wrote *Wuthering Heights.* I also read some of the novels of Thomas Hardy at this particular period, and I was taught these novels. But the question of the twentieth-century experimentation—the kind of sensibility which was going into Joyce and into Hemingway and Gertrude Stein, a number of such people who wrote in English—hit me just by exploring on my own. One reason for the "studying" came because I had no one to explain to me what was implied. Because—for instance, Hemingway always had intrigued me since I used to buy the stories or read them in the Negro barbershops, and the pages of *Esquire* magazine. I read these stories, well they weren't "stories" for the most part; they were reports from Bimini. They were reportage on bullfighting and so on and very exciting for me. But when I began to read the novels, the question of the style, the what-was-not-stated in the understatement, required study.

GRAHAM: The way he could throw something down and seemingly walk away from it, but you knew you had seen it.

ELLISON: You had seen it, and you knew that some great crisis of courage had occurred and was just not said. And I related this to jazz.

GRAHAM: This is what I want to get at. I want to get at your music and your writing, and the whole idea of the total form that you obviously concern yourself so much with in *Invisible Man*. Did you not do work in sculpture also?

ELLISON: That was a very brief thing, and was part of the minor experiences which are seized upon and given a significance which it really didn't have. I turned out to have had a certain sort of facile ability to handle natural forms in clay, although I couldn't draw anything. I could look at you and if you sat still long enough, do a reasonable study. But I only did this for a brief time.

GRAHAM: Would you go back to the jazz then? I'm so interested in this crosscurrent business of the arts, the interrelationships. You were about to say something to the effect that the suggestiveness of jazz, the unstated implications . . .

ELLISON: One thing about jazz is that it was eclectic. It is eclectic at its best. It had no hierarchical respect for music outside of its own particular area, and, in fact, it made the whole world of music, of sound, its own. And it took what it needed from those areas. You hear references to opera, to church music, to anything, in something by Louis Armstrong or any other jazzman of the thirties, forties, and fifties. So this acquaintance with jazz made me quite aware that allusions to ideas and to other works of art were always turning up in Hemingway.

GRAHAM: He's very conscious of painting.

ELLISON: Very conscious of painting, very conscious of languages, very conscious of ceremony and ritual. Just by reading as though I were *listening* to it, as though I were listening to music I wasn't too fully aware of, I began to get a little closer to what was being implied. Much of the art of jazz lies in subtle allusion.

GRAHAM: I guess we'd say a major distinction between good writing and bad writing is that bad writing hits you over the head when you don't need to be hit over the head.

ELLISON: When you've gotten the point, and are saying, "All right! Let's keep going."

GRAHAM: I find this particularly true of poems. I often get a sense that—let's say it's a four-stanza poem and we don't need that fourth stanza. The man has done his work, and all of a sudden he's coming onstage saying, "Now this is what I've been doing up here." We don't need it. It's home.

ELLISON: Like the formula that they used to give the kids in high school debating societies: You say what your point is, you make your point, and then you say that you have made your point.

GRAHAM: I'm afraid I have led many a young man, in directing debate, up that garden path. They may be rather good debaters, but as artists they leave a little to be desired. It would seem to me that the thrust of contemporary writing, right now in the seventies, must be a difficult one for the young artist (or the mature artist) to handle because there is such a tendency toward shrillness, toward polemic. It would be difficult, especially, I think, for the black novelist, to write an honest novel and at the same time avoid trying to change all of the world. I mean, the tone of the time is a tone of manifesto, of organizations and activists.

ELLISON: But this was also the tone of the time when I first came to writing during the thirties. The ideology was different, but you had many exponents of shrillness and people who did not believe that literature had its own function (and I might even say sacred function) in the lives of people and thus had implicitly its own social reason for being.

GRAHAM: We know, too, that so many of those socially aware novels of the thirties . . . There were something like nine novels written on the Scottsboro Boys. And who reads them now?

ELLISON: And who can remember one of them?

GRAHAM: But I think this must be a kind of a dangerous temptation.

ELLISON: I think it's a dangerous temptation. I think for black writers it's especially dangerous. It's dangerous to all American writers, in fact, writers of any cultural background, but it's especially dangerous for us because the realities of our social and political condition—economic condition—are so real and so productive of personal as well as group disaster, that we tend to see the whole world in those terms. The real point is somehow, if you're a novelist, to put it into some sort of human perspective, and a perspective which can be communicated to other people who cannot have the immediacy of what is now called "the Black Experience."

GRAHAM: Have you any particular young black writer that you feel is here now? Is there anyone I can read? I'm thinking of novelists now. I've read a lot of polemicists. Who do you read?

ELLISON: I've found the work of James Allen McPherson, who has not written a novel but is working on one. He had a book of poetry called *Hue and Cry,* which is the work of a sensitive young man, a black man. He is interested in using his experience as a means of insight into the human condition. And he is not, by any means, neglecting what they call the "Black Experience." In fact, he's written some stories which make use of the very rich folklore which has accumulated through the experience of dining-car and Pullman porters. He's right in the groove of an American experience which, say, Stephen Crane sort of touched on in the story "The Bride Comes to Yellow Sky." Crane mentions the fact that the bride and groom were subjected to a terrific form of snobbery throughout the train, but they really got the business from the dining-car waiters who were perhaps the most sophisticated people on that train, you know. In the center they got the very wealthy, as well as the poor, the very sophisticated as well as the relatively naive.

James Dickey

BIOGRAPHICAL

Born: 2 February 1923 in Atlanta, Georgia.

Education: B.A. Vanderbilt 1949, M.A. Vanderbilt 1950.

Occupational: Two hitches (World War II and Korea) in the service, a stint as an advertising man; teacher and poet-in-residence at Rice, Florida, Reed, San Fernando Valley State, and Wisconsin; Poetry Consultant of Library of Congress 1966–1968; presently Poet-in-Residence and Professor of English at the University of South Carolina.

Books: Poetry—*Into the Stone* (1960), *Drowning with Others* (1962), *Interpreter's House* (1963), *Helmets* (1964), *Two Poems of the Air* (1964), *Buckdancer's Choice* (1965), *Poems 1957–1967, Eye-Beaters, Blood, Victory, Madness, Buckhead and Mercy* (1970); novel—*Deliverance* (1970); nonfiction—*The Suspect in Poetry* (1941), *Spinning the Crystal Ball* (1967), *Babel to Byzantium* (1968); *Self-Interviews* (1970), and *Sorties* (1971).

His prizes, in America and abroad, are many, from 1958 to the present. Most notably, he received the National Book Award in 1966. Wrote the screenplay for *Deliverance.*

SNAPSHOT

Legends, myths, fables and fabliaux, anecdotes, quotations from, hard and funny sayings, true and false, wheel and flock about him, a shrill invisible halo of birds explosively circling the edges of his wide-brimmed Warner Brothers sheriff's hat, the one he probably sleeps in (they say). No, not once upon a time an ad man for nothing at all, and he can *do* some splendid impersonations, best of all (I think) King Kong and Marlon Brando. Yes, more masks and costumes than a whole Halloween party, more hidden rabbits and aces than a magician. Something else! But . . . but behind all obvious shucks and colorful charades is the powerful dedicated poet and a complex man burning alive in pure intensity. Not even his big, strong, long-legged body can deny his curious gentleness, his clear vulnerability. His head-high easy swagger does not disguise his suffering. Jim can be like a carnival pitchman because the truth is so precious to him and always so threatened. To know him, the only way, look for him, truly tall and strong and all alive, in his poems.

I. *I mean, I'm really not very good as a pure lyric poet, someone who isolates and makes a particularly poignant comment about a moment in time, a timeless moment, I guess you might say.*

GRAHAM: I've been reading a lot of Mr. Dickey's poetry, and there's a good bit of it out now, isn't there, Jim? It adds up as the years move along.

DICKEY: Yes, probably a hundred and fifty poems.

GRAHAM: *Eye-Beaters, Blood, Victory, Madness, Buckhead and Mercy* is a title to serve as a long introduction to the book. I'm interested in the "size" of your poems. We've talked from time to time about the needs for control and compression; do you have to have room? I've seen very few short poems by James Dickey.

DICKEY: I've written a few short ones, but to be really excited about working on a poem, I would prefer to have something that unfolds over a relatively long space. I realize people don't have time to read long poems now, but the effect that I like the most in any poem is essentially cumulative.

GRAHAM: It seems to me to establish an image and turn it around and offer at times alternatives for extended readings of a situation for yourself.

DICKEY: Well, perhaps. One of the most anthologized poems of mine is a poem called "Falling" which has to do with an airline stewardess falling out of an airplane, and what her thoughts are on falling through the air in the middle of the night, onto the farmlands of Kansas.

GRAHAM: In that poem one of the things you managed to do is sustain the narrative drive as she falls through the strangeness of space, in some curious way free of her body and yet very conscious of her body. You hold the story. But the realer thing that I found was that you hold that *fall*. You keep the girl from falling. You keep her up in the air.

DICKEY: Well, what I wanted (maybe I shouldn't be so conscious about explaining my intentions; I mean that usually isn't something that I do), but in that poem I wanted to use a kind of Bergsonian time shift, in which time itself, that is as we know it, clock time, would not be real time. What we have in that poem is what Bergson referred to as *durée,* duration, lived time, rather than clock time, where things seem to stretch out longer than they ordinarily would. It seems to take an eternity to reach the earth, as it would do, I'm sure.

GRAHAM: Within that eternity, it seems to me you control the rhythms, the pace of your lines, or, better still, your groups, so that you keep the girl in the air rhythmically. The sounds hold her up there, and I'm interested also in what I would almost argue is your use of—not a new form of punctuation—but your use of spacings. Do you "design" your pages? All these spacings?

DICKEY: I'm thinking mainly in terms of the phrase. When I began to conceive of using that gap technique, I guess . . . and everybody's doing it now. Almost every new poetry book I pick up is using that or a modified form of it, usually not very effectively. I mean, people will fasten on a new gimmick very quickly because they think that's going to solve all their expressive problems for them. But this is a device, a technique like any other, and it has its effective uses and its ineffective uses. It's not going to solve all problems for all poets. But what I intended, though, was to try to conceive a use of poetic line which would be like a small line within a large line, to set the lines apart not by printing them one above the other, or one below the other, but by putting them parallel and leaving white spaces between them. Because this seemed to me more nearly to approximate the way the human mind really does work and associate. It goes in jumps instead of a regular linear progression.

GRAHAM: I've read a great deal of poetry over the last ten or twelve days, and you're the first man who, in effect, "forced" me to read out loud. I took some of your things, with these spacings. After I had read them silently, then read aloud, I found that you were telling me, really, in an additional way, besides the vowel, consonant, and concept length, you were telling me through those spaces how to read your play. Because I think a lot of times you're writing plays in your poems.

DICKEY: Most of them are. Most of them deal with an action of some sort. I mean, I'm really not very good as a pure lyric poet, someone who isolates and makes a particularly poignant comment about a fragment or a moment in time, a timeless moment, I guess you might say. I admire those poets enormously, someone like Wilbur, Richard Wilbur, who can do that, but I'm not primarily a lyric poet. What few lyric moments I have ever been able to conceive of were not self-sufficient in themselves, but were imbedded in some sort of larger structure which was not lyric, but essentially dramatic.

GRAHAM: Yes, this is what I see in this poem that I'm interested in. Would you mind reading just a chunk of "Messages to and from My Sons"—the butterflies section? I realize this is a particularly large example of your use of space, but I'd like to hear you control with your voice that little section that begins at the bottom of page ten.

DICKEY: I guess the context probably should be commented on very briefly. It's a poem about a father playing with his son in an open field, kind of like a pasture, where there's a lake, and the boy goes to sleep on the earth dam that makes the lake and the father continues his—this middle-aged man continues to play. His son is asleep and he's looking for something to play with. I think play is awfully important at any age. He finds a skeleton of a cow and he sits down and gets playing with the bones and the head and the horns and so on.

I picked up the head
And inside the nose-place were packets
And whole undealt decks
Of thin bones, like shaved playing cards.
I won the horns.   They twisted loose from the forehead
And would not twist back   as I gambled and rocked
With the skull in my lap,
The cow not straining to live.   In that car I rode
Far off
and in
and in
While you were sleeping off the light
Of the world.
And when I came
From the bone dust in pure abandon, I found you lying on the earth
Dam, slanted in the grass that held back
The water, your hands behind your head,

Gazing through your eyelids into the universal
    Light, and the butterflies were going

  . . . Here

                                            here

          here
          here

                                    from here

   madly over

                    to
here

                                      here.

    They went over you here and through you
    Here no yes and tattered apart,
       Beat out over water and back
        To earth, and over my oldest
     Son asleep: their ragged, brave wings
  Pulsed on the blue flowers shook like the inmost
  Play and blazed all over and around
        Where you slept holding back
 Water without strain.
              That is all, but like all joy
On earth and water,
        in bones and in wings and in light,
    It is a gamble. It is play, son, now
  As then. I put the horns beside you in the grass
And turned back to my handsprings and my leaps.

GRAHAM: You're taking chances in there. I mean, six, eight, ten *here*'s as you're trying to establish the movement in space.

DICKEY: Of the butterflies. It's typical of the way they do, they're so erratic.

GRAHAM: They're almost spookily erratic in tall grass. I'm thinking in part of concrete poetry and the famous emblem poems of the seventeenth century or, for that matter, simply good typography.

DICKEY: The poem creates the shape of what it's about, like George Herbert's "Church Monuments," or things like that.

GRAHAM: Right, "The Altar" and "Angel Wings," "Easter Wings"?

DICKEY: Yes, some of that. I wouldn't really be interested in that myself. A contemporary of mine, John Hollander, has a hang-up about that. He makes poems in the shape of swans and the Empire State Building and the map of New York State. That's interesting, but I don't have enough of a graphic sense to be effective at that, and it doesn't interest me that much as a device. But I love to read his.

GRAHAM: I remember the book very clearly. He's got a wonderful sense of language, but that does seem as if it is imposing. Oh, it's a little like playing football in high-top shoes or something. It's an interesting challenge, maybe.

DICKEY: It seems gimmicky, in the end it seems gimmicky. The great master, of course, is the French poet Apollinaire, and his *Calligrammes,* where he makes poems that are like the shape of a man smoking a pipe or like rain falling.

GRAHAM: There's a wonderful one like a necktie, but he's kind of playing a joke on us in most of those.

DICKEY: I think most of the time it's a put-on. But I love Apollinaire and I read all of those, where you have to turn the book upside down and it reads in a circle, and all that sort of thing, and you keep turning the book around to get the words. But the thing that makes Apollinaire a wonderful poet is the same thing that makes e. e. cummings with all his typographical hijinx a fine poet. It's not that at all, it's not that rather obvious use of those devices or overuse of devices, it's the quality of

phrase which makes the phrase good no matter what shape it's
in.

II. *The thing is that any given poem is a collaboration
between the poet and his memory bank, and his interpretation of his experience, and the reader's interpretation of his own experience.*

GRAHAM: Your book *Buckdancer's Choice,* which was issued in
1966, won what I think is the greatest honor in America, certainly, the National Book Award. The basic thing, I think, that
attracted me to your poetry, was the rhythm of it, that and the
observation. But this rhythm serves as a kind of control. But
as you were mentioning casually, there's more to trying to control the reader than just pleasing him with music. And I like
your word *surprise* there, because there were times when I didn't
know what was coming next simply because you broke a rhythm
and then sort of pushed me off balance and pulled me back. The
other thing is this business of observation. Do you consciously
press yourself to look? Do you keep a notebook, for instance, of
things you see? And by "see" I mean anything sensory.

DICKEY: What I do, and it's done in a very dilatory fashion, I
note down some things from time to time. What I really would
like to do—I mean, after all, one lives in the twentieth century,
and I would like to avail myself of some of the mechanical con-
trivances, like cassette tape recorders, carried around with me
all the time and talk to it, talk to the machine, all the time, and
have somebody transcribe it off.

GRAHAM: As a storage, memory bank for you?

DICKEY: Why not? It's just like the airplane. You want to get to a place, you get on a plane and go there.

GRAHAM: This is one of the attractive things about your poetry. It's not extraordinary that you write about butterflies and children, and yet you also write about very contemporary things. You see, you experience, a lot of machinery. I'm involved in this whole idea of the poet or the painter, this whole business of stripping the veil of familiarity off things. I've seen a million butterflies. But your poem in which the butterflies play a part, that is a memory bank for me really, because I not only read your poem, but I'm pulling this experience in because of the expression of the poet.

DICKEY: That's the true magic of poetry, I think. The thing is that any given poem is a collaboration between the poet and his memory bank, and his interpretation of his experience, and the reader's interpretation of his own experience. If I say the word "tree," you and I don't see the same tree. Let's just try it out as an experiment. What tree do you see?

GRAHAM: I've got a kind of . . .

DICKEY: What kind is it?

GRAHAM: I've got a funny oak that'll never let go of its leaf.

DICKEY: That's fine, but I see a pine tree. So what's wrong with you? But I said "tree" and you do see. You bring the tree to the poem out of your experience.

GRAHAM: So we work together on the tree.

DICKEY: It's a collaboration, sure. And what the poem does, and if it's good, and the right poem and the right reader, it's an enrichment of his own life, through the poet's life, which can't be known to you.

GRAHAM: You know, during the Hollins Conference here, I've been reading a lot of poetry, and talking with you poets, and something that's happened with me is that I'm looking at people more carefully. I'm looking at the landscape here at Hollins, which I find a very attractive college. I know I'm seeing, hearing, things with a kind of acuity, through the poetry, I believe.

DICKEY: That's right, that's what it's all about. I mean, we just have to take a couple of things as axiomatic or as taken for granted, that it's better to live deeply and passionately and to observe deeply and passionately and to feel deeply and passionately than it is to live shallowly and noncommittally.

GRAHAM: As some of these people in your new novel, *Deliverance,* they want to live shallowly.

DICKEY: Yes—it's easier that way.

GRAHAM: If you don't go mad.

DICKEY: It allows you to avoid the pain, because all this deep and passionate experience which we all so much hope for involves a terrible sense of pain. And the main thing that it does, too—that one probably would want to avoid, that everybody wants to avoid at one time or another—is the sharpening of the sense of time passing.

GRAHAM: This is what the poet seems to me to know more about than the novelist does, in some curious fashion.

DICKEY: I think the most beautiful phrase that indicates this doesn't come from poetry at all, but from basketball games on television when they say, "The clock is running . . ." Which it is, it is, it always is.

GRAHAM: In terms of observation, one of the poems—this is not a typical poem—but would you mind reading that little one, "In the Pocket"? This is one of the teasers in this gathering of your poetry, this business of staying with all kinds of life. And I'll tell you the line I like best in this after you read it.

DICKEY: That's a bargain. One of the things I'm coming more and more to write about and to pay attention to is the dependency of men on each other. You find this in wars, in forward-zone combat action, probably at a more intense level than anywhere else. But how long has it been since you called somebody your "buddy"?

GRAHAM: When you were in a little squad tent, they were your "buddies."

DICKEY: Yeah, there's a marvelous kind of basic language that soldiers use. Say two enlisted men get drunk in a town and one of them's arrested. You look up the major, wherever he is, or somebody who's responsible for your unit, and you say, "Major, would you come on down to the jail? My buddy's in trouble." How long has it been since you had a buddy that you felt like that about?

GRAHAM: It's been a long time.

DICKEY: This is a poem about that, except it's football instead of soldiering. Where the linemen form this pocket for the passer and everything. And they trust him; so it's really a kind of condition of trust. And they're going to keep the opposing linemen out until he can find his number one receiver, number two receiver, number three receiver. The first two may be covered, but the third one, even if he's got half a stride on the defensive halfback. . . .

GRAHAM: And that's a pretty thing to watch, that half-stride.

DICKEY: It sure is. It's like that. The poem's called "In the Pocket," and it's written from the standpoint of the quarterback.

Going backward
All of me and some
Of my friends are forming a shell   my arm is looking
Everywhere and some are breaking
In   breaking down
And out   breaking
Across, and one going deep   deeper
Than my arm.   Where is Number One hooking
Into the violent green alive
With linebackers?   I cannot find him he cannot beat
His man   I fall back more
Into the pocket   it is raging and breaking
Number Two has disappeared into the chalk
Of the sideline   Number Three is cutting with half
A step of grace   my friends are crumbling
Around me the wrong color
Is looming   hands are coming
Up and over between
My arm and Number Three: throw it hit him in the middle
Of his enemies   hit move scramble
Before death and the ground
Come up   LEAP STAND KILL DIE STRIKE

Now.

GRAHAM: I just saw in your reading this sense of the sea, almost
—"it is raging and breaking." That's the way you talk about
water coming in.

DICKEY: Yes it is, and I felt that.

GRAHAM: All this confusion.

DICKEY: Surging. . . .

GRAHAM: In terms of this business of observing: one of the
tricks I've played on myself in watching football is to try to
isolate, not the quarterback, but isolate from his shoulder to the
ball, really. And so your line, "my arm is looking everywhere"—
all of a sudden the sense of—almost the *football* itself.

DICKEY: Sensory object.

GRAHAM: Right, right! And it's got to find where it's going.

DICKEY: That's it, that's it!

GRAHAM: Let's pretend the whole poem weren't there. Of course that line can't live without the rest of it. But that line is going to make me look at football even more differently, now. And this is part of the function of the poet.

DICKEY: Yes, it is, it surely is, as I see it. It's that intensification of ordinary experience, something that anybody can do, something that anybody can see, but which becomes through the office of the poet, the poet's craft and art—strange and wonderful.

GRAHAM: This temptation for people to suggest that one steps into a world of language and stays there, and therefore, someway, you don't meet life, is so naive because actually the language . . . you *do* live in a world of language. But then it thrusts you back in the actual world.

DICKEY: This is the whole point. We were talking in class today about Walter Pater's statement, "All the arts aspire to the condition of music." What he intended, I suppose, was that the arts want to be as self-sufficient as music is. It has its own universe, its own laws, and refers, or need refer, to nothing outside itself. Poetry's not like that. Poetry is a referential art. I was talking about the poem referring to the tree earlier, but, if there were no real trees, that would be meaningless as poetry.

GRAHAM: We wouldn't have any experience to bring to it or to thrust out of.

DICKEY: Or to go back into, by means of the poem.

GRAHAM: With this business of subject matter: you've written a lot of poetry about the war, some of it terrifying in its picturing of the depersonalization. In your reading have you found the great novel out of World War Two?

DICKEY: No, but I think the best novel I ever read about World War Two is James Gould Cozzens' *Guard of Honor*, which is not about combat at all, it's about a training base.

GRAHAM: All right, I'll go at that. You know, I'm thinking of *All Quiet on the Western Front,* for instance—and that is World War One.

DICKEY: I think that's a wonderful book, too.

GRAHAM: I reread it and it holds up.

DICKEY: But I think the best writing about World War One— and everybody's interested in World War One now. Why would you suppose they are? I mean I have some ideas, but . . . I mean, the fascination with World War One and everything that pertains to World War One, not just the combat, but the temper of life, the quality of life there. People are awfully interested in all that.

GRAHAM: Some of it is this business of the destruction of a generation. We're seeing *that,* rather than the atomic bomb, as a watershed.

DICKEY: I also think that people are fascinated by the fact— which is a fact—that the war was fought in the most bestial, and humanly-depraved, uncomfortable, agonizing situation that men have ever had to cope with. That trench warfare, that must have been. . . . I mean, Vietnam is bad enough; or the New Guinea campaign in World War Two was bad.

GRAHAM: But they can fly you out if you're hurt.

DICKEY: That's right, and you get a medic's aid. But that tragic floundering around in the slime, and those rats, and no-man's land and . . . men will never have to do anything worse than that.

III. *What I need is freedom to do work, whether it's novels, poetry or whatever.*

GRAHAM: We have a fairly recent shift in your activities. I want to say, Jim, that the novel writing comes as no real surprise to me. In your poetry you like to have a little room, your poems are long, and you like to work with an action rather than a stasis in your poetry. You don't just look at a landscape. There's a fox moving through it, or a butterfly dancing around it, or an airplane, or that poor stewardess who falls or is sucked out of the plane at ten thousand feet. There's always action, though. But with *Deliverance,* the recently published novel, what led you to it, finally? You had to make a decision as to whether you'd write a poem, or many poems, maybe, and the novel. What happened in your mind?

DICKEY: That's precisely the point, and *Deliverance* is about the only idea that ever came to me that was capable of novelistic treatment. So I figured I had better seize the day.

GRAHAM: So it's a new experience, and you had to get it out in a special way?

DICKEY: I had intended to write, in fact I did write, several of the episodes which occur in *Deliverance* as poems. The thing about the chicken heads and all that was a poem called "On the Coosawattee." And going through the fir forest and the canoe, I wrote as a poem. And some of the whitewater scenes on the river I wrote as poems. But the whole action of *Deliver-*

ance was something that seemed to me to gravitate toward fiction rather than toward poetry. There's an unusual sensation for me, because nearly everything else gravitates toward poetry. And I don't have any ambitions at all to write fiction and get on the great novelistic hit parade or anything of that sort. But this material seemed to declare itself as a novel, and so I figured I'd better try to help it out as I could.

GRAHAM: This is not unanalogous to Pirandello's *Six Characters in Search of an Author*. And the thing that you're saying here is, in a way, that the observations you have made, and these observations permitted themselves to be made in poetry, but they wanted to break out a little bit, and you needed the novel?

DICKEY: No, not quite, that's partly it. But it seemed to demand or at least implore the author to employ a novelistic form. And since I had not done any of this, and since the sense of the untried has always been very strong with me, I just thought I would give it, as they say in Australia, "give it a go." And so I did give it a go, and with results as you know.

GRAHAM: You are working with men, at least some of the men, who've either kind of died in life, some unconsciously, some very deliberately not getting involved in life. Your narrator here is with an advertising agency and he knows—he's a vice-president —he's not the big deal. It's a little outfit doing commercial stuff and he knows it, and he chooses almost to not be disturbed.

DICKEY: That's right, to insulate himself against anything intense, because he feels that he doesn't require that, and it's so much easier without it.

GRAHAM: Then he takes his chance. One thing that occurred to me in the reading: these men, four of them, go into the deep woods, into this canoe trip on rather dangerous or mysterious water. They don't quite know where it is on a map. They don't know what is there. It struck me that a word like a "test" or a "retreat," a retreat in the religious sense of stepping back for three days with an examination of conscience, contemplation. Is this some of what you were doing?

DICKEY: A couple of them have kind of a romantic notion of getting back to the primitive, getting back to the wilderness before it's destroyed. And we all have a great nostalgia for things that we've destroyed. We'll miss our world as it was, made by something else than me, you know. And we see so much of this in the popular media, print and television and so on, so much emphasis now on ecology. If I asked you to go on a canoe trip with me, John, and I said that this is the most beautiful valley in Appalachia, which is beautiful generally, and it was going to be dammed up and destroyed, you would feel a kind of moral constraint to go.

GRAHAM: Have to catch it before it's gone. It's like waking someone up and saying the sunrise is magnificent. You can't let them sleep.

DICKEY: And that's why they go, that's why three of them go. I mean, they don't have any great compulsion to go. But Lewis is different. He's a kind of a suburban maniac.

GRAHAM: Yes, he's a dangerous man, obviously. He's an upsetter of things.

DICKEY: But these fellas are crazy about him, and will follow him, up to a point, in anything he wants to do, because he's so unusual. He's the only one of them who's self-determined, who can do what he wants to do. And this is what he wants to do.

GRAHAM: They smile at him once in a while in his intensity. I remember the very wonderful opening scene. They're looking at the map—it's out on the bar table, held down by the glasses of beer—and they're talking about it. And they certainly smile at him, but his intensity is demanding.

DICKEY: Because that's something that nobody else in their experience has.

GRAHAM: The whole thrust of a long narrative, did you find that difficult? I mean, you had all this experience in narrative poetry. Did you find that long narrative hard to sustain in the writing of the novel?

DICKEY: The first draft that I did, I just kind of wrote it like I used to write poems. I was impatient with what a really great novelist would be most interested in, that is, the nitty-gritty of the details. I was impatient with that. I just wanted to write the big scenes. I wrote those, and then I had to go back and fill in the extra stuff, and that was what was difficult about it for me.

GRAHAM: One thing that I was watching for—this is not kind—but I was watching the novel to see if you wound up sliding into a kind of poetic compression that might not function for the novel. But I did not see this pop out. Was this a control problem?

DICKEY: No, no. That was a labor of five or six years, to take all that out—the conventional kind of Updikey writing, like the perennial A student in the creative writing course. That's what I didn't want to do.

GRAHAM: Was this a constant act then of discipline, to be— frankly, to be James Dickey, novelist, rather than James Dickey, poet, working at a novel?

DICKEY: Well, I don't really know. I don't really concern myself about those considerations, the kind of thing you read in the contributor's column of a magazine. You know—"he is now working on a novel." I didn't really think about that. I wrote *Deliverance* pretty much by fits and starts, something that I toyed with for a while and it interested me but did not over- whelm me. On about the fourth draft of it, the thing caught fire in my mind, when I saw that it would actually be possible to finish it. If I pushed on it, I really could finish it. I began to like some of the stuff in it so much I thought it would be unforgivable—I would never forgive myself—if I didn't go ahead and do my best to realize it.

GRAHAM: With this new experience in your writing, do you get any sense that—I'm not going to say, that you've changed as a result of writing the novel—but that maybe your poetry is going to be a little different?

DICKEY: That really would not be given to me to say, John. I would have to cite the same sort of thing that happens to Ed in the end of *Deliverance:* he's changed, but nobody knows it but him. He's changed only in secret ways.

GRAHAM: Does he have an idea at the end of the novel what he's going to do with the change, or is it still a mystery to him too?

DICKEY: No, he just has it.

GRAHAM: He's come a little closer to the heart of life.

DICKEY: Right. He has it. He doesn't have to explain it. He doesn't have to kill anybody again, but he knows that when he had to do it that he was capable of doing it, and he did it.

GRAHAM: An ultimate act?

DICKEY: That's right . . . only once. You only have to do it once.

GRAHAM: With this whole business of control, you say you don't feel now as if you were going to get on the novel production line. Do you feel that more has to be said in prose? There must, however, have been spin-offs, other novelistic ideas while you were en route with *Deliverance?*

DICKEY: I have a kind of vague idea building up in my mind, but I don't know whether I'll ever write it or not. But I don't want to be committed to the American success syndrome where

I've got to produce a best-seller every three years or something like that. I don't need that. What I need is freedom to do work, whether it's novels, poetry or whatever.

GRAHAM: Back to the whole problem you were talking about earlier. What the poet makes us aware of is the moment of time. What was it you said about the basketball game?

DICKEY: "The clock is running . . ."

David Slavitt

BIOGRAPHICAL

Born: 23 March 1935 in White Plains, New York.

Education: B.A. Yale 1956, M.A. Columbia 1957.

Occupational: Was (briefly) instructor in English at Georgia Tech; served as an associate editor (book and film critic) for *Newsweek* 1958–1965. Presently writes full-time and describes himself, according to his mood, as either "unemployed" or "retired."

Books: Poetry includes *Suits for the Dead* (1961), *The Carnivore* (1965), *Day Sailing* (1969), and *Child's Play* (1972); also (translation) *The Eclogues of Virgil* (1971) and *The Eclogues and Georgics of Virgil* (1972); novels are *Rochelle, or Virtue Rewarded* (1966), *Feel Free* (1968), *Anagrams* (1971) and *ABCD* (1972).

As "Henry Sutton," the following popular novels: *The Exhibitionist* (1967), *The Voyeur* (1968), *Vector* (1970), and *Crash* (1972).

SNAPSHOT

With a great tangle of dark curls and (sometimes) a beard as thick as a hedge, barrel-chested with a lightfoot, almost tiptoey walk, he comes on like a large shaggy dancing bear. Or a big kid in a bear suit. A growl like a bear, too, in a rich baritone (now gravel, now clear as woodwinds) when growls seem in order. One of his children wrote a poem about it which tells it beautifully:

> When in trouble
> Or in doubt,
> Run in circles
> Scream and shout.

But laughter's his true music, with trumpets and trombones declaring a range of wit that runs, easy, graceful and astonishing, between, say, early Medici and late Lenny Bruce. One of the very few really good and gifted poet-performers on the circuit, but could also have been among the first of standup comics. Words, all creeds and colors of them, all shapes and sizes are his wealth. He owns more than anyone and is their benevolent, generous, courageous slavemaster, always audacious never exploitative. He beat Kurt Vonnegut easily in a big showdown of anagrams. He was also the one, offhand, at first sight and in a wink, who invented and summoned up Levy, the Oculist, whose ghost haunts Hollins College.

I. *So, it's like arranging fruit in a basket. You put the good ones on top, and then, for the suspicious housewife, you put a couple of good ones at the bottom.*

GRAHAM: Mr. Slavitt has a lot of strings to his bow. I know that during the Hollins Conference, he's been talking on film criticism. I'm not going to say, David, that I'm not interested in that, but what I am very interested in is your poetry. I have here in front of me these volumes in the Contemporary Poetry

Series: *The Carnivore,* which was 1965, and then a recent one (and quite bluntly, I like the newest one best)—*Day Sailing.*

SLAVITT: All writers like to hear that "there's been a terrible falling off in your work." It's an awful thing to hear. You seem to have become stupid as you get older.

GRAHAM: What about *The Carnivore?* Now you've got some distance on it, is it like having a lot of children? You sort of love them all differently, but as much? Or do you walk away from a book when it's finished?

SLAVITT: I don't think of them as "books," really, because they aren't. You don't sit down and write a book of poems. You write a whole lot of poems and when the pile is thick enough, it's a book. There are poems in *The Carnivore* that I like. There are poems in *Day Sailing* that I like. There are poems in *Suits for the Dead* that I still like. I'm much more interested in the newer things, the things since *Day Sailing,* because those are fresh, and I'm still trying to decide if I like them or how much I like them.

GRAHAM: They're still part of your life, I mean those observations, aren't they?

SLAVITT: No, not really, sometimes, not . . . I don't know. They're artifacts. How well did I do and do I really like it? Even the good ones, say in *Carnivore,* which is a long time ago —yes, they are good, and I know that now. Having decided this, what else is there to say?

GRAHAM: This word "artifact" triggers something with me. I realize that this seems like almost an artificial question, but with making up a gathering of poems such as *Carnivore* and *Day Sailing,* do you really choose with great care the order of appearance of poems in a book? Must a book be read in sequence? But even more important than that, do you in a sense build by putting two poems back to back? Do you build some kind of a tension, maybe?

SLAVITT: There is an interesting three days that I spend—I think any poet spends—trying to figure out what the order is going to be. There are certain obvious things that you do. You want a good one at the front and you want a good one at the end because most people will read either the first or the last poem to see whether they are going to buy the book. Or, if they've been taken out of a library, whether they are going to read it or just bring it back unread. So, it's like arranging fruit in a basket. You put the good ones on top, and then, for the suspicious housewife, you put a couple of good ones at the bottom. The other poems, all the ones in the middle, you sit there trying to find some plausible order for that reader—there aren't very many of them, I think—but for the reader who does sit down and read the poems sequentially. I don't do it that way. When I have a book of poems, I sort of find titles that appeal to me or first lines that wander around vaguely. But there are people who do that; so, you have at least an occasion for seeing what the order ought to be. And it's kind of interesting to find out because it's the first absolutely necessary time to do this, to find out what you've been talking about the last two or three years.

GRAHAM: Is there any pattern there?

SLAVITT: To see what the patterns are, what poems actually go together and what things can be brought together in interesting ways. It's not a very high level of intellectual activity, it's about the same sort of thing as determining what order the acts ought to go on, say, an Ed Sullivan show. But you find out odd things occasionally. Like, "Gee, I seem to have been interested in birds these past two years," or something like that.

GRAHAM: Or planting bulbs as you seem to have been.

SLAVITT: Or planting bulbs. . . . Well, after I moved out of New York and White Plains, and went up to the Cape, and I got involved with gardening and landscaping, I found myself knowing more about that. And you're interested in things that you know about.

GRAHAM: One of the "gatherings" I enjoyed in *Day Sailing*, in particular and it sort of started me off, it was about two-thirds through the book, you've got a little grouping called "Ideas of Disorder," where you talk about a pond and a—

SLAVITT: That was conceived that way as a suite.

GRAHAM: You write about a great many different things. In this particular case, it was an "idea of irregularities," really, where you hit on a number of things—whales, sounding and blowing in the night, and building and planting and discovering that bulbs are best planted by just throwing them and planting where they fall. But it seems to me that this was a gathering that was a fruitful playing of poems off against each other. Of course, they are physical, but the *idea* was dominating. It might have been the title. But I see you also writing poems of experience, action of self, of others, of nature, a lot of history, and a lot of art. There's a wonderful little poem, "Sapphic Fragments." The relationship between the poet and the painter is one that intrigues me. Is it an imaginative thing you're doing?

SLAVITT: There are a lot of poems in my work about painting. There are a lot of things about music, because the strange thing about poetry is what it always wants to be—something else. In certain ways, it wants to be musical, in certain ways it wants to be intellectual, in certain ways it wants to be visual and feely. And if you want to go to the limit of the circle of what's possible in poetry, you find yourself into all kinds of things— even mathematics.

GRAHAM: I'm interested in the little poem on the Rousseau painting. You're commenting? You're not trying to "reproduce" a painting?

SLAVITT: No, I can remember about how this one happened. I was reading the *Anathemata,* and there was a footnote somewhere about how lions were fond of lavender. There's no source for this, and it had nothing to do with the page that it was a footnote for. That seemed to be somewhat negligent because an idea as bizarre as that wanted to be in something. And so I thought I would remedy that defect or fill the hole. And what could you do with lions liking lavender? They had nothing to do with each other, so irrelevant and incongruous. I began to think about what the thing would look like and the look would be sort of like those sort of crazy Rousseau-tropical-jungle things.

GRAHAM: Those crowded jungles!

SLAVITT: Those crowded jungles. He used to paint those from the top down, almost like a wallpaper. Go across the top and do the top third, and then the middle third, and then the bottom third, and he wouldn't know . . .

GRAHAM: What he might find under the bush . . .

SLAVITT: Large cats, in the middle of it! He would start doing ferns. Some of them would stay ferns and some of them would turn into the tops of trees. They would have big trunks.

GRAHAM: One of the crazy things about writers, and now you're suggesting painters too, is this sense of discovery. You evolve into a poem, you start following your nose.

SLAVITT: Oh, I think this is what Frost meant when he said that a poem "begins in delight and ends in wisdom." No surprise for the writer and no surprise for the reader. What you do—and again, this is painterly—is after you've made the first stroke on a canvas, you are as much responding to that stroke as you are taking an idea and putting it on to the canvas. You get into a dialogue situation of what can be done with the possibilities, of what can come out of what is already there. Which is why poetry is so much more fun to do than novels. You don't get that in novels until one hundred, one hundred fifty pages in. It takes that long to establish your stroke. I like to play around in all the games in *The Carnivore*. In plays you get this classically in the second act curtain, where suddenly all this "has to be." You have enough development and complication. There must be a dénouement, and the dénouement must come out of what's already happened. But the characters must stay alive. This is what Forster was talking about in *Aspects of the Novel*. If you go in and bully your characters, and say, "Look, it says in the outline that you must go off to Africa and be a missionary, do this," the character starts to sound like a puppet. If you allow him to do what he wants, which is to run away with the house-keeper and live in Finland, well, that's nice, but it has nothing to do with your novel which has been raped. So you have to sit down with this character and decide there must be something that you can do that is in some way congruent with the notion you had of the book, but perfectly acceptable to you. And, when a novel works, it's because of this third thing, something that you hadn't thought of, isn't immediately obvious from the character, that has come out of it, come out of this discussion. It's better usually than anything you could have intended.

GRAHAM: You're talking about the search for options.

SLAVITT: But this happens in poetry. Yes, this happens in poetry like the beginning with the second line. Because, already by then, you're starting to think of rhymes, and rhymes are occasions for invention. I mean, if the word doesn't have a rhyme that's obvious, then you've got to think of some other word to rhyme with, some other pre-rhyme, or, you've got to take one of the possible rhymes and incorporate it somehow, in the direction that you've got to go in to incorporate this. This may be better than anything that you could have planned up front.

GRAHAM: And the poor poet is the poet who gets trapped by his rhyming and will not explore enough options. I mean where a poem starts one way and where the rhyme may dictate . . .

SLAVITT: If he insists too much that the poem goes the way he wanted it to, or, if he doesn't insist enough and is led by the nose by his rhymes, either way, he's dead. There has to be this continual negotiation. It's like trying to persuade a series of red ants, you know, one hundred of them to stand in a line and behave like Goldwyn Girls. It can be done for moment, but they do scamper off.

II. *To do a sestina is deliberately to noodle around and then see if you can overcome the circularities of the form and appear to be making a linear statement of any kind at all.*

GRAHAM: Now, *Day Sailing* is the later of the two that I've read, David, and I've been reading a lot of loosely put together poetry over the last ten days, a tremendous amount of poetry. And I am interested in the variety of *forms* that you're working in. How do you feel about variety of form? Do you stumble on it?

SLAVITT: Well, I think the first question is, before variety of form, is form itself. I was a little shocked a couple of years ago by "form." I guess it was at San Francisco State, when I was there doing a reading, and all of these West Coast woollyheads were kind of belligerent really, because they had all of these crazy ideas about poems should be *in process* and they shouldn't have beginnings, middles and endings and they should be "you know, like biological." It just struck me as being (a) *rot* and (b) *too easy*. And the whole idea of a poem, if McLuhan and all of that means anything, is that it's a *made thing*. What poems are about, first of all, is that they are poems. This isn't really as fashionable now as it should be, or Wilbur's reputation would be higher than it is.

GRAHAM: He's a man fascinated by traditional forms.

SLAVITT: He is, I think, perhaps after Auden, the best poet going in the language. His latest book, I think, came out . . .

GRAHAM: *Walking to Sleep* was very recent.

SLAVITT: *Walking to Sleep,* right. It was about ten months ago and it was reviewed only about a month ago, in a roundup review in the *Saturday Review* and then in a sort of impertinent, snippet thing in *The New York Times,* and then silence. Because he has what Frost used to call "good manners" and does not confess to all kinds of terrible personal problems and he's not politically involved. But it's all there. It's full of life and it's full of stuff, but it's not strident, and he doesn't grab by the lapel and breathe in your face, and spray you with spittle.

GRAHAM: I'm interested in your poetry because of a kind of complication that I see in Wilbur's. You'll be talking about very serious things very seriously. Let's go to "Precautions" or the "Sestina for the Last Week of March," all of them in *Day Sailing.* What you are doing in there, I think, is talking about things, about yourself, about your reactions to things, and this is very serious. But, it also seems to me you've got a reserved mock of that seriousness in there, a kind of distance-keeping, or maybe just a complicating aspect of your life. I think Wilbur does this.

SLAVITT: I think what happened, or I hope what happens is this. There's an initial something that starts you thinking, "maybe I ought to do a poem about it," or "maybe it's a poem" or "maybe it could be made into a poem." The "Sestina for the Last Week of March" was a visual experience. I was up on the Cape, and I was shaving. Right next to the mirror is a window that looks out, among other things, onto great elm trees. There's a huge old elm tree, and that last week in March was when you could see very clearly even at the distance of thirty or forty yards, the swollen buds ready to go "pop" and become leaves.

GRAHAM: It's almost a haze over the tree.

SLAVITT: And all of that imminent: yes, the tree begins to look blurry, the quality of light around the tree is different and affected, and it's all terribly juicy. Something wanted to be done with this. Okay, so fine. Nothing particular . . . in fact, to do a sestina is deliberately to noodle around and then see if you can overcome the circularities of the form and appear to be making a linear statement of any kind at all. Now with all those technical problems to deal with, I mean the problem of writing a sestina—the most difficult form, I think there is—you can't really be too concerned with what you're talking about. You only find out what you're going to say when you've read what you've written. You can function in a sort of preconscious way, rejecting things that seem to you either false or boring, or strained or tiresome. I mean, there are a lot of things that you won't let through because you don't like them. But so long as you are talking interestingly or writing interestingly, and the thing seems to be alive and you're responding properly to the occasions of the rhyme and the patterns of the words and listening to them and the stuff is alive, you've got enough to do.

GRAHAM: In other words, grace is important.

SLAVITT: Grace is important. Grace is most of it. Then, at the end of it, or, as we spoke of last time, at the end of a book of poems, you look back and see what you've said and find out who you are and what you think. I don't think it's coyness or perversity that keeps poets from sitting down to say, "Well, in this poem, I meant," because they didn't know what they meant. They are as interested to find out as anybody else what it was that they meant and who they are. The wit, the humor, the irony that come in are just perfectly natural and comfortable to me. Seriousness, pursued for too long, becomes deadly.

GRAHAM: It's boring and it's rather lacerating and one pushes it away.

SLAVITT: A poem ought to be as well run as a good drawing room.

GRAHAM: I'm interested in some of the breaks in the "Sestina." Could you read some from that now?

SLAVITT: The thing about a sestina is that you don't have very much choice, because you've got those six end words, "yielding," "breath," "ladies," "trees," "abandon," and "cities," which lock you in.

GRAHAM: Those are your perimeter.

SLAVITT: That's the perimeter. And then you try to appear as linear, and as conversational and rational as you can, given an utterly loony constriction that you've voluntarily assumed.

GRAHAM: It's a three-legged race.

SLAVITT: It's a six-legged race. Then, you've got to use all six legs each time you take a step!

> Suddenly the ground is flesh and yielding
> as if one walked on a body, and air is breath
> and the woods are full of delicate, naked ladies

Now that was the first phrase that popped into my head, looking at this luscious elm tree . . .

> and the woods are full of delicate, naked ladies
> who hide in bushes and beckon behind the trees
> in all the tempting attitudes of abandon
> of the famous streets of certain infamous cities.
>
> Who has not read the erotic promise of cities,
> or walked in squares with the light abruptly yielding
> to shadows of unimaginable abandon?
> But here, in the daylight and fresh air, the breath
> of gin hangs on the juniper, and trees
> carefully pose themselves like elegant ladies
>
> considering some indiscretion.

That, I suppose, is the break that you mean?

GRAHAM: That's the turn that I enjoyed in particular, that leap right there.

SLAVITT: That was fun because the stanza form is another thing that you are locked into and what can you do with enjambment, and run-ons of lines and stanzas and keep the thing going.

GRAHAM: It is a jumble. That's the jumble I enjoyed. It was a surprise because with the spacing of the poem I had to have some natural stop there. My eyes would not let me carry that run on and then your little phrase "considering some indiscretion" . . . that was part of the big joke and that's what I'm talking about.

SLAVITT: It's like in a film. The characters are still there, talking about the same thing, but somehow, the light has changed, and it's suddenly ominous. Or it's suddenly, you know, "carefully posed themselves like elegant ladies" which is all kind of neutral, "considering some kind of indiscretion," and it's all . . .

GRAHAM: The background music changes and underlines it differently. Go ahead and read some more.

SLAVITT:

> Ladies
> learn to conceal such thoughts in civilized cities.
> Oh, sometimes, in a formal park, the trees
> will make their improper suggestions, conversation yielding
> to difficult silences, the very drawing of breath
> becoming absurdly physical: "Abandon
>
> pretense, civilization, cities. Abandon
> all the constraints by which you live as ladies.
> Strip naked, lie in the grass, pick baby's-breath
> bouquets, and flee for your lives, flee the cities . . ."

But they never do. That week of spring yielding
yields itself to summer. Leaves clothe the trees.

And yet, some must have gone. Behind the trees,
those delicate creatures of our fancy's abandon
must have begun somewhere. There are myths yielding
many examples—reasonable ladies
of the kind one meets in fashionable cities
once, in the woods, struggled to catch their breath

and changed in the time it takes to draw a breath,
turning into, melting into trees.
Their stories are embroidered back in the cities,
tamed for us who can hear only so much abandon.
They have been refined, no doubt for the sake of the ladies
who know their truth and long for such a yielding

and for gentlemen of the cities, lest they abandon
fine careers, fine ladies, and run off, yielding
to the whispered breath of nymphs, behind the trees.

GRAHAM: Very nice.

SLAVITT: And there I was with my elm tree up there.

GRAHAM: I've talked with a lot of poets about their poetry and occasionally on the program, they will read it. But, they won't interrupt themselves. And this is part of the fun.

SLAVITT: If the poem works and if the program works, then, perhaps this will not have been the only experience that our listeners will have with the poem, and they will be tempted to go and read it for themselves. If they are not, then that's their worry.

III. *One writes poems for oneself, and one's wife, and eleven friends.*

GRAHAM: Mr. Slavitt is extremely well known for his novels, but, quite frankly, David, I did not know about the poetry until maybe two or three weeks ago when you were introduced to me by your poems, by George Garrett.

SLAVITT: I'm well known for the Henry Sutton novels. They sell a lot. The David Slavitt novels are nearly as obscure as the poems.

GRAHAM: I'm going to get at your fiction. I've got three or four of your novels; the last one is *Vector,* is it not?

SLAVITT: That's a Sutton book. It's not bad, but Longines does not, for whimsical reasons, call some of their watches Wittnauer.

GRAHAM: We'll get at the fiction later, but I'm very, very taken with your most recent book of poetry, *Day Sailing.* I hear a lot of voices in the book of poems, and I'm interested in—well, your lack of pressure on the reader. I think for instance of a poet I'm very keen on, James Dickey, who controls his reader very strongly through his rhythms. He "demands," almost, in the visual as well as audible effect of his poems, so that you can't move very much.

SLAVITT: I like his recent thing. It's better than most of the earlier things that his reputation was mostly built on. He's not, essentially, a very musical guy.

GRAHAM: Essentially?

SLAVITT: I mean he plays the banjo and guitar and all this stuff because it's popular to do, and it fits in with his *persona*. But the intricacies of counterpoint are not the kinds of things that I should think turn him on. From reading him, and from having met him maybe a couple of times in my life, he's not that sort of ear. It's a different kind. All those old poems of his that are trimeter. It's when the spoon is banged for the third time on the table, go back to the left-hand margin. It's a kind of bongo-drum insistence, which would be terrible if it weren't coupled with a kind of sensibility that can use this, profit from it.

GRAHAM: It's difficult for me to describe what I think he has, but it is a long line of rhythm—"pacing" is really the word I want.

SLAVITT: Even there, you see, it's a long line which allows certain kinds of variations and different tunes, but it's a line which is too long to be musical. You can't be musical in English for more than six beats.

GRAHAM: I constantly see this material as "musing," really, and in that sense I'm probably saying that it is not musical.

SLAVITT: It's not musical, it's visual, from the way he sets up on the page. Each time there's a break, often in the middle of a line, down, or just a space in a line, left. You know, this is the equivalent of one of his famous podium gestures when he's doing a live reading. It's a look, a take, whatever, an emphasis —it isn't musical.

GRAHAM: It's not built deeply into the poem?

SLAVITT: I don't think his poems depend on that kind of musical intricacy which is, you know, not a pejorative remark. It's just that it's that kind rather than this kind. My things play off against each other, not necessarily out of choice, but because my genesis as a poet was peculiarly fortunate. I went to Andover and I studied with Dudley Fitts, the poet and translator. He's dead now, but he was a sort of friend of Ezra Pound's, and had the most articulate and the most highly developed and sensitive ear of any critic or of any poet or of any translator, practically, within the last fifty years.

GRAHAM: Richard Wilbur was close to him, was he not? Wrote a poem on his death?

SLAVITT: Yes, well, I'm in that sort of New England mandarin school. I was too young to have any choice about it, but by the time I graduated from Andover and went off to Yale, my technical equipment was as good as that of ninety-five percent of the grown-up poets writing then or now. I didn't have anything particular to *say* maybe—bracket "I'm glad you admit of a small doubt as to your own divinity, Mr. Slavitt" unbracket— I didn't know who I was, and I was too facile in copying gestures of other people, because I could do that easily. But the ear was trained.

GRAHAM: Was it trained in—I know you've done a lot of translations, and don't you have a book, as a matter of fact, of translations, just about ready to come out?

SLAVITT: *The Eclogues of Virgil,* which aren't so much translations as essays on *The Eclogues,* in poems. I mean the poems themselves are kind of literary essays. It's very difficult to explain, but they did that a lot during the Renaissance, where you would convey what the poem was about and incorporate in this your comments upon what it meant. Sort of like the ideal—anything can be a poem, even a literary essay. This is a series of ten literary essays, one on each of the eclogues, where

I quote from the poems occasionally. I mean in English, I've translated that.

GRAHAM: This gives you an enormous fluidity, doesn't it?

SLAVITT: It's wonderful. You can run back and forth, and it's an equivalent way of getting the same shape of experience of what the *Eclogues* were. It's sort of complicated. Virgil wasn't really writing about shepherds at all. The shepherds were figures that stood for various people in the literary world of Rome at the time. They were all friends and other poets and guys like this. The lit biz has always been a tough game, even then. So one of the things that you do is that you insult certain people, praise other people, but disguising them as shepherds. And the very tawdriness of the literary racket is such that the shepherds become almost real, if only by virtue of longing for that kind of simplicity and openness. But the people who were reading these poems—or hearing them, because they were performed—would be able to translate back from this shepherd to that guy sitting over there. Watch him squirm! And it became an experience like a seven-layer cake, where the interleaving of cake and icing was—you know, an artistic act and a virtuoso thing in and of itself. And I've managed the same kind of intricacy of experience by being able to slip back and forth between 1970 and about 45—not *1945,* but just 45, whenever Virgil was writing—and incorporate all this stuff, occasionally talk about them as shepherds and occasionally talk about them as literary types.

GRAHAM: Do you think for a young poet that the exercising of oneself through translations—whether very loose, these essay-like things, or through a fairly precise translation—do you think this would sharpen my ear, for instance?

SLAVITT: I don't know. Fairly precise translation is never interesting, because it's just a matter of—well, I shouldn't say even that. If you do it very well, then you are really writing your own poem, like Pope's Homer or Wilbur's Molière.

GRAHAM: No, if Wilbur had done nothing except those translations of the plays . . .

SLAVITT: Oh, monumental, just monumental! Securely brilliant!

GRAHAM: Have you seen them? Those lines bounce back and forth even with simply amateurs. Those lines just hop.

SLAVITT: The kinds of translations that I do, and the kind of playing around with the classics that I do, are the same sorts of things that are in the history poems. I think there may be a couple of them in *Day Sailing;* there are a lot of them in *Carnivore*—where I take a paragraph, or even more frequently a footnote, in Gibbon or some place, or in the Procopius' *Secret History,* and embellish this, as if . . . this is the given. It verges toward narrative verse, or dramatic lyric, the Browning kind of thing. If Browning had been a better poet, he would have been a great poet, because all the things he was doing were very interesting and, even given his occasional deficiencies and grotesqueries, he's still most rewarding to read. One can learn a lot more from Browning, I think, than Wordsworth.

GRAHAM: What I'd like to do again—I haven't read it now for too long—but I think *The Ring and the Book* is one of the great poems.

SLAVITT: It's too long. But it's great.

GRAHAM: Well, you have to hang in, there's no question about it.

SLAVITT: I mean, by the time you've heard this story the eleventh time, from the eleventh guy, and it's different again, you just don't care—"Throw all these people out, they're lying."

GRAHAM: Let me switch off here just a little bit into this whole idea of voice. This is almost a dumb, practical question, but in the book we had before, *Day Sailing,* it suddenly struck me maybe it's because I know you and do know George Garrett, that you've dedicated this specific poem to a friend. It's a kind of letter to a friend on receiving a book of his poetry, it's a reply. Do you, as poet, often have a very specific person in mind that might be listening to your poem while you're en route— to kind of focus?

SLAVITT: No. Not even in there. I mean, the poem was written on the occasion of George's giving me a copy of *For a Bitter Season,* and, as it says in the poem, that same day a friend had come by, and we hadn't seen him for years, and he did bring this elegant crystal bowl. And that's how you flick it, find out how good it is: Dinnnnggg! Marvelous! I just wrote the poem, and it was his book that was the occasion for it—"For George and on the Occasion Of"—but the reader is still me, and those of my friends who are sufficiently close to me to enjoy the kinds of mumblings that I do. One writes poems for oneself, and one's wife, and eleven friends.

IV. *Lots of games! Sure! The world is a game!*

GRAHAM: We've been talking about David Slavitt's poetry, and I am afraid, David, I have not read the novels, but I'd like to talk about them anyway. Back on my desk I have two fairly fat ones: one, *Feel Free,* and the other, *Vector.* And I've seen your name in five thousand magazines, but I still haven't read the novels. What can I expect?

SLAVITT: I don't know. I have the advantage over you, see? I can say anything at all.

GRAHAM: First of all, I guess you're going to tell me they're terrific novels.

SLAVITT: No, the Sutton novels, which are *The Exhibitionist*, *The Voyeur*, and *Vector*, are *public* novels. They were originally conceived of, executed as, and intended to be, and were "bestsellers." The idea was to make a lot of money, wide audience, big sales. Not hard to do.

GRAHAM: A lot of people are trying. But then this gives you time?

SLAVITT: There are fools and damned fools. I'm merely foolish. It's a way of buying time so I can write the other novels and the poems, which don't pay all that terribly well. And it saves me having to spend seven, eight, nine months a year pretending to teach, wearing tweeds, getting into arguments with faculty committees.

GRAHAM: That's what breaks your back. I'll meet twenty classes before serving on a committee.

SLAVITT: I have no classes and I have no committees. I have no appointments, and I don't even have to commute to an office.

GRAHAM: I'm sure you have examined this problem a million and one times. Are you able to keep these things apart, your public novels and your private novels?

SLAVITT: I had, again, a very fortunate training for that kind of thing.

GRAHAM: How so?

SLAVITT: Well, if you put in seven years working for *Newsweek*, you know what writing for millions of people is. And then you go home and you write poems. And you know what writing for dozens of people is. They're different. Faulkner was able to go out to Hollywood and write Howard Hawks' screenplays and come back to Mississippi and write William Faulkner novels. It can be done.

GRAHAM: Don't a lot of people drown in the attempt, thinking they're going to preserve some pure intention, while doing another job.

SLAVITT: I never thought of the Slavitt stuff as being all that pure in intention anyway. I do that for fun. Because I like it. Because it amuses me. Because it's fun to do it well.

GRAHAM: I see this in the poems.

SLAVITT: And the novels, too. Now, the novels are kind of interesting in the way they've developed. The first novel was *Rochelle, or Virtue Rewarded,* which is still around in a Dell paperback—I think the hard cover can be got from bookstores, but you have to bully them because they have to order it from Delacorte, and Delacorte has to find it somewhere in a warehouse in nether Nebraska. But it exists, it's there. That was a novel that I wrote in my twenties, and there were several things that occurred to me—up front, you know—cautionary things for guys writing a novel. First of all, all the great novels are written by men—men and women—in their forties and fifties. Poets and musicians and chess players and mathematicians bloom early. Poets can survive, some, but mathematicians have all of their original work by the time they're thirty and then they just elaborate on it. Novelists, because of the nature of the novel and what's involved, have to be familiar with the texture of the world, and it takes a long time to get familiar.

GRAHAM: Just plain lots of experience.

SLAVITT: Lots of experience, and, you know, for lack of any more precise word, "wisdom," something like that. Well, I obviously didn't have any of that when I was twenty and I was at least shrewd enough to know that I didn't. So the point was to make the novel as much of a game, as much of a closed system, as much of a bright bauble as I possibly could, and it's a novel about a remark. There's a couple with a cousin, and the cousin is thirty and sort of homely and sweet, but not married. And she's boring. And one of the characters says of her, "Well, the trouble is that Rochelle is virtuous but dull. Now, if we could make her vicious, but interesting, she would do much better." So for her own good they set out to corrupt her. By the end of the novel, of course, she's vicious and dull. So with the novel, it's not quite so precious, perhaps, as Ronald Firbank, but it's very limited in what it supposes to do, what it attempts to do. The next novel was *The Exhibitionist,* which is, you know, big money and all, and you write that as though the nineteenth century was still here. You come on straight, flat-footed, and dirty. It sells. The next novel after that was *Feel Free,* which was kind of like—well, I thought of it as my master's essay in the craft of the novel.

GRAHAM: How do you mean?

SLAVITT: To do a novel with no tricks, where the language itself was not the interesting thing, but a character, what was happening to him. I'd never done that before. This is about a guy who goes bankrupt—Bernie Lazarus. And, obviously, "Lazarus," "bankruptcy," he comes back from his bankruptcy, but legally his corporation is dead so he's dead because he was the corporation. Nobody in his family understands him any more. He's a small time Prince Mishkin. And he winds up as a professional Hebrew prayer-sayer in a Jewish cemetery. The next novel was *The Voyeur,* which was like *Son of the Exhibitionist—The Exhibitionist* was not about the Fondas, and *The Voyeur* was not about Hugh Hefner—which is the big difference. It had a plot, which was also new, because *The Exhibitionist* was a *Bildungsroman.* After that I did *Anagrams* which will be published— well, first in London by Hodder and Stoughton, and then sometime after that in the spring [1971] by Doubleday. *Anagrams* is really my first novel. Or what most novelists do when they're writing their first novel. I'd been around the track enough, so

I knew what to use and what not. It's a novel about a guy who comes down, like, to a poetry reading, and it's based roughly on a literary festival that was at Hollins and at the University of Virginia some years ago. During the course of this, the guy is writing a poem, so it's really a novel about the writing of a sonnet. That cut the ground down and cut the competition down a lot because there are very few people who can do that. Most poets are incompetent as novelists, and most novelists are incompetent as poets. So the only possible guys in the world to do this would be me; Robert Penn Warren; maybe George Garrett, if he wanted to do that; Nabokov, certainly he'd come pretty close in *The Gift;* Anthony Burgess, maybe; John Wain, perhaps. But instead of having thousands of competitors you have a—dozens. If it's even a plural dozen.

GRAHAM: In *Anagrams* do we get, at the end of the novel, a produced sonnet?

SLAVITT: Oh yes, a produced sonnet, and not only that, but you see the changes, you see the emendations, you see the corrections, you see it change direction. And the fun part is that I didn't write the sonnet. I let the guy do it, Jerome Carpenter. And you watch the experience of what happens in this two-and-a-half-day weekend, filter through his head and come out into the poem. Nobody's ever done that before, and if the novel is a tenth as good as what I think it is, it's probably one of the great achievements of, like, the last twenty years.

GRAHAM: Why not make it the twentieth century?

SLAVITT: Well, because we've got *Ulysses* and some of those big fellas back in the twenties.

GRAHAM: I'm sorry, but what about Nabokov's *Pale Fire?*

SLAVITT: *Pale Fire,* yes, *Pale Fire* is after all a novel. That's a game too, but a more arrogant game, where the novel is in the

maniac footnotes to a poem. He wrote the poem first, and then—
I mean, it could be most any poem, it just had to be long enough
to support enough footnotes to put a novel in.

GRAHAM: Something suddenly occurred to me, it's not unlike
the movie *8½*—in that the movie is its own self-creation.

SLAVITT: Kind of, except that at the end, you have fourteen
lines of the sonnet, which exists in a way independently of the
novel. I mean, you can read it as a sonnet, and it's not bad. It's
not the kind of sonnet I would write myself, but not bad at all.

GRAHAM: But it is a sonnet that the protagonist wrote.

SLAVITT: It is a sonnet that this guy wrote, and it's about as good
as he ought to be writing, 'cause he's in his twenties, he's still
finding his voice. There're two poets in it, a young poet and a
sort of old poet friend, lots of funny things in it, all kinds of
games. At one point he loses his poems, and he has to come on
to a reading but he doesn't have a poem. He goes to the library
to steal one. I'm able to settle a lot of scores. There are a lot of
poets that are not worth stealing from, he discovers. Finally he
steals one from a literary magazine. The poem is an undergraduate poem by D. Martyn Vattlis, which is an anagram on D. Ryt-
man Slavitt. And it's in fact a poem of mine that I wrote and
published in the *Yale Lit* that wasn't good enough to keep.
There are things wrong with it. So I have my character steal
that poem from me, fix it, and then do it fixed at the reading.
Of course, the character, who I've suddenly changed into a girl,
because with "Dee" it could be anything, comes up and says,
"But I wrote a poem almost exactly like that, a lot of the words
were . . ." And he says, "Yeah, I know, I fixed it for you, and
this is supposed to be a learning experience. It's not just a show-
and-tell." And he gives it to her. It's a sort of generous, decent
act, but of course it's hideously misunderstood by everybody.
And they think of him as a crook.

GRAHAM: You're going to play games with your language.

SLAVITT: Lots of games! Sure! The world is a game!

GRAHAM: Let me ask you this, because I'm fascinated with what you're up to. How long does it take you to turn out a "public" novel? I mean four or five hundred pages?

SLAVITT: *Vector* took three months to write.

GRAHAM: That fast? Do you dictate?

SLAVITT: I dictate into a tape machine and then I edit the tapes myself, I mean transcribe—at night when I'm less alert. I do the dictation in the morning and I try to get a full reel of tape, one side, at 1⅞ inches per second, and when I transcribe that, depending on how much dialogue there is, it will be anywhere from twenty to twenty-seven pages. As Henri Peyre said back at Yale, "Writing a novel is not very difficult: you simply write ten pages a day for a month and then you have a novel."

GRAHAM: (laughing) Oh shit!

William Harrison

BIOGRAPHICAL

Born: 29 October 1933 in Dallas, Texas.
Education: B.A. Texas Christian 1955, M.A. Vanderbilt 1959, studied at Writers' Workshop at Iowa in early '60's.
Occupational: Various jobs, including a stint as a preacher and evangelist; since 1964 has directed the graduate writing program at the University of Arkansas.
Books: Novels—*The Theologian* (1965), *In a Wild Sanctuary* (1969), *Lessons in Paradise* (1971). His short stories have been widely published and anthologized and a collection of them is coming.

SNAPSHOT

He has the perfect build, the flawless complexion, the extraordinary handsomeness, accented and finally dominated by light and light-thrilled "Paul Newman" eyes, to be an old-timey, but young movie star. First impression is Captain Charisma, cool and controlled and probably admirable all the way. Then he smiles and flashes a splendid gold tooth up front, proudly and a little mischievously. You remember that because he's very serious, very disciplined, not cautious by any means but never off-balance. A streak of the gambler (and he won big once in Las Vegas) with the gambler's calm courage and weighty patience. His brief days as a preacher of the gospel are not so much a secret or a closed book as simply . . . long gone. But whatever his religious faith may be, he carries still a priest's unsentimental charity and compassion for the suffering and trouble of others and so is often most powerfully gentle in bad times, can direct a bad scene into some felicity without effort or even seeming to. Evangelical fervor and inspiration have not been banished, but as artist he holds these powers in almost savage check. The result, in life and art, seems to be a superb control, brightened by an over-brimming of power, energy, purpose and dedication. The result is, in life and art, a genuine authority which can be at once a comfort and a model for aspiration.

It seems natural, then, that he has been a great teacher from the beginning.

I. *I like to write into enigmatic areas.*

GRAHAM: Bill, I'm halfway through the first novel of yours I came on, *In a Wild Sanctuary,* and I'm intrigued, since we're hyperconscious here at the Hollins Conference about the "how" of writing. I'm intrigued by the form that you've evolved or established in *In a Wild Sanctuary,* a novel about four rather keyed-up graduate students at a large university.

HARRISON: The University of Chicago.

GRAHAM: Oh, it's Chicago. But each one of these—we've got a botanist, a mathematician, a psychologist, and an English major —is working on the others, especially this mathematician, the talker, Clive. He talks like a big reader, lots of literary allusions, and he sets the tone of this novel, at least for the novel as far as

I've gone, because the air is certainly superheated. This is a pushing human being.

HARRISON: Clive is a very malevolent and provocative character. I felt that if he was really going to convince the other students in what turns out to be a suicide and murder plot, he was really going to convince them that it may be a sanity to take their lives in these times, then, he's got to convince the readers, too. And so a lot of his sort of neo-Freudian, Brigid-Brophy-type borrowings . . . I mean to be deliberately provocative, and I want the readers to begin to say "yes" to Clive along with the other characters. Of course, he's a fantastic liar, a fantastic con man, but irresistible, a sort of an intellectual killer.

GRAHAM: I was very taken with the little interlude on his early life, when he's a little grubby boy playing chess.

HARRISON: He became a chess player, a manipulator, very early. As he says in the novel, he becomes a player, now, of a greater game; for he finds it much more exciting to move people around than chessmen.

GRAHAM: Do you remember that little story that we read when we were fourteen years old, called "The Most Dangerous Game," about the man who goes hunting men?

HARRISON: We've got a sense of that here. One of the things that got me to writing *In a Wild Sanctuary* was the idea of suicides. There was a real suicide pact, at the University of Kansas. And I was working on another novel at the time, which I immediately scrapped; because I was taken with this notion. Suicide is just such an enigmatic subject. I find that our psychologists, for example, know so little about it though they have a great deal of data, statistical data, mainly. And I like to write into enigmatic areas.

GRAHAM: That prompts your imagination, just as did this University of Kansas story?

HARRISON: Also it keeps me from being investigated too closely. The novel I've just finished is about a young prodigy, a genius. We know a great deal about genius and high IQ, and yet, on the other hand, we don't. After all the studies, after all the investigations into the nature of the child prodigy, it's a mystery to us still.

GRAHAM: We don't know what to do with them, what to expect of them, and very often they don't seem to know what to expect of us or do with us. The new novel is called . . . ?

HARRISON: *Lessons in Paradise.*

GRAHAM: Is this a chunk of your theology background that's drawing you toward enigmatic subjects?

HARRISON: Oh no. My first book, *The Theologian,* I think I sort of gave my readers, few as they are, a bath of theology there. I'll never return to it.

GRAHAM: Could I go back to *In a Wild Sanctuary* again, to the making of it? Did you have trouble with the multiple voices? Each one of the four major figures speaks at length, for himself really; and then we have this enormous variety of almost summary of a situation from a variety of points of view, very tightly bundled together, almost as if it were a kind of poem.

HARRISON: Well, it's really in third person. But what I'm trying to do technically is to gear down into a sort of first-person intelligence at times on the part of almost all the characters in the novel. So I'm trying to blend first and third into a kind of central intelligence format. I slip into Clive's mind, and into Stoker's, and Pless's, and the Colonel's. This is the style I think I'll probably continue to work in for a number of years.

GRAHAM: You feel, then, you're getting the advantages of third person plus the immediacy of the first person?

HARRISON: Think what fiction is. It's a genre that allows the artist to slip into a character's consciousness, and even subconsciousness, which the theater can't do, which some poems do, but traditionally poetry has not done; and so the peculiarity, the uniqueness, of fiction is this ability to be a psychological, an interior drama, that at times is a kind of counterpoint to the drama that's going on. For instance, in a novel I can simply have a character do or say one thing, but I can show my readers that inside of his head he's thinking quite something different.

GRAHAM: Perhaps very much at war with the apparent actions. Then you've got the game, to go to one of your terms, the game of the reactions of everyone else to trying to get inside of his mind with the reader.

HARRISON: Right, and they simply can't know. If they had known what Clive really thought, the book would have come out a different way. It's a pretty bleak book, as it comes out this way; for Clive is a manipulator, and at a time when there are many manipulators he's one of the best, I hope.

GRAHAM: With *Lessons in Paradise,* the new novel, now, is your prodigy protagonist a manipulator or just trying to survive?

HARRISON: This is a light happy book, and the story of his coming out into the world of flesh and blood and people and love and commitment. My character there was raised by his mother as a prodigy, spent some years at the University of Chicago before he was sixteen, where, by the way, he had finished his Ph.D. for all intents and purposes. He goes out into the world, but he is a cold fish, a piston-like machine. The story is how his mother plots—indeed, even after her death—to thrust Baskin back into a real world. In fact, she sets him up with a young woman who is also her protégée. So it's the story of his first love affair.

GRAHAM: Is the mother a manipulator or is she a lover?

HARRISON: Kind of a manipulator, but a happy one, and, I hope, one of my better women characters, maybe my first and only one.

GRAHAM: Just as a sort of offshoot, some of *Lessons in Paradise* is being issued—is it serially or just a big chunk of it, in *Playboy?*

HARRISON: I'm delighted, because it's really about Sarah, and she's a good and full woman. I'm surprised really that *Playboy* took it. Their usual portrait of the woman as object is going to be dispelled by Sarah's presence there. I'm happy about it.

GRAHAM: Do you do work in short story, too?

HARRISON: I have a collection of fifteen stories. And after *Lessons in Paradise,* which will be out in March of 1971, the short story volume will be issued. So I've got a lot of things going. Another novel is growing now, which is set in the Arkansas prison system. You know the infamous prison system where they recently, last couple of years, discovered the bodies?

GRAHAM: Bodies in unmarked graves and what-have-you? You're getting your data from the newspapers there again?

HARRISON: Some, but I live in Arkansas and have been down to the prison. The nice thing about living in a small state, and there are only about two million people in Arkansas, is that you can have a lot of freedom and flexibility, and you can call up friends of friends who know the director of prisons, and you can have an inside view. And that's what I've enjoyed.

GRAHAM: You've got next year planned as a writing year, don't you? What's your target date with some of this stuff? It sounds like you're juggling a lot of balls at once.

HARRISON: I don't know, I seem to have a lot of books in the air, all at once. I'm going to Europe, ironically, at the time when I have an Arkansas subject to write about.

GRAHAM: That's what I was working at. Is that a good distance?

HARRISON: I don't know, I don't know. I doubt that the book will be finished before I return. I'll probably go back to Cummins prison and investigate some things again before it's finished.

GRAHAM: A curious thing happened to me when I spent a year in Europe studying at one point. I was forced, in part because of the Europeans, I was forced in part to look at my society in a very different way, sometimes rather defensively.

HARRISON: Someone asked me if I was going to get perspective on America, and I said, "I don't know." Maybe I have enough or too much perspective on America. Maybe I'm going to get a little on Europe, since I haven't been, and it's high time to go and see it.

GRAHAM: What you're basically doing, then, is buying time, which is what writers just plain have to have. How long, Bill, did *In a Wild Sanctuary* take? It's not a fat book, but it's three hundred pages.

HARRISON: It took me three years, but I wrote *Lessons in Paradise* in eleven months. And so who knows? I also wrote it at a time when I was not complaining about my working habits. I was teaching full-time. I seemed to be home with the family a great deal. My life seemed to be going smoothly and I had a few ten-page days. I'm not a cantankerous writer, I can write anywhere. I don't have any real problems with writing. I don't have any myths that I have to go through, any sort of rituals, to set up for myself that enable me to write. That's kind of a silliness.

GRAHAM: It's a danger of self-indulgence, isn't it? Because sometimes it's a 75-watt bulb instead of a 100-watt bulb in the lamp and then if you believe that you live by 100-watt bulbs, you're a dead duck that day?

HARRISON: I had one friend that spent all last year going over the country hunting for a place, a mountain top, a lake, a certain locale, where he felt like he could write a book, and he wrote two pages last year.

R. H. W. Dillard

BIOGRAPHICAL

Born: 11 October 1937 in Roanoke, Virginia.
Education: B.A. Roanoke College 1958, M.A. University of Virginia 1959, Ph.D. Virginia 1965.
Occupational: Since 1965 Dillard has taught at Hollins College, where he is presently Associate Professor of English and Director of the Graduate Program in English. He was Director of the Hollins Conference in Creative Writing and Cinema.
Books: Poetry—*The Day I Stopped Dreaming About Barbara Steele* (1966), *News of the Nile* (1971), *After Borges* (1972); anthologies—*The Experience of America: A Book of Readings* (with Louis D. Rubin, Jr., 1969), *The Sounder Few: Essays from the Hollins Critic* (with George P. Garrett and John Rees Moore, 1971).

Some of his critical essays are widely recognized as of major importance. His essay on Nabokov, "Not Text, But Texture: The Novels of Vladimir Nabokov," is regarded as one of the finest pieces written about that master; "Even a Man Who Is Pure of Heart," dealing with the horror film (which Dillard has taught with joy) is a classic.

He co-authored the script of *Frankenstein Meets the Space Monster.*

A number of his highly original short stories have been anthologized. It is (in the considered opinion of the editor) a crying shame that no publisher has yet seen fit to publish his collection of short stories—*Dance, Wolf, Dance.*

SNAPSHOT

An almost impossible task for me, here and now, because Richard is one of the people, in life and art, I admire most and with next to no reservations.

Once, in an anthology headnote, I described him as "half hillbilly, half Nabokov." True, as far as it goes. Pale and dark-haired, he has always looked (long before *A Hard Day's Night*) like the Fifth Beatle. He also looks *just* like Edgar Allan Poe, only without the mustache.

He has suffered a lot of physical pain, but you would never know it. Because joy, both given and earned, is his natural element. He communicates joy (is a *great* teacher) and brings forth a joyous response. He can make all learning (even pure bibliography, which he's good at) a pure delight.

Outwardly the most *original* of the writers here, he is also, perhaps, the most deeply (inwardly) traditional. That is, oldest and newest are happily simultaneous.

What else? Well, his poem, "Meditation for a Pickle Suite," *really was* set to music and performed in concert by the Pittsburgh Symphony.

I. *It's because old ladies stop me on the street and tell me I look like Edgar Allan Poe. Perfect strangers grab me by the sleeve. It's terrifying.*

GRAHAM: I have before me what I think is a very handsomely designed book of poetry, *The Day I Stopped Dreaming About*

Barbara Steele. Richard, I've known you for a good while now and so I think I'll go ahead and ask. I don't know who Barbara Steele *is.*

DILLARD: The truth is I'm still dreaming about her.

GRAHAM: Well, who is she?

DILLARD: Barbara Steele is a movie actress who was in Fellini's *8½* and a great number of horror films. She is known as the queen of the horror films, and she is very beautiful, dark-haired, and is always tortured horribly. And in this book she comes to be a kind of representation of that dark side of the self—Shakespeare's Dark Lady. Mine is Barbara Steele. I always compare myself to Shakespeare early.

GRAHAM: Well, all right, so did Keats, and he died young.

DILLARD: Watch it!

GRAHAM: One of the things, right there, is my lack of knowledge of your world. I see the little headnote from Robert Herrick is "Dreams," the idea that we are each hurled by dreams into a several or separate world. I have trouble with your poetry, in the sense of the allusiveness. Now when you give me a note to Shakespeare, as you do in "Ancient Pistol's Stolen Home," a poem I like very, very much, I'm all right. But the Barbara Steele blocked me—your opening line—"The drizzle shifted"—right there, you see. . . . Your poetry is difficult. Who's your audience?

DILLARD: I begin to suspect my audience is primarily composed of me. It's a great horror when you've been writing for years and you discover that people that you've always assumed to be your audience don't understand a word you say. It all seems very clear to me—crystal clear.

GRAHAM: Well, look, I'm . . .

DILLARD: Part of the . . .

GRAHAM: See? I'm reacting to your poetry. Take this—I have to call it "strange"—poem called "Why Were the Bandit's Eyes Hidden Behind a Green Mask?" Now, I react to this; and yet, if I were asked by a student to help him through it, I don't know quite where I would start. Would you want to read it and talk about it a little bit?

DILLARD: Okay, I'll do that.

GRAHAM: Again, I *like* it. I have some sense of sort of knowing the poem, Richard, and yet I couldn't talk for a straight minute on it.

DILLARD: I heard a comment, someone said after reading this poem, once—"Who does this guy think he is, Edgar Allan Poe?"

GRAHAM: Well, that wasn't the direction I was going in.

DILLARD: I try to think of this as a book, a unit, constructed in a certain way, as a movement from, say, Barbara Steele and what she represents, to . . . light, whatever. . . .

GRAHAM: Yes, to light, to love.

DILLARD: There's a set of love poems in it designed to kind of indicate the shift of that movement. The middle section of the book, which the bandit poem is in, is a kind of *false history*. I've always intended it to hold together as a unit. I called it "The Turn of the Century," meaning the turn of any century, or the fact that the century is turned.

GRAHAM: Or the turn of your century, maybe?

DILLARD: Yes, and one reason it seems allusive, I sort of consciously did it, not in the sense of T. S. Eliot's allusiveness. Many of the things that seem to be allusions in here are not allusions to anything. People are always asking me, what city is this poem about? It's no city; the theory being that all history is primarily imaginary anyway, and as we sit in a room and look at our documents, we create a past. St. Augustine warned us that the past isn't real, but we don't pay any attention to that. We treat it as if it is real.

GRAHAM: And leading up to us, as George Garrett saw, we're the only real pin in the whole long ribbon of history.

DILLARD: Right. So I thought, why not do a set of poems that are concerned with a history? That if I imagine it honestly enough, carefully enough, and write carefully out of that imagination, that history should then be true. It will at least be true to my understanding of the present. And that's about all we can ask of any history, I suppose. This is not to deny that we do gain a kind of factual history that is very useful and helpful.

GRAHAM: Well, this history, though, that you want to do, is a personal and necessary forming of your reality.

DILLARD: Sure, it's based upon experience. The time that I wrote this book was right at the end of six years in graduate school, college before that, high school before that. The great bulk of my experience was literary, things I'd read. So this book is probably a great deal more allusive because of that. And this false history is, needless to say, based upon real history, fact. You want me to read this?

GRAHAM: Yes, I would like you to go into details about what you're talking about.

DILLARD: Well, this is a very small poem. And I will tell you the hidden secret. We hermetic poets should remain sealed, or else we go bad.

GRAHAM: (laughs) All right.

DILLARD: Okay: "Why Were the Bandit's Eyes Hidden Behind a Green Mask?"

The stuttering bishop,
The midwife,
And there were the children
Strung across the highway
Like Christmas festoons.

The carriage was of gold
And gleamed,
And the peasants bore rakes
To ravish the ladies.
(That year was a time.)
The leaves fell early.

The dust lay low.

The horse's ears were back,
His beribboned tail,
The pinwheels of his eyes,
The foam,
His teeth were flat and wide,
And the bridge we never reached.

GRAHAM: All right, I can see the Apocalypse, you see? No, go ahead. Why a stuttering bishop? Is this the breakdown of things?

DILLARD: What I was primarily concerned with . . . Maybe this is why the person wondered if I thought I was Edgar Allan Poe. I *do* sometimes think I'm Edgar Allan Poe. It's because old ladies stop me on the street and tell me I look like Edgar Allan Poe. Perfect strangers grab me by the sleeve. It's terrifying!

GRAHAM: I would think—when you're having a hard enough time trying to find out who Richard Dillard is—for someone to tell you you're someone else is a little difficult.

DILLARD: Poe's primary feeling about the way to understand a poem is through *effect*. And that's what I was concerned with here. Simply, I needed an effect to fit into the movement of this whole sequence, and it is—I mean, Apocalypse is the "right answer." It's the time when things have gone bad. But beyond that, I don't think there's any explanation for it, it's just a set of images put together to evoke that particular feeling, a feeling that you can translate into idea if you like. And you could interpret it, I suppose, that the bishop stutters because it is a bad time, religion is not the answer. You have a midwife in it, and the idea of birth. But then the children are strung across the highway. I can tell things about people who read this poem, perhaps more than they can about me, by how they interpret it. Were the children hanging by their necks or were they holding hands?

GRAHAM: I had an accident, even with the image of "like Christmas festoons." They were in danger.

DILLARD: Well, that's the feeling I wanted.

GRAHAM: I mean, "strung across" tips the hand.

DILLARD: That's what I want. Christmas is bad, it's gone bad. The bishop stutters. If the midwife produces children, the children come to no good end. And in the second stanza, you have this image of a kind of elegant, worthless world—gold carriages. The peasants, again birth, are bearing rakes. That's a kind of a bit of foolishness. I don't know if it's proper or not, but the idea is that their children become rakes who in turn ravish the ladies. And in turn, I just closed with the image of the horse, trusting to instinct, that a horse is very easy to use to strike the kind of feeling I wanted, because its eyes are so huge. And you never reach the bridge.

GRAHAM: Now I'm into your logic problem, which you've been forcing me toward. I've often rather wondered how a book is made, a book of poetry, and I rather presumed that it would be set up chronologically. But you're telling that this book has to be read as a book, then, not as individual poems.

DILLARD: I would hope so. Wallace Stevens, for example, worked for years constructing *Harmonium* and moving the poems around 'til they were in precisely the order he wanted. And later I think he got the idea that no one was reading it that way, and his later books are all simply chronological.

GRAHAM: Then, of course, I am inclined, in reading poetry, to pick up the book and thumb through it, and read a poem here and a poem there, not recognizing that a writer is perhaps forming a development: from dark to light in your particular case, in *The Day I Stopped Dreaming About Barbara Steele*.

DILLARD: The first two books I've done, I've arranged later to try to make them into a book. The third one I'm going to do chronologically because I worked from the very start with the idea of it as a single book. That's like writing a novel.

GRAHAM: Right there, you've reached a point in your development where you know better what you are, probably.

DILLARD: Could be. Could be the fourth book'll go back to the first. There's another thing, a book always arranges itself.

II. *I suddenly have a feeling that I've just wrecked my whole life right here on the air.*

GRAHAM: I have read, and frankly I enjoyed very much, Richard, *The Day I Stopped Dreaming About Barbara Steele and Other Poems*. I was wondering, this was published about four years ago now, so how do you feel about *The Day I Stopped Dreaming About Barbara Steele*? I mean, you've changed, you've grown. What do you think of the book now?

DILLARD: I haven't looked at it. I always used to believe, when I read interviews with writers in which they said they didn't remember their books, that they were lying. And now I've learned that it's true. It seems very far away. Well, the fact of the matter is, it *is* kind of far away.

GRAHAM: Is it not true that the act of writing poems is more important to you than the continuing existence of the poem, or something like that?

DILLARD: That's true. The real pleasure is the part where you're all alone making the poem. After that you take pleasure in seeing people respond to it, or hearing that they do.

GRAHAM: You still are writing regularly. What are you up to now?

DILLARD: That's another reason it seems farther away. I'm going to have a second book out in the spring of 1971. And I'm about halfway through a third book which I hope to finish around the time the second one is published.

GRAHAM: If you reread your own things, you could get trapped. I don't mean to mock, at all, now, but you could almost fall in love with themes that actually you've finished with.

DILLARD: Raymond Chandler said that when you read your own work for inspiration, you know you're through. You've had it.

GRAHAM: There's a great legal term that says if you serve as your own lawyer you have a fool for an attorney. The analogy may work. But what have you been doing? You say you have a book just about ready. What's it going to be called?

DILLARD: *News of the Nile.*

GRAHAM: Are you patterning your poems in this particular book the way you did with *The Day I Stopped Dreaming About Barbara Steele?*

DILLARD: It's in two parts. The first I call "Old World," and the second part, "New World." And I hope it's a distinction between, say, grammar and geography. So it has a movement. I think it's a movement away from idea and a kind of abstract way of looking at things, toward the real and living moment. And I also have another theory—not only if you read your own work for inspiration are you wrecking it, but if you talk about your own work, you're only destroying yourself. I suddenly have a feeling that I've just wrecked my whole life right here on the air.

GRAHAM: Well, of course, I know that if you talk about a piece of writing that you are trying to do, you may sort of exhaust the psychological need to write and therefore never write it.

DILLARD: There's also a fear of explaining. That is, if you put a book together, and set it up in a certain way, it's not fair to the book or to yourself to explain them. You've cheapened it somehow.

GRAHAM: Let me ask one other thing. I was reared on a lot of what might be called philosophical poetry. I think, very specifically, of someone like T. S. Eliot of the *Four Quartets,* as a kind of—oh, I don't quite want to say goal, an apex type of poetry. But in a way that's true. Am I not correct in thinking that younger poets now, aren't they shifting more back toward the imagists, really?

DILLARD: I think so.

GRAHAM: Rather than the argumentative.

DILLARD: I can quote Raymond Chandler again, who also said, "Ideas are poison." And he was thinking of the business of writing. That is, if you start out with ideas you're probably never going to write anything. I'm always accused of being an academic poet, too concerned with ideas, being too allusive.

GRAHAM: I don't think being allusive in literature is by definition. It's part of experience.

DILLARD: I like to think that I wouldn't be a teacher if I weren't interested in ideas, or in the process of thinking. The poems come from the same source, but, I hope, in a different way. That is, not so specifically concerned with idea as Eliot's. I think it's one reason why Wallace Stevens and William Carlos Williams are rising in the esteem of younger people.

GRAHAM: I hear young people talking about William Carlos Williams all the time.

DILLARD: He was a very intellectual poet, in his own way, but the way he handled his ideas was less explicit. He was more concerned with the projection of ideas through form than through statement. That is, the way a series of events moves in a Williams poem contains an idea.

GRAHAM: Maybe I'm thinking of the type of poem that we were stuffed with in grammar school, or better, really, in high school where they have the moral tagged on at the end. Now this is what all these images really "mean." And I have, in reviewing books of poetry, found often that I'd like to strike about the last two or four lines of a poem, where, in effect, the poet shows his hand a little too broadly.

DILLARD: It was a late nineteenth-century tradition. Like Longfellow would write a beautiful poem, and then explain it to you at the end.

GRAHAM: Not so different, maybe, from Thackeray's stepping out. Of course, Fielding did it, and got away with it very successfully in *Tom Jones.*

DILLARD: It shifted our idea of art somewhat into the idea of a communal experience, with author and reader joined together to create the work. Nabokov can say that a book is like a chess problem. The author sets the puzzle, the reader solves it, and until the reader does solve it, the puzzle doesn't really exist.

GRAHAM: Of course this has been building, at least in aesthetic theory, certainly from the very early nineteenth century, and especially in German aesthetic theory. And we get it, of course, in the Impressionist painters, the idea of that cooperation. Well, look, with the new book, *News of the Nile*—are you doing different things, now?

DILLARD: Wish I could tell you. You might be able to see the difference. It's hard for me to say. They grow one from the next.

GRAHAM: A friend of ours here at Hollins keeps urging me to get you to read the pickle poem. Could we?

DILLARD: Now *there's* a poem that is fraught with ideas! I'll explain it, or just read it?

GRAHAM: Why not just read it?

DILLARD: It's called. . . . Oh, the title calls for a slight explanation. It's called "Meditation for a Pickle Suite" and it was written to be a part of a piece of music to be entitled *Pickle Suite*. It was commissioned by the symphony in Pittsburgh. And I was told to write a poem of a certain number of lines on the subject of "The Pickle."

GRAHAM: I like this. This is indeed setting a chess problem for you, to switch Nabokov's explanation.

DILLARD: So this is just a poem describing the passage of a day in terms of pickles, and it brings curious reactions from people.

GRAHAM: Go ahead, Richard.

DILLARD:

> Morning: the soft release
> As you open a jar of pickles.
> The sun through the window warm
> And moving like light through brine,
> The shadows of pickles swim the floor.
> And in the tree, flowing down the chimney,
> The songs of fresh birds clean as pickles.
> Memories float through the day
> Like pickles, perhaps sweet gherkins.
> The past rises and falls
> Like curious pickles in dark jars,
> Your hands sure as pickles,
> Opening dreams like albums,
> Pale Polish pickles.
> Your eyes grow sharp as pickles,
> Thoughts as green, as shining
> As rows of pickles, damp and fresh,
> Placed out in the afternoon sun.

I would say that poem is about the struggle between the Augustinian and the Thomist. . . .
(Both laughing)

GRAHAM: What it *does* remind me of, is William Carlos Williams, especially those last few lines.

DILLARD: It's curious. People have read it on the page and have sometimes thought that it was an odd poem, but one that was sort of quietly descriptive. Whenever it's read out loud to an audience, people get hysterical. I guess it's simply the sound of the word "pickle" that does it. You learn something about the difference between sound and sense, I guess.

GRAHAM: Of course, here's the strange business of seeing a movie on television and seeing it with a group. . . . Well, obviously, everybody knows this because of the use of canned laughter, or a claque at an opera, to get the applause going. But to the poem. In a way, I would want to argue that the poem proves that almost any metaphor will suggest meaning, any comparison, *any* comparison. If you were to substitute cherries there, to get away from what is a comical word, pickle, if you were to substitute cherries, you could get something of the same effect. What was it, your eyes are—how does it go?

DILLARD: "grow sharp as pickles."

GRAHAM: Well, you could substitute cherries or new potatoes, and this could get a suggestion of meaning.

DILLARD: Crazy to some degree, but it interests me about the power of metaphor, and I think maybe that's what poets in preceding generations haven't worked with as much, especially not recently. They've been so concerned with the *rational* metaphor. When you say, "Your lips are like a rose," well that means red and soft.

GRAHAM: But if you say, "Your lips are like pickles," where are you?

DILLARD: Somewhere strange, but then you find out all kind of things. You may learn something about something.

GRAHAM: It's almost like an experimentation with nonsense.

DILLARD: What interests me in the poems of Crashaw is he attempted to press metaphor far beyond where it had been before. And it quite often ends up ludicrous. You know, "the eyes of Mary Magdalen are like walking bathtubs."